El Anís del Consul
Alberto Gironella

Swinging the Maelstrom

New Perspectives on Malcolm Lowry

EDITED BY
SHERRILL GRACE

McGill-Queen's University Press
Montreal & Kingston • London • Buffalo

© McGill-Queen's University Press 1992
ISBN 0-7735-0862-7

Legal deposit first quarter 1992
Bibliothèque nationale du Québec

Printed in Canada on acid-free paper

Canadian Cataloguing in Publication Data

Main entry under title:
Swinging the maelstrom
Includes bibliographical references.
ISBN 0-7735-0862-7
1. Lowry, Malcolm, 1909-1957 – Criticism and
interpretation. I. Grace, Sherrill E., 1944–

PS8523.O96Z87 1992   823'.912   C91-090605-X
PR9199.3.L69Z87 1992

Typeset in Bembo 10/12 by Caractéra inc., Quebec City

For David Markson
and the Virgin

"for those who have nobody them with"

Contents

viii   Contents

Acknowledgments

It is a pleasure to acknowledge here the many funding organizations and individuals who have made this volume possible. For their financial support of the 1987 Lowry Symposium: the Social Sciences and Humanities Research Council of Canada, the Leon and Thea Koerner Foundation, the University of British Columbia Alumni Association, the British Council, and both the President, Dr David Strangway, and then Dean of Arts, Dr Robert M. Will, of the University of British Columbia. For financial support in the preparation of this volume it is a pleasure to thank the Social Sciences and Humanities Research Council of Canada, symposium delegates, and Dr Jane Fredeman, who generously contributed computer funds for the preparation of the original hard copy. This volume is made richer by the inclusion of various visual materials, and I would especially like to thank Teresa de la Rosa and Alberto Gironella for permission to reproduce *El Anís del Consul* and Peter Matson for permission to quote from both published and unpublished work and to reproduce the manuscript materials that accompany Suzanne Kim's and Victor Doyen's studies. I am grateful also to the Lowry Estate and the Royal University Library of Oslo, Department of Manuscripts, for permission to reprint Lowry's letter of September 1931 to Nordahl Grieg. For her permission to reprint "Not with a Bang" and for his permission to reprint the text of his keynote address *"Hear us O Lord* and the Orpheus Occasion," I would like to extend warm personal thanks to Jan Gabrial and Robert Kroetsch. Finally, it is a pleasure to thank Gabriele Scardellato of the Centre for Textual Studies in the English Department at the University of British Columbia for his patience and care in producing the original hard copy of each text, Debbi Onbirbak for typing revisions, Cynthia Sugars and Rohan Spratley, who chased down several elusive references for me, Stefan Haag and Rohan Spratley, who helped me proofread the "whole bolus," Susan Kent Davidson for her editorial hawk's eye, and John Grace for his generous support. For their good cheer and collegiality at all times, my thanks to all the contributors.

S.G.
Vancouver 1991

Abbreviations and Editions

With the exception of the editions noted here, contributors have used those editions of Lowry's works available to them and have identified these editions in their notes.

DAG   *Dark as the Grave Wherein My Friend Is Laid*
HOL   *Hear us O Lord from heaven thy dwelling place*
OF   *October Ferry to Gabriola*
SL   *Selected Letters of Malcolm Lowry* (New York: J.B. Lippincott 1965)
SP   *Selected Poems of Malcolm Lowry* (San Francisco: City Lights Books 1962)
UV   *Under the Volcano*
UBC SC   The Lowry Archive in Special Collections at the University of British Columbia, followed by box number: folder number, page number.

Swinging the Maelstrom

Putting Lowry in Perspective: An Introduction

SHERRILL GRACE

Why can I play it over and over again? As many times as a Beethoven quartet, save that I'm not going to compare the two, since jazz isn't music perhaps so much as a form of expressionism, maybe actually more analogous to literature or poetry, than music? But where the heck in what passage or movement of prose can I find the selection, the discipline, unselfishness, spontaneity, freedom, and final concision, and form of this darn thing? As well as the chaos, mournfulness, despair? These qualities ought to be manifest in any interpretation of the modern world.[1]

Malcolm Lowry was one of the great interpreters of the modern world, and forty years after the publication of his masterpiece, *Under the Volcano* (1947), his vision of that world seems if anything more urgent, more compelling, more frightening – and more beautiful – than before. Because he was a meticulous, obsessive reviser (some would say that revision *was* his creative process), and because he worked and thought constantly in interdisciplinary, interartistic, and syncretic terms, he produced only a few "finished" texts. To what degree he ever thought of anything (in the text or the world) as finished is, of course, a peculiarly Lowryan *topos*. Even the "unfinished" texts – those corrupt editions put together by other hands and published posthumously – however, constitute encyclopaedic explorations of the modern world. Whether that world is the dense, churrigueresque one that his Consul prays to have destroyed in *Volcano* or the richly mystical one celebrated by his jazz-composer protagonist in "Forest Path to the Spring," Lowry's aim throughout was to interpret the world for us and, by doing so, to render it a home for the human imagination.

The complexity of Lowry's texts, with their multi-layered, densely woven texture, has made the scholar's interpretation of his material a challenging process and one, moreover, that is far from finished. In interpreting Lowry to ourselves and others, we must listen to the political discussions, recognize the literary allusions and myriad references to films, music, and painting; we must be alert to the wide scope of his historical references and be prepared to pursue a host of details, hints, or echoes drawn from familiar or arcane areas of philosophical and religious knowledge. Above all we must listen to his language, for here is a writer obsessed (as perhaps only Joyce was too) with the "musicating" word. Deeply immersed, more often enmeshed, in this modern world, Malcolm Lowry *interpreted* it (elucidated, construed, performed, translated it) in the words that generate our own interpretations.

Literary scholars, however, are not the only Lowry interpreters. From early on, Lowry and his *Volcano* began to attract a cult following of general readers and aficionados. More recently, especially during the last ten to fifteen years, Lowry has been interpreted, rewritten, and reinvented by a large number of fellow artists: poets, fiction writers, playwrights, filmmakers, painters, graphic artists, and musicians. The scope of this artistic interpretation bears testimony, of course, to Lowry's tremendous impact on younger generations. Terrified yet fascinated by his own precursors, Lowry has become an archetypal precursor in his own right. One wonders what he would have thought of such a state of affairs. One wonders because this is an author who resists Roland Barthes' formulation and refuses to die.

On the occasion that inspired most of the articles in this volume, Lowry's *presence* was acknowledged on all sides. The 1987 International Malcolm Lowry Symposium held at the University of British Columbia brought together more than one hundred delegates from around the world and represented friends, devoted readers, students and established scholars, bibliophiles, amateur photographers, translators, writers, and other artists. Activities at the conference, from papers, panels, and workshops to related artistic events, demonstrated conclusively just how wide and varied have been both Lowry's impact on us and the spectrum of his interpreters. Given the nature of this conference and of the volume of essays published here as a result, two editorial parameters require some explanation. One is mechanical: the reader needs information about the principles of selection (for *Swinging the Maelstrom* is not a proceedings) and some brief remarks about the collection as a whole. The other is substantive: no collection of words alone does justice to Lowry's texts or to the variety of material presented at the conference; therefore, something must be said – and shown – of Lowry's interartistic context. To "put Lowry in perspective," then, is to identify him as the primary interpreter, to situate his work at the centre of a set of interpretations, and to constitute a multiplicity of "Lowrys" – all walking the wibberly, wobberly walk – from the poetry, drama, painting, and music of others. Here and in the second part of this introduction I outline editorial considerations and introduce the volume; in the concluding section I place Lowry in the larger interartistic context evoked at the symposium.

Of the twenty individual papers (selected from over forty refereed submissions), three panels, and two workshops at the conference, thirteen pieces were chosen for revision and inclusion here. Since all the work presented was very good, it was indeed difficult to make yet another selection from it. For understandable reasons, however, it is not always possible or desirable to publish "proceedings," which are inevitably less unified than a carefully designed volume. My task has been to choose essays, each of which represents a new examination of Lowry, that constitute as comprehensive a discussion of the work as possible. I regret that there were no submissions (hence no papers) on *Ultramarine* or *Lunar Caustic* to choose from, but Victor Doyen and Elsa Linguanti are both interested in the novella, so it may not be long before new work is available on the latter. The article by Cynthia Sugars on *Dark as the Grave* arrived too late for refereeing, but given its quality and the paucity of good work on that text, it seemed sensible to include it here. Jan Gabrial's fine short story, "Not with a Bang," occupies a special place and reappears in print here for the first time in over forty years.

The selected articles do, however, cover most *aspects* of Lowry studies: biography, correspondence, *Volcano* and post-*Volcano* fiction, translation, manuscript editing, poetry, and interartistic comparisons. Although two of Lowry's favorite films, *Sunrise* and *The Cabinet of Dr Caligari*, were screened at the symposium and many references were made, *en passant*, to Lowry's cinematic propensities, no one submitted any new investigations of Lowry and film. However, Wieland Schulz-Keil's paper, presented at the 1984 Lowry conference in London and describing the production of the sixty-seventh screenplay of *Volcano*, has recently appeared in print, and the Mota/Tiessen edition of the Lowrys' screenplay for *Tender Is the Night* is now available.[2] One fascinating new area of investigation explored at the Vancouver conference was the translating of *Under the Volcano*. Interest generated by translation problems – and the light they throw on Lowry's language – suggest that here we only touched the tip of the iceberg, if not the volcano.

Because the contributors to this volume represent international Lowry scholarship, a variety of mechanical problems that cannot be easily standardized arise. As much as possible I have tried to create consistency in stylistic and bibliographic matters while not, I hope, muting the contributors' individual voices. Since there are several editions of most Lowry texts (notably *Volcano*), with no one edition readily available to all, each author refers to his or her own editions. There are, however, two exceptions to this rule: *The Selected Letters of Malcolm Lowry*, ed. Harvey Breit and Margerie Lowry (Philadelphia and New York: J.B. Lippincott 1965), and *Selected Poems of Malcolm Lowry*, ed. Earle Birney, with the assistance of Margerie Lowry (San Francisco:

City Lights Books 1962). These two standard texts are referred to throughout as SL and SP, followed by the page number.[3] Many of the contributors quote from or work closely with the extensive Malcolm Lowry Collection housed in Special Collections at the University of British Columbia. Over the years there have been many additions to the collection, and recently one complete restructuring of the catalogue.[4] Where possible, references are keyed to the 1985 Combs–Sugars inventory, which renders the 1973 one obsolete; not all contributors, however, were able to make the complex conversion from 1973 to 1985 inventories. Unless otherwise indicated, all unpublished material (manuscripts, correspondence, etc.) referred to is held in the Lowry Collection.

Swinging the Maelstrom (the title Lowry gave to an early version of *Lunar Caustic* and to a jazz composition in "The Forest Path to the Spring")[5] is organized into four parts that proceed from biography (the so-called facts of the life), through the fictions and beyond, to what poet Sharon Thesen calls the "confabulations" of and with Lowry by other artists.[6] The "tintinnabulations" (a word, so Aiken protested, that Lowry stole from him!) in part 4 ring us back to the beginning and Alberto Gironella's mixed-media variations on a theme by Malcolm Lowry. The collection, then, is a composition for seventeen voices that displays, I hope, something of the "discipline," "unselfishness," "freedom," and "final concision" that Lowry loved in jazz.

Jan Gabrial, who married Lowry in January 1934, shared a few exciting, creative, yet difficult years with him in Europe, New York City, and finally in Mexico. The story of these years is told in her forthcoming memoir. "Not with a Bang," which first appeared in *Story* 29 (September–October 1946), concentrates on their last moments together in Mexico City in December 1937, and in Michael she has captured something of Lowry's complex sensitivity, childishness, and destructiveness as perceived through her efforts to help him and her private pain. Hallvard Dahlie and David Falk also explore "the life," but from very different perspectives. Beginning with the known "facts" of Lowry's friendship with the Norwegian writer Nordahl Grieg, Dahlie traces the outlines of Lowryan fictions about Grieg only to return to some new "facts" that do not necessarily solve the puzzle. (Several factors led me to include an edited, annotated transcription of the extraordinary letter that Dahlie discovered – but it should be read *after* Dahlie's essay as the culmination of his Poe-esque detective work.) Falk bridges the life and art by what he calls Lowry's "aesthetics of salvation." He conjures up an image of Lowry *after* the *Volcano*, "groping his way through a labyrinth of paper" in the attempt to salvage himself and his texts. Falk's shift of critical attention from the "life" to the "works" (despite the symbiotic relationship of the two) prepares the way for the literal maze of manuscripts left behind by Lowry and entered by Victor Doyen, in part 3, for salvage operations of another sort.

In "Genus Floridum", as in all the articles in part 2, *Under the Volcano* is subjected to close scrutiny. This study represents an amalgamation of information about problems in translation. It further demonstrates – dramatically, I think – the degree to which the translator must be an interpreter and co-creator. This glimpse into the "Máquina Infernal" of translation leaves the lay reader impressed by the sheer enormity of the task. Hilda Thomas's political "reading" of *Volcano* is a more astute analysis of Lowry's method and achievement than any similar reading to date in that she dismantles sentimental, romanticized approaches to the novel by demonstrating that the text performs a "remorseless" critique, not only of the brutal aspects of fascism but also of the most seductive features of bourgeois nostalgia and individualism.

With Frederick Asals' lucid discussion of the semiotic system of *Volcano*, the articles in part 2 move farther away from more traditional forms of literary scholarship towards the application of new methodologies to Lowry texts. The necessity for revision led Lowry to develop what Asals describes as a set of techniques through which he created "unsettling lacunae and ghostly presences" in the text, strategic indeterminacies that problematize the narrative, and cunning misreadings of it that become destabilized signifiers within the system." *Volcano*, as Asals observes, is a "semiotician's dream or nightmare." Approaching the ruptures in the text from the perspective of speech-act theory, Joan Mulholland illustrates the centrality of speech acts for a Lowry text, and she goes on to speculate that Lowry's unusual use of them permits him to "cannibalize" life at the same time as he creates a tension and separation between speech and silence, reality and artifice, signifiers and signifieds.

Sue Vice and Donald Jewison work within a wider framework of post-structuralist theory drawn from Bakhtin, Derrida, Jameson, and others in order to address the problems Lowry critics face with his so-called plagiarisms and ambiguous periodization. Both articles argue strongly for a *post*modernist Lowry who liberates discourse, in part through intertextuality, without ever merely playing metafictional games with his reader. Jewison links Lowry with Canetti, Borges, and Eco, thereby reminding us of the deadly serious import of *Volcano*'s interpretation of our modern world. Vice works deftly with its textuality and, like Asals, anticipates the elegant play with texts in part 3.

The studies in part 3 have two things in common: they all deal with post-*Volcano* writing, and they all must face the textual problems that arise from that fact. Probably the most "finished" of the late work is *Hear us O Lord from heaven thy dwelling place*, and it too was published posthumously. Elsa Linguanti argues, however (and few, I think, would disagree with her), that these stories rank near *Volcano* as the finest things Lowry wrote. As does Jewison, she proceeds by isolating the intertextuality at various levels of the discourse: those embedded allusions and passages from extratextual sources that link *Hear us O Lord* with *Volcano* and *Lunar Caustic* constitute the macrotext; those that derive intratextually, from within Lowry's own system, constitute the microtext. The successful "musicating" of these texts is, Linguanti suggests, akin to jazz.

Where Cynthia Sugars works closely with the edited *Dark as the Grave* as published, Victor Doyen returns to the earliest manuscript drafts of *October Ferry to Gabriola* and works forward towards the published novel. To read these articles together creates a strange sense of double exposure, rather like observing the same object through a still projected on a moving shot. Sugars' synchronic reading uncovers an informing structure for Lowry's interrupted text; Doyen's diachronic reading allows us to watch a structure unfold or exfoliate through a sequence of foliations. But the text is always already Lowry's. By taking *Dark as the Grave* seriously *in its own right*, Sugars tells us how to read it as a lesson in *ecdysis* (Lowry's term), while Doyen's meticulous analysis provides a wealth of fascinating evidence for Lowry's incremental creation of those key *topoi* that concern Suzanne Kim and Mark Thomas.

Lowry's poetry presents the Lowryan with some very special problems. On the one hand, it is not earth-shattering; on the other, it has much to tell us about one of the greatest prose stylists of the century. The poems are often impossible to date, embarrassing to read, and apparently plagiarized; certainly, Earle Birney and Margerie Lowry came to a parting of the ways over what was, properly speaking, Lowry's and could be safely published under his name. While not dismissing these problems, Kim and Thomas begin from an entirely different *point de repère*. Using the techniques of genetic criticism, Kim analyses Lowry's creative processes and the significant "figures" within the poems. Not surprisingly, these "figures" are familiar from Lowry's other work, and one constellation of these – the Self – proved virtually fatal for him. Kim reads Lowry as striving for the integration of his "multiplicity of reeling selves" and as unable to achieve release in a Derridean *dissémination*. This is the other side of that coin explored by Vice and Jewison in part 2 and by Doyen in part 3. Thomas returns us to the question of precursors, and his analysis of inter- and intratextuality demonstrates how Lowry remade his sources and carefully constructed an allusive complexity that deliberately opens what Asals (speaking of *Volcano*) calls the breaks or gaps in the text. Like Kim, Thomas does not claim the poetry as high art but as serious literary production.

In part 4, two of the artists who made major contributions to the symposium provide the closing words. Robert Kroetsch, of course, is a master speaker, a master of word-play, a writer who finds in Lowry a kindred spirit. When he delivered the original text of this essay as the symposium's keynote address, his audience was spellbound. Using Lowry's texts, chiefly from *Hear us O Lord*, he weaves the Lowry voice into his own celebration of the anguish and ecstasy of creation; invoking the Lowry spirit, he evokes the *jouissance* of reading, of writing, of being written; he confabulates with Lowry, and with us. Musician, composer, and teacher, Graham Collier discusses the compositional similarities between Lowry's texts and "free jazz" in order to illuminate that some-times obscure but often clear rhythm that runs through everything Lowry wrote. Although his essay cannot recapture the intense excite-ment of the North American première of "The Day of the Dead" at the symposium on the night of 11 May 1987, Collier explains the jazz parallels with Lowry's work, thus enabling the reader to appreciate the power of his prose and something of the fascination he holds for another artist. If Lowry was correct in thinking that "jazz isn't music perhaps so much as a form of expressionism" (see the opening quotation to this introduction), then Collier's extraordinary work would not only have delighted and moved him but also justified this belief.

Quite naturally, on its last page a Lowryan text should return the reader to its beginning, and *Swinging the Maelstrom* begins with Alberto Giro-nella's *El Anís del Consul* (see the frontispiece). Gironella, who has done several mixed-media/collage works inspired by Lowry (one of which is in the private collection of Octavio Paz), designed the cover for Raûl Ortiz y Ortiz's 1964 Spanish translation of *Volcano*.[7] But Gironella is by no means the only painter to be drawn to or inspired by Lowry; perhaps the internationally best-known example is Belgian painter Pierre Ale-chinsky.[8] What is of paramount interest to the literary scholar in these visual responses to Lowry is the painter's relationship with the verbal medium of the novel. Does the painter respond to Lowry's subject, thereby using his text in a manner that parallels Lowry's own thematic use of a painting such as Hieronymous Bosch's *The Prodigal Son* (c 1510)?[9] Or does the painter rework Lowry's imagery in pictorial terms?

Gironella's *El Anís del Consul* responds to both subject and imagery, and then moves beyond these to create a complex, multi-layered pictorial image in which Lowry's *Volcano* functions as a literally collaged inter-text. What Gironella's piece achieves is a fascinating semiotic equivalent to the novel. Fastened between outer and inner frames, and marching around the edge of this large, nearly square composition, are three even rows of round bottle-caps. These caps serve as an ironic "frame" for the central image: visually they mirror the blue and yellow spots on the white ground of the painting, at the same time as they duplicate (their shiny surfaces adding a dizzying suggestion of endless reduplication, of vertigo, that echoes Lowry) the motif of the black ferris wheel. This is Lowry's (and Ezekiel's) wheels taken to their highest power.

At the hub of Gironella's wheel is the Consul's anís – or rather the squared, circular label announcing it. From this dead centre the eye is drawn in a number of directions towards other pieces of the Consul's (and our) world: labels for tequila, for cigarettes ("Alas!" *UV* 52),[10] and signs – BOX, QUAUHNAHUAC. Beginning, then, with one of Lowry's subjects (alcohol) and pictorializing a central Lowry image (the wheel), Gironella goes on to embed Lowry's words within his own text until the painting/collage becomes an intertextual parallel to *Under the Volcano*; as viewers we can read Gironella's work as a gloss on Lowry's text, or, to reverse the process, we can read *Under the Volcano* as embedded in *El Anís del Consul*. But Gironella's infernal machine does not stop there. At the lower right of the inner image we see the jacket cover of the Spanish translation of *Under the Volcano* – the cover originally designed by the painter Alberto Gironella. Above the words *Bajo el Volcán*, in tiny white letters (the smallest font image within the piece) on a black ground we can just make out the sign of the *originary* force behind this intertextual *tour de force*: Malcolm Lowry. By incorporating himself within the painting through this oblique gesture (duplication of cover), Gironella achieves two striking effects. First, he comments intratextually on his own work and his own activity as an artist. Second, he duplicates the Lowry system – its multi-layered intertextuality *and* its obsession with origins, translation, interpretation, and biographical fabulation – to create a subtle and complex semiotic parallel to *Under the Volcano*. From fabulator in his own right, Gironella becomes a Lowry confabulator: he talks with Lowry and us.

Lowry's relation to film, as I suggested earlier, is equally complex. Inspired by many films whose themes, characters, and techniques he wove into his narratives, Lowry and his work have in turn haunted and bedevilled filmmakers. Huston's 1984 *Under the Volcano,* while attempting to capture something of a reputedly filmic novel on the screen, is in many ways a record of John Huston's own passionate involvement (not to mention that of the producers and screenplay writer) with the book and its author. The film is not Lowry's *Volcano*, nor mine or yours, but Huston's, and it reflects his insights, decisions, and responses; it recreates Lowry's Day of the Dead and brings the (a?) Consul back to life while playing out (what Lowry always called, speaking of himself) Huston's and Finney's "hysterical identifications."

But another filmmaker has tackled Lowry and his fiction from an entirely different perspective. In his 1977 National Film Board of Canada documentary *Inquiry into the Life and Death of Malcolm Lowry,* Donald Brittain narrates his exploration of Lowry's private hell while simultaneously incorporating Lowry's fiction into the film through powerful voice-over readings by Richard Burton. The film's impact and success derive from Brittain's skilful layering of fact and fiction, his juxtaposing of violent, expressionistic camera-work and wheeling visual effects, with static interviews, and his disorienting interspersal of matter-of-fact narration and dramatic readings (that only the viewer familiar with the texts will identify immediately as "readings") with a variety of nameless interviewees' voices. The final effect is one of submersion in an overwhelming intertextuality of life and art where the portrait of the man Lowry emerges as an inextricable part of his own and the film-maker's imaginations.

After constant rereadings of Lowry's fiction and an increased understanding of its levels of meaning with the many links to Lowry's life, Graham Collier began composing his Lowry-inspired jazz cantata "The Day of the Dead" in the mid-seventies. The commission to do the piece arrived, according to Collier, at a point in his musical development when he felt he had "found a way of controlling jazz improvisation within a compositional framework."[11] Thus, his "Day of the Dead" provides what Collier describes as "another layer" in the already densely layered composition we call Malcolm Lowry, but it is a layer that includes, while extending beyond, the Lowry-text, thereby translating, transforming, interpreting it in new, exciting ways. After rejecting the temptation to describe or re-create *Volcano* in musical terms, with "solos all round" to convey Lowry's four points of view, Collier claims that what he wanted to create was "the addition of *another layer*" to the jazz (a musical language that is always already layered) by introducing the human voice and words "into the music."

Like Gironella's visual composition, Collier's jazz, itself heavily layered with reprises, voice-overs, and doubling effects achieved by synchronized taping, becomes another intertext in the Lowry macrosystem, and its creator another confabulator. And it is this that Collier, Gironella, and Brittain (to a lesser extent Huston) have in common: despite their different and non-verbal media, each begins with Lowry's language, with the semiotic richness of his words, the rhythms of his sentences, the proliferating associations of his images, the exquisite parataxis of his discourse and of his narrative forms; and each introduces the Lowry voice/text into the new work.

The danger of Lowry's attraction for another writer is, of course, much greater than for the composer or the painter. Whether the impulse is merely to allude to a Lowry text or to identify with and emulate the author and his style, the writer runs the risk of being cannibalized by Lowry, of being absorbed in the labyrinth of Lowry's imagination or trapped by his or her own "hysterical identifications." There are, however, two distinct categories of Lowry inheritors. The first comprises those who have been influenced by him to one degree or another, those whose work bears a sign, a trace of Lowry's presence along with the signs of other great writers who are part of the tradition. Robert Kroetsch, David Markson, Russell Haley, Tony Cartano, and John Williams represent this type of literary inheritor, but Gabriel Garcia Marquez perhaps speaks for them all when he protests that, having read *Volcano* more often than other books, he would prefer never to read it again, "but I know that is impossible because I will never rest until I have discovered where its magic is hidden."[12] For many writers today Lowry and his fictions have become part of the imagination's baggage and touchstones for a host of associations.

It is the second category of Lowry literary inheritor, however, who interests me here. Like the painter, composer, and filmmaker, this writer is a confabulator. He or she is, moreover, a confabulator in the full sense of the word. The primary meaning of confabulate is to converse, discuss, talk together with, but in psychiatry confabulation also designates the replacement of a gap in memory by a verbal falsification that the subject accepts as correct. Lowry's literary confabulators (beginning with his own eponymous heroes) not only converse with Lowry; they also re-create him. Their con*fabulations* of Lowry fill the gap in their and our memories by adding to the fictions/falsifications that we accept as somehow *correct*.

This confabulating began with Charlotte Haldane and Jan Gabrial, continued with Conrad Aiken and Al Purdy, and has reached new heights of independent artistic and literary complexity in the last decade.[13] In his 1984 play *Goodnight Disgrace* Michael Mercer reimagines a young Lowry haunting the memory, filling the narrative gaps in the life of an ailing, aging, and forgotten Aiken in two acts largely devoted to Aiken's reluctant recollections of their increasingly sinister confabulations. Whatever reasons Mercer may have had for this approach (his own interviews of Aiken clearly left him with feelings of ambivalence and guilt), the play explores that Freudian "anxiety of influence" anatomized by Harold Bloom. Mercer's Lowry seeks to devour and supplant his elder and mentor; he is the Oedipal artist (like Aiken's Hambo) par excellence, the embodiment of Aiken's most secret desire and fear – the "son" who will take over his characters, his themes, and his language until he writes the "father" out of existence. In the final moments of the play Mercer's Lowry summarizes their relationship "*quietly, coldly*": "I've absorbed you. I've killed you finally, drained from you all the knowledge you were unable to use ... for lack of courage or conscious-ness. Or, even, perversely enough, by your own design. Because, after it's over ... and you've always known it as much as you feared it ... I will be the one they remember. I am as much their tragic flaw as I am yours. And I will make art of it."[14]

Victor-Lévy Beaulieu's Lowry is also the Oedipal artist, but within a much more duplicitous, metafictional structure. From his essays and reviews collected in *Entre la sainteté et le terrorisme* (1984), Beaulieu makes it clear that Lowry is one of his own kindred spirits and that, like Marquez, he accepts the fact that, with *Volcano*, "on ne finit jamais la lecture."[15] One essay from 1970 (though it is scarcely an essay so much as a double commentary), called "Melville-pot en finale Lowry," jux-taposes Beaulieu's observations on Melville with those on Lowry, quot-ing from each, setting one voice off against the other (and both against his own) in a miniature example of the narrative strategy he would use for his extraordinary biographical fiction *Monsieur Melville*. In the essay Beaulieu remarks that *Dark as the Grave* is the work "que j'aime le mieux puisqu'il est déjà tout plein de mort" (*Entre la sainteté*, 193). In *Monsieur Melville* he creates a fictional Lowry who doubles as Meville's "camar-ade" and his son, Malcolm.[16]

Malcolm Lowry is by no means the only author with whom Monsieur Melville converses – Flaubert and Hawthorne appear at greater length, in fact – but his first name affords him a special importance for Melville/ Beaulieu. At times, of course, the actual son (Melville's first son, Mal-colm) appears in his own right, but when Beaulieu brings his Melville, via discussion of Redburn, to Liverpool, filial identities blur. Touring the city with his "camarade Lowry" (143), Monsieur Melville reflects: "Le Liverpool de Père n'existait plus. Un autre Liverpool avait pris la place. Et si un jour mon fils Malcolm devait entreprendre le meme voyage, il n'y verrait pas davantage que moi: le monde se meurt et le fils ne plus rester le fils. Il devient le Père ou il se tire une balle dans la tête" (144). Son/friend/inheritor/precursor – Beaulieu's Melville's Lowry can be seen (by Melville, by Beaulieu, *en finale* by us) from time to time in the voyaging, in the dying, in the confabulating of this strange text that inscribes, with terrible precision, Lowry's own "hys-terical identification" with Herman Melville and echoes Lowry's remark to Jonathan Cape that he was firing "a shot" that would "probably go straight through my brain" (see the quotation on page 15).

Together with the novelists and playwrights, poets have often attempted to address, invoke, celebrate, or lay to rest the ghost of Malcolm Lowry. In his 1983 volume *Die Einsamkeit der Männer, Mexikanische Sonnette* (*Lowry-Lieder*), Wolf Wondratschek follows the steps of Lowry and his Consul through the Mexican landscape of *Volcano*.[17] Sometimes the poet addresses these characters of his own imagining, but at others he overhears them (as Laruelle did) when they – Geoffrey and Yvonne – address Lowry; occasionally Wondratschek speaks directly to Lowry as a brother, a *Doppelgänger* ("Fliehende sind wir, die sich festhalten," 14). But Lowry's only response is: "Ich, Malcolm Lowry, habe nie gelebt"(36). Wondratschek's Lowry Lieder celebrate not so much the writer's achievement as the man's life and death – his drinking, his loneliness, his betrayals, and his self-destruction.

Sharon Thesen, whose title supplies my concept of "confabulation," creates a very different Lowry. In her 1984 volume of poetry *Confabulations: Poems for Malcolm Lowry*, which she read to symposium delegates and guests before Collier's "Day of the Dead" première, Thesen *talks with* Lowry as artist, and in the process she adds "another layer," introduces another voice into the conversation. Daring to meet Lowry on his own ground – the word – she articulates both his need and her own, but in her own voice, as well as his:

Language the mask –
pelado – peeled –
now it takes me
up to a whole afternoon
to find the word I need.[18]

The result is less an absorption, let alone a killing-off, of the precursor, so much as a dialogue, a talking together with, a double-voicing, and a filling of the gap in memory that we accept as never-ending. Thesen's poems, like Gironella's art and Collier's music, textualize Lowry, constructing him in languages – verbal, pictorial, musical – contextualizing him by inserting his texts into their own, which in turn become part of an expanding Lowry-text.

Language is the key to Lowry. He was obsessed with words and with the anxieties of verbal influence from other writers. Being extraordinarily sensitive to the multiplicity of voices surrounding him from literary tradition (Shakespeare, Chaucer, Marlowe, Coleridge, Melville, Tolstoy, O'Neill, Poe, Kafka, Cocteau, Baudelaire) and in his immediate milieu (in newspapers, bars, films, music, painting, or the inconsequential sign or document), he transformed these voices and his "hysterical identifications" into art. As a result, his writing is an orchestration of voices within the fictions created by his protagonists. On one level, all Lowry's heroes (even the Consul) are writers – writers who fear they are being written, writer-characters in search of their author, writers whose story is life itself, and writers "who are no de wrider [but] de espider" (*UV* 371)! Like the Spanish philosopher José Ortega y Gasset, whose work he admired, Lowry believed that the best image for man was that of the novelist who makes up his life as he goes along.[19]

To read Lowry, then, is to enter a world where art and life overlap, a universe full of voices, and a system where the writer is continually reborn within his own story. In this manner Lowry at once lays to rest the ghosts of his own identifications, does homage to, elegizes, eulogizes, confabulates with others, and constitutes himself. He does, with consummate skill, what others are now doing with him. His work is always about the layers of language – *pelado* – about writing and being written, about origins and the nature of the imagination.

When he wrote to Jonathan Cape in that exegetical letter of 1946, he insisted that "in our Elizabethan days we used to have at least passionate poetic writing about things that will always mean something and not just silly ass style and semi-colon technique: and in this sense I am trying to remedy a deficiency, to strike a blow, to fire a shot as it were, roughly in the direction of ... another Renaissance: it will probably go straight through my brain but that is another matter" (*SL* 80). The Renaissance, however, has taken a form he could not have foreseen or predicted, for in the writing and the reading of these confabulations and interpretations, it is Lowry's words that are reborn as we improvise another phrase in *Swinging the Maelstrom* and participate in an ongoing interpretation of the modern world.

NOTES

1 This passage is from an unpublished letter to Robert Giroux, 11 Jan. 1952, in the Lowry Collection, and I would like to thank Stefan Haag for bringing it to my attention.

2 See Schulz-Keil's article "The 67th Reading: *Under the Volcano* and Its Screenplays," *Apparently Incongruous Parts: The Worlds of Malcolm Lowry*, ed. Paul Tiessen (Metuchen, NJ: Scarecrow Press 1990), 129–45, and *The Cinema of Malcolm Lowry: A Scholarly Edition of Lowry's "Tender is the Night,"* ed. Miguel Mota and Paul Tiessen (Vancouver: UBC Press 1990).

3 For the assistance of readers, the Cape (1965) and Putnam (1969) publications of the *Letters* are reprints of the original with identical pagination.

4 The first Lowry Collection inventory was compiled by Judith O. Combs in 1973. Since that time the library has acquired many additions to the

collection, and a new inventory incorporating the Combs material was produced in 1985: *Malcolm Lowry 1909–1957: An Inventory to the Malcolm Lowry Collection in the Library of the University of British Columbia, Special Collections Divisions*, prepared by Judith O. Combs (1973), revised by Cynthia Sugars (1985).

5 Lowry's first version of the novella about New York's Bellevue Hospital was called "The Last Address"; when he revised it during the early forties, he called it "Swinging the Maelstrom" (a title for a jazz composition which he used again in "Forest Path"), thereby shifting attention to his musician protagonist's profession and to a comparative note of hope. By 1946 he had settled on the title *Lunar Caustic*, but he did not live to complete his combinations of the two versions and their revision for *The Voyage That Never Ends*. See Douglas Day's description of the text in *Malcolm Lowry* (New York: Oxford University Press 1973), 197–99, and my discussion of its place in the *Voyage* in *The Voyage That Never Ends: Malcolm Lowry's Fiction* (Vancouver: UBC Press 1982), 13–14.

6 I owe the discovery of this word to Sharon Thesen's volume *Confabulations: Poems for Malcolm Lowry* (Lantzville, BC: Oolichan Books 1984). In these poems Thesen skilfully explores the primary sense of the term "to talk together" and its other associations, which I discuss below; therefore, since my first reading of these poems early in 1985, "confabulation" has come to signify for me a central concept in Lowryan discourse.

7 I would like to thank Alberto Gironella for his kind permission to reproduce *El Anís del Consul* in *Swinging the Maelstrom* and for the information he has supplied about his work in our correspondence.

8 The best English discussion of Alechinsky is *Pierre Alechinsky*, by the artist, with an introduction by Eugène Ionesco, trans. Michael Fineberg (New York: Harry N. Abrams 1977). As a man steeped in art history and literature, Alechinsky is fascinated by words, texts, and allusions that, together with his strong COBRA-like (he was a close friend of Asger Jorn's and an associate of the group) colours and images, constitute his distinctively postmodern, neo-expressionist style. Wandering Jew, left-handed painter of hallucinatory canvasses, jazz enthusiast, "joker and ontologist," writer/poet, Belgian-living-in-exile-in-France, visitor to Niagara Falls, to Mexico, to New York, etc., erudite, allusive, ironic, and fascinated by volcanoes – Alechinsky is the quintessential Lowry artist. An example of Alechinsky's work inspired by *Under the Volcano* is *The Shadow of Malcolm Lowry* in the Modern Art Museum in Mexico, and he misquotes the Consul in the margins of his 1965 *Central Park*, the first work with the cartoon-like marginalia for which he has become famous; he writes: "(As Malcolm Lowry said: Everything's in Brer Rabbit.)" It is, in fact, the Consul who "liked to say 'Everything is to be found in Peter Rabbit'" (*UV* 178), but one imagines Lowry being pleased with the painter's altera-

tion. Gironella, a friend of Alechinsky's, shows the influence of the Belgian painter in his techniques, and they have exhibited together on several occasions, most recently in 1982.

9 For a discussion of Lowry's use of this painting as a *mise en abîme*, see my article "'An assembly of apparently incongruous parts': Intertextuality in Lowry's 'Through the Panama,'" in Tiessen, *Apparently Incongruous Parts*, 187–228.

10 All references are to the 1963 Penguin edition of *Under the Volcano*.

11 This and following quotations of Collier are taken from the record jacket for *The Day of the Dead* (London: Mosaic Records 1978).

12 In a letter to me dated 14 Feb. 1984 Paul Tiessen confirms Ronald Binns's discovery of the following advertising blurb in the 1981 Bruguera paperback edition of the Ortiz translation of *Volcano*: "*Bajo el Volcán* es tal vez la novela que más veces he leído en mi vida. Quisiera no leerla más, pero sé que no será posible, porque no descansaré hasta descubrir dónde está su magia escondida. Gabrial Garcia Marquez." See also Tony Cartano's *Malcolm Lowry: Essai* (Paris: Henri Veyrier 1979) and two of his novels, *Le Singe hurleur* (1978) and *Le Conquistador* (1973); William New's "Russell Haley's Lowry," *Malcolm Lowry Newsletter* 4 (Spring 1979): 20–2; and John Williams' comment in *Interviews with Black Writers*, ed. John O'Brien (New York: Liveright 1973), 233: "In terms of form, my single influence has been Malcolm Lowry in *Under the Volcano*. I tried to emulate him in *Sissie* and improve on what he did with the telescoping of time. But I think I did it much better in *The Man Who Cried I Am*."

13 To the best of my knowledge these re-creations of Lowry began well before his death with Charlotte Haldane's novel *I Bring Not Peace* (1932), Jan Gabrial's story "Not with a Bang," *Story* 24 (Sept. – Oct. 1946): 55–61, and Conrad Aiken's *Ushant* (1952). Canadian poet Al Purdy has evoked Lowry in poems and fiction, as have Vancouver writers William McConnell and Frances Duncan.

14 *Goodnight Disgrace* (Vancouver: Talonbooks 1986), 111. Mercer calls for a non-realistic production and sets with slide projections and drumbeats to reinforce the central situation: Aiken, dying in a retirement home, is haunted in his final days by this character/son/usurper "Malcolm Lowry."

15 "Sur Malcolm Lowry," *Entre la sainteté et le terrorisme* (Montréal: VLB éditeur 1984), 329. In "Melville-pot en finale Lowry," 189–94, Beaulieu praises *Dark as the Grave* for its "conscience," "morale," and "théorème": "C'est ainsi que *Sombre comme la tombe où repose mon ami* est un grand livre, peut-être celui de Lowry que j'aime le mieux piusqu'il est déjà tout plein de mort." I would like to thank my colleague Eva-Marie Kröller for bringing Beaulieu's enthusiasm for Lowry to my attention.

16 *Monsieur Melville*, 3 vols. (Montréal: VLB éditeur 1978). Further references are included in the text.

17 *Die Einsamkeit der Männer* (Zürich: Diogenes Verlag 1983); for a discussion of the volume, see Stefan Haag's review in the *Malcolm Lowry Review* 21–2 (Fall 1987–Spring 1988): 113–20.

18 Thesen, *Confabulations*, 23. My review of *Confabulations*, accompanied by a reproduction of Ron Bolt's lithograph *The Cape Sable Man,* which carries a Lowry quotation, appeared in the *Malcolm Lowry Review* 17–18 (1985–86): 59–66 and in *Essays on Canadian Writing* 34 (Spring 1987): 18–23.

19 I discuss Lowry's debt to Ortega in "'Consciousness of Shipwreck': Ortega y Gasset and Malcolm Lowry's Concept of the Artist," *José Ortega y Gasset,* ed. Nora de Marval-McNair (New York: Greenwood Press 1987), 137–42.

PART ONE

Lowry and the Fiction of Life

Not with a Bang*

JAN GABRIAL

In 1945, some eight years after I left Mexico and five years after filing for divorce from Malcolm Lowry, working from notes made during our ultimate weeks together, I wrote "Not with a Bang." The scene in the hotel room took place as written and the dialogue was ours. The episode of the puppy was indeed part of that cataclysmic night, though the drama in the bar is fictional, and Malcolm somehow divested himself of his sad-eyed, misbegotten little dog.

In spite of Arthur Calder-Marshall's fanciful account of a robbery-that-never-occurred, our house in Cuernavaca was totally gutted of all save manuscripts and Malc's grungier apparel. Deprived of clothes, typewriter, and even bed-linen, devoid of funds for their replacement, and with Malcolm on a binge of discouraging proportions, I saw no escape but to seek work. When offered a post as editorial assistant in a Hollywood agency, I snapped at it, neither of us recognizing then that such severance might prove terminal.

As for Malcolm, unready to relinquish the locale of his nascent book, he had fixated on Oaxaca, perhaps because Lawrence, an early and important influence, once lived there. For some while I continued urging that he join me, pleas duly modified by continuing reports of his intemperance and incarcerations in the carcels of Oaxaca. From Malc himself I'd received only a bombardment of wires and letters threatening suicide should I fail to discard my job and wamble back to Mexico. But warnings such as these had punctuated our relationship. With over-use their devastating power had been muted. As Malcolm's tequila-laden rampages continued unabated, my resolution firmed: life on his terms could only plunge us both into his engulfing alcoholic seas. Travel had been my escape mechanism of choice: to trade it for a progression of lost weekends was not good enough.

Though there was never an actual break, our union disintegrated as we drifted through succeeding months, and drifting, shed old loyalties. Love was still there, but encrusted now by bitterness and pain. In 1940, when our divorce was finalized, Malcolm remarried, consigning me to limbo. Not until *Under the Volcano*, conceived and fleshed during our stormy year in Mexico, would I again meet the man who had so captivated me in Granada that distant May of 1933.

His incandescent love letters, passionate, whimsical, and lyrical – a few only several lines in length, others ten pages long – echo the morning years we knew together and keep alive the memories we once shared.

J.G. (1990)

A sound of fumbling and stumbling and shuffling began outside the door (all her life Catherine would associate such sounds with Michael) and her heart pounded wearily, and she turned in the bed, her mouth half open in protest and her brows drawn close together.

A key was fitted into the lock and then the door swung inward and two bellboys appeared, half propping Michael up between them. They stared roundly and sheepishly at her, the pale hair covering her shoulders, the robe on the other pillow.

"Here is the Señor," one of them said proudly. "Here he is once more Señora, the Señor."

Michael drew himself up and flung them off, straightening his shoulders with drunken dignity. "What the hell do you think you're doing?" he shouted, and stalked over and sat heavily on the bed.

Catherine roughed back her hair with one hand and the other bellboy said confidentially, "We could hardly push the Mister into the elevator."

"That's a goddam lie," Michael said. His mouth was heavy and loose in his swollen face.

Catherine looked in between the bellboys and said carefully, "Thanks very much. He'll be all right now. You can go."

"Just a proper tin Jesus, aren't you?" Michael said.

The bellboys bowed and swung out.

"I might have known it," Catherine said without bitterness. "I might have known the one night I'm tired enough to go to sleep at nine o'clock I'd be honored by a visit. I haven't any money, if that's what you want. We're out of money. We don't get a check until tomorrow. Tuesday, remember? You get your father's checks on Tuesdays."

Michael stared at her analytically. His sea-blue eyes were almost buried in the liquored flush of his cheeks. "A wife," he said. "A wife is a legally kept woman who eats you out of house and home. So I have to have a wife."

"It's the luxury of it," Catherine said. "After you hocked both my working cameras, I settled back into a life of ease." She waved her hand around the disordered room. "Mexico City," she said. "The Paris of the Western Hemisphere."

"You're a great woman," Michael said extravagantly. "You're the greatest woman in the world, but why the hell do I have to listen to you?"

"I'm the tiredest woman in the world," Catherine said. "Period."

"Tired!" Michael echoed. "Tired, oh my God!"

"Why don't you come to bed?" she asked him reasonably. "Why don't you get some sleep?"

"Sleep?" Michael said, shuddering. "But that I should answer a cry of yours with a counter cry must show you how fast nailed I am to the eagle-baffling mountain."

She sighed and edged down further in the bed. "Night life," she said. "I don't know how I do it. Last night you came in at one, the night before you came in at five, the night before that you didn't come in and I waited for you. If it means anything," she said, studying him gravely, "you look like Saint Sebastian when they'd been shooting arrows at him."

"I feel like Saint Sebastian," Michael said, "when he was very dead."

He had been holding his coat bunched up on one side, and now he drew it apart and peered within and turned back to her and laid a finger on his lips. "Don't talk so loud," he said warningly. "You must be very quiet. It's asleep."

She was beginning to shiver in the badly heated room. As she reached for her robe she watched him. His face had taken on a look that was profound and sly. "It's asleep," he said again, very tenderly.

A feeble wheeze came from beneath his coat, belying him.

"Michael," said Catherine, "what have you got there? What is it, Michael?"

He smiled gently at the coat and her heart contracted.

"It's a dog. A little, little, little dog who is cold and tireder than you will ever know how to be."

He opened his coat and laid on the bed beside her a small black-and-white puppy, a few weeks old, a puppy with black ears and a black nose and nervous, agonized black eyes. It lay where he had put it, shivering.

"A man on the street," Michael said thickly, "was selling it. I bought it for you."

The puppy had started to sniff about the bed; suddenly it planted its four small legs more firmly. Catherine snatched it up and dropped it on the floor, where it whimpered loudly.

"Look," Catherine said, "you don't have to sleep here. You practically never sleep here. I do."

"It's such a little, little dog," Michael repeated.

"It isn't a question of size," Catherine said. "It's a question of I have to sleep in this bed and they only change them once a week."

"You are a bitch," Michael said violently. He bent over and picked up the puppy and held it in his arms. "It's everything I have in the world to love," he said. "Everything I have in the world and that's all I have. My wife is a legally kept woman who is only after what she can get, with an eye on every man who passes."

Catherine put both hands to her head and shut her eyes. "There are all kinds of women," she said harshly. "Some of them like dogs. Some of them like husbands. I'm funny that way. I don't want a small dog that isn't housebroken in place of a husband whose whereabouts I don't know for days at a time."

She was beginning to cry inside and she knew that the need was there, as it was always there; that she wanted Michael, wanted his nearness and his tenderness. But he wouldn't give her that. He would give her a dog, a symbol, saying in effect, "This innocent, helpless, gentle creature is your husband Michael; look after it and mop up after it and cherish it and give it your protection."

"Michael," she said, "oh but Michael, don't you see – "

But he was already getting up, bundling the puppy back underneath his coat, swaying a little on his feet.

"I love you," he told her with excessive firmness. "God damn it, how I love you, because you are a wonderful woman. I am not doing anything destructive. If you would only understand that I am not doing anything destructive."

He began to make his way carefully toward the door.

"Michael," Catherine said remorsefully, "stay, Michael. We'll keep the dog. Don't go."

He didn't answer her. He pulled the door open, teetered back on his heels for a second, then strode out into the hall, slamming the door upon her.

When he had gone Catherine sat in the bed, very still, feeling as though the world had gone away and left her in emptiness.

The picture of him striding out the door, with his face set and lonely, rose up a dozen times so that the empty, quiet room was filled with Michaels, turning in misery from her on her seat of judgment.

And crying a little with weariness and pity, she thrust the covers away and slid from bed.

When she went out of the hotel, the bellboys stared at her, and the night clerk half leaned across his desk as if to ask her to call upon his competence. But she pushed through the doors of the hotel into the bitter night of the Avenue of the Fifth of May, and stood, holding her coat about her face, deliberating: just where would Michael be?

A list of bars had formed within her mind and one after another she visited them: the hotel bar, a near-by saloon, Mac's, Paolo's, Butch's Manhattan Café. Michael had been to none.

Then she remembered a cantina they had sometimes gone to, in the small streets back of the Teatro Nacional, where children lay at night, huddled upon the pavements, with posters torn from the walls and newspapers gathered from the gutters piled over them for a memory of the warmth of sunlight. She hailed a cab and gave the address of the Maria y Marta.

Her emotions were suspended within her now, suspended in anxiety like a foetus in alcohol, stillborn, insistent, waiting. The night took on an unreal quality and the taxi, as if in a dream, sighed through the streets of the great quiet city.

As it pulled up she saw Michael sitting on the pavement a little to one side of the cheerlessly lighted entrance, his coat bundled beside him. His head was in his hands and he looked forlorn and somehow inevitable, as though all the days of his life had prepared him for this moment of sitting on a curb on this street of violence and tragedies, as though there were no further place for him to go, as though the pages stopped here and there wasn't any more.

Catherine walked over and touched his shoulder; he didn't move, didn't raise his head.

"Michael," she said, and squatted down beside him.

When his white gaze had focused on her he stared, but he still said nothing.

"You'll be cold," she said. "Put on your coat, you'll be cold. I followed you, Michael," she said, putting her hands upon his knees, trying to hold his stare. "Why do we do these things? why do we do them to each other, Michael?"

"You're a good person, Cathy," Michael said. "But you can't tie the wind to a cliff. The rock has claimed your Sisyphus."

"Michael," she urged him, "oh Michael, please. I get so desperate. I'm lonely. You shut me away from you."

His brow puckered and his voice came faint and lost, bewildered. "I?" he said. "I shut you away? Oh, little Cathy, oh, God, help me then."

"I can make you happy if you'll let me," she cried out to him. "I can. I have. I don't know why I want to go on doing it, but let me, Michael, try."

But he shook his head, so slowly that every movement seemed to cost a tremendous effort. "It isn't any good," he said. "The trimmers, not good enough for heaven, poor devils, not bad enough for hell. It isn't any use."

"Oh, Michael, you're so *wrong*," Catherine said desperately. But he had set his face backward in time.

"Michael," she said, speaking now very softly to him. "Michael darling, remember the good things, the good parts of our life together: our winter in Taos; the old reading rooms in the library where we worked; the party Ben gave for your first book of poems; Martha's Vineyard, where you taught me to play tennis ... Oh, Michael, all of it, like a tapestry – you can't renounce it, it's woven all through us. It's a part of us."

Michael's hands covered hers. His finger tips were icy. "The hotel room at Lake Patzcuaro." Now he was looking at her.

Her laughter pleaded with him. "And when we turned, the bed sighed like a wind, and we could see the butterfly boats out on the lake."

"Tzintsuntzan," Michael said. "Place of the Humming Birds."

He caught up her hands and put them across his eyes. She could feel tears behind them. They might have been children abandoned together in hostility.

"Won't you come home now?" she asked almost humbly. "Won't you come home at last? I can't go on asking you, Michael. Please come with me; we won't talk about anything that's happened."

He sighed and she could feel the tortured breath against her wrists. And then he put her hands away from him.

She waited, and she could feel him going past her, the moment going past.

"No," he said. "No," clinging to this resistance because resistance meant that he was still a man. "No," he said then more loudly like a child.

She let her hands fall in between her knees. "Well, put your coat on. Please put your coat on anyhow."

He looked down at his coat. "The little dog," he whispered. "It's asleep."

She had forgotten about the dog. She started to open the folds of the coat, but he checked her, trembling. "No," he protested. "No. Don't you understand, it's asleep. You must let it be asleep."

"It must be smothering, Michael. Let me just look at it."

She pulled the folds back and the little dog, its head on its paws, peered at her, moaning plaintively.

"It isn't asleep," Catherine said. "Michael, it's sick."

"It's asleep, I say. Oh, damn you, it's asleep."

She laid her hand on the dog and was shocked at the cold tremors of its body. "Michael, feel it yourself, it's too chilly for it here. Take it into the bar, then. Please, Michael, take it inside, please."

"I love it," Michael said, beginning to break, his voice beginning to break, to sing with tears. "It's all I have to love. I'm all it has. It's my little dog," he sobbed. "It's my little dog. I love it."

"You have me," Catherine said. "Don't you know you have me, Michael?"

"You?" he said. "But you want it to die. You want everything I've ever loved to die. You've always wanted it. God and I and the pigeon who is the eye of God, we see through everything, we see through you."

She tried to pick up the dog but he struck her hand away. "Let it alone," he shouted. "Let it alone, you hear? You think you can control me, don't you? You think you can manage me, don't you? You think I don't see it? Well, let me tell you, I know everything. Because I am a great person, you see? I am a great person, all my life I am a great person, even though the stupid, mealymouthed crumbling little bellboy people will want to destroy me for it." He grew a little quieter. "You are a great person too," he said, "but you waste yourself. God, how you waste yourself!"

"Oh, all right, then," Catherine said. "So I waste myself. But take the dog inside, anyhow. Or put your coat on. Or something, Michael, *please.*"

"Oh, to hell with your chatter," Michael said, stumbling to his feet. "Chatter, babble, chatter, babble, that's all you do." He gathered up his coat, holding it and the dog closely beneath his arm, and scowling and muttering, staggered into the bar.

After a moment Catherine followed him.

It was a small cantina that had seen several murders and that stank of urine. Four booths lined one wall and there were scattered tables in the center; unshaded bulbs glared from the ceiling. Michael went directly to the bar and put down his coat upon it and summoned the bartender.

"Tequila," he said loudly. Then he looked at the man next to him and put an arm on his shoulder. "And one for my friend here. Two."

The man had a stubble of beard and wore the blue jeans of a workman. He looked surprised but pleased, and he smiled at Michael ingratiatingly.

Catherine sat at a small table that was near by. I could use a drink, she thought. I don't have to get drunk but I could certainly use a drink in the worst way.

"Parras," she called, and the barman brought her a small glass and a larger one that held carbonated water. She looked about her as she drank the liquor.

It was early but there were already a few people there. Michael was pointedly ignoring her, but at a near-by table a dark good-looking man, probably half Indian, was staring with interest, and when he caught her glance he smiled.

She looked away, but the man's face stayed in her mind, hanging there in the foreground of her thoughts like the grin of the Cheshire cat.

I could show Michael, she thought. It would help me to put up with Michael and I might get a night's sleep for a change. I could show Michael, she thought again, bitter because he had resisted her when she was open to him. Then she thought, I'm really too tired to drink. So I'd get back at Michael. I'd wake up tomorrow in a strange room with a guy I couldn't talk to. It isn't much good if you can't talk to him afterward. I ought to know.

She knocked on the table and the bartender brought her another drink. The dark man was looking at her half expectantly. She frowned at him, and his glance grew hurt and surprised, and he looked abruptly away. There, that was that. She had frowned at him.

Michael was telling the man at the bar that he had flown in the Battle of Britain. Every time he gets drunk enough he flies in the Battle of Britain, she thought; it's a substitute for action. He always comes down in flames because even his visions must be couched in self-destruction.

Then as she looked at him, she noticed with an awakening shock that while his right hand, holding his glass, was waving, his left hand and arm were leaning on the coat. And she was sure that in that moment she could hear the pitiful gasping whimper from within. She set down her glass and ran up to the bar.

"Let me alone," cried Michael as she tugged at his arm. "Let me alone," he cried, suspecting fresh rebuke, and he pressed his left hand more firmly on the coat.

The puppy was suffocating; she could hear its gasps, its long faint struggling breaths.

"The dog" she said. "The dog, Michael – you're hurting it, Michael, you're choking it!"

He raised his left arm then and struck her; the back of his hand caught her across the neck so that she staggered backward and grabbed at a chair to save herself from falling.

The man in the blue jeans seized Michael's arm, looking shocked and unhappy.

While they were struggling, Catherine flung back the top folds of the coat; the puppy was shaking terribly; suffering stood out in every line of its tiny feeble body; its mouth was open, and its eyes – looking at nothing – were partly shut and dull; the piteous sounds came irregularly from its small wet throat.

"It's dying," Catherine cried, feeling the horror in her. "Michael – it's dying – don't you understand?"

"It's thirsty," Michael said desperately. "That's all, it's thirsty. Water!" He turned to the bartender. "A little water," he called, "for my little dog."

But as the puzzled bartender turned for the water, with the other man standing watchful in case Michael should break out once more, the puppy struggled and its head sank forward against the roughness of the coat; the noises ceased, and it lay still, and alien.

"It's asleep now," Michael said. "Never mind the water."

"Michael," Catherine whispered, "don't you see – it's dead."

"That's a damned lie!" Michael shouted in agony and loathing. "It's asleep, I tell you! Look!"

She gazed in desperation at the bartender. He touched it and looked at Michael firmly. "*Muerto*," said the bartender. "Dead. Dead, Señor. Yes."

Michael's mouth opened childishly. He looked as though he were about to cry. "But I loved it," he insisted, as though that could make all the difference. "It's my little dog. I was going to look after it."

Catherine turned her white face toward him and stared at him, at all the things in him she had cherished, which had grown stretched and loose in his flight headlong from the meaning of his life, his backward flight to a lost world on which the walls of history were closing.

And she thought. Already it is happening to me. I catch myself thinking that if I sleep with the man in the dark shirt I can get back at you.

He turned on her, his voice harsh with his own fear. "You wanted it to die," he stammered, "you want to destroy everything that loves me, you think I don't know – "

The dark man at the table had risen, as if in readiness; the man in the blue jeans was standing watchful; the bartender looked tense. But Catherine stared dispassionately at Michael, as though he were an enemy whose strength she was now gauging to protect herself.

" – You think I don't know you are destroying *me!*"

One day all of it cracks, just like this, and falls away, and you discover yourself enmeshed in a jelly of pity for the man you married, and making that your life ...

"But God and I," Michael said, "and the pigeon who is the eye of God – "

She walked over to the table and put down the payment for her drinks. Then she went out into the street without another look at him.

She wanted to think ahead to life, but the thoughts wouldn't come.

And then, across the surface of her mind – I hope they don't steal Michael's coat ...

She stopped, staring before her into the night. But I don't have to worry about that any more, she told herself. I don't have to worry about Michael any more at all.

And harshly, violently, she began to cry, because she knew that the boat that was Michael had slipped its moorings in her life, and was even now putting out to the darker sea to which she could not follow him.

"A Norwegian at Heart": Lowry and the Grieg Connection

HALLVARD DAHLIE

From his transforming of his maternal grandfather into a Norwegian sea captain, through his enigmatic relationship with the Norwegian writer Nordahl Grieg, to his utilization of Norwegian names, words, and phrases in many of his works, Lowry from the outset of his career demonstrated a fascination with elements of the Nordic world. Sigbjørn Wilderness's plight in "Through the Panama" of an "Englishman who is a Scotchman who is Norwegian who is a Canadian who is a Negro at heart"[1] can with little modification be applied to Lowry himself, for he frequently addressed himself, both whimsically and seriously, to the question of his own nationality, which from time to time manifested itself in his seeing himself as "a Norwegian at heart." Obviously, in a writer as complex and inconsistent as Lowry, this element is but one of many and offers in itself no simplistic key to his works, but it recurs consistently enough to warrant a closer look.

In this examination I want chiefly to look at the relationship between Lowry and Grieg, which to this day presents more unanswered questions than absolute facts. Grieg's own works, his letters, and the recollections others have of him give some indication of the nature of this man and help to explain the bases of Lowry's attraction to him. That Grieg's *The Ship Sails On* had a strong impact on Lowry's *Ultramarine* has long been recognized, and I have dealt with this elsewhere,[2] but it is worth noting that Lowry's use of Norwegian in this novel, which he did not borrow from Grieg, both underscores the novel's realism and embodies an aesthetic experiment that anticipates the stylistic qualities of some of his later works.

The extent of the "Norwegianness" of Lowry, as is true of many of the supposed facts of this man's life and career, remains in the area of speculation, and there are many questions to which there are no firm answers. When did his interest in things Norwegian first begin? When did he learn the Norwegian language? Was there a Norwegian ancestry on his mother's side? Where and when did he meet Nordahl Grieg? If he did meet him, why would he not inform his family or his close friends of this experience? All we know for a fact – that is, if we can believe what Lowry said in his letter to Grieg (SL 15–16) – is that he received a letter from him sometime in 1931 and that there were some "extraordinary coincidences which led up to [their] meeting." If the two in fact did meet, why did he not on that occasion tell him about these coincidences, instead of saying that he wished he could someday tell him about them? Even if Lowry knew little or no Norwegian at the time, Grieg was totally proficient in English, so there would have been no language barrier between them.

If we accept that they did meet, the question of where and when has not been clearly resolved. Margerie Lowry's 1962 statement for the revised edition of *Ultramarine* – that Malcolm went to Norway in the summer of 1930 – seems to constitute a starting-point for every critic who has addressed this issue, although there are different versions of just how these two writers got together.[3] There is general agreement that Lowry signed on as a fireman aboard a Norwegian freighter bound for Norway, but some have this ship bound for Oslo while others have it heading for Archangel. In this latter case they apparently depended on Margerie Lowry's biographical account as given to Lippincott, which represents a modification of Lowry's 1951 comments to David Markson: "The ship never reached Archangel; they stopped at a small town in northern Norway, Aalesund, hoping to take on cargo; the captain failed in this and the crew was paid off. While in this town Malcolm learned that Nordahl Grieg was living under an assumed name in Oslo. So he went by train to Oslo, where he met Grieg by another coincidence, and they became fast friends."[4] According to Margerie, Malcolm somehow learned that Grieg was living on a street called Bygdø Allé and, asking the first man he met there, was directed immediately to Grieg's door. This is a point I will return to later.

Muriel Bradbrook is not sure "whether Lowry met Grieg in Oslo or in a mountain hut,"[5] while Douglas Day quotes Lowry's story to James Stern about how he had discovered that "Grieg lived not in Oslo at all, but ... many scores of miles away in the north of the country," and arming himself with a map and compass, "set off into the foreign land on foot through snow," finally finding Grieg in "a remote mountain cabin in the middle of the night."[6] Lowry's brother Russell is under-

standably skeptical of all these versions: he maintains that he and Malcolm were both "based on Inglewood that summer of 1930," but
concedes that if in fact Malcolm somehow did get to Norway, it was as
a paying passenger out of either Leith, Scotland, or Newcastle.[7]

Up to a point we can undoubtedly blame many of these inconsistent
details on Lowry himself, but it should be noted that it was Margerie
and not he who said that the ship bound for Archangel stopped in
Aalesund. What he said in his long letter to David Markson was that
the ship went "to a port in northern Norway that oddly *has the same
name* as one of the principal characters, though not the hero, of X's
novel" (SL 202), X of course being Nordahl Grieg. There *is* a character
in *The Ship Sails On* by the name of Aalesund, it is true, but more to
the point, there is also one named Narvik, so presumably it was from
the northern port of this name that Lowry made his way to Oslo.

Clearly, Margerie has taken Malcolm's fictional inventiveness here
and turned it into biographical fact, which is true also of her reference
to the assumed name under which Grieg was supposed to be living.
There is no evidence I am aware of that in 1930 or 1931 Grieg used
anything but his real name; certainly, there is no indication of this in
the letters he wrote to his family during these years. Interestingly
enough, however, he had in 1923, in conjunction with his friend Nils
Lie, published a parody called *Bergenstoget Plyndret Inatt* "The Bergen
Train Will Be Robbed Tonight") under the pseudonym Jonathan Jerv,[8]
but he had long since abandoned that stance. It is my understanding
too that the identity of Jonathan Jerv was not widely known, even in
Norway, until the publication of Harald Grieg's book about his brother
in 1956. The reference to the assumed name, therefore, is likely another
manifestation of Lowry's desire to shroud this relationship in some sort
of mystery, a device that simultaneously worked as an appropriate fictional element for the plot of *In Ballast to the White Sea*.

Letters from the two individuals involved are not much help in clarifying the situation. Aside from his 1938 letter to Grieg, Lowry wrote
to Conrad Aiken from the Hotell Parkheimen on Drammensveien in
Oslo, though when he wrote is not certain, for the letter carries no
date. He tells Aiken that the ship he arrived on, the s.s. *Fagervik*, "has
been laid up and I am here waiting a few days for another ship. It is a
swell place; but the swellest place in it, up in the mountains, is called
Frognersaeteren."[9] No mention here of Nordahl Grieg, which is
strange, if to meet him was the express purpose for his trip to Norway;
he mentions only that he is very much taken up with reading the American novelist Julian Green.

Nordahl Grieg did write a brief note to Lowry, which may or may
not be the 1931 letter Lowry referred to in 1938, for Grieg's note bears

only the date 17 September, with no year and no address. "My dear Malcolm Lowry," he wrote, "I am very sorry, but I have to work as hell these days. I have got no chance to accept your kind invitation. My nights and days are crowded with work. As a fellow-writer I know you will understand and forgive. Yours, Nordahl Grieg."[10] (It is interesting to note that Lowry picked up Grieg's unidiomatic expression and used it in *Ultramarine*, where the Norwegian cook Andy tells Hilliot that he'll soon find out what things are like: "It's just a question of working as hell.")[11]

What we don't know is whether Lowry was in Oslo when he received this note; if so, and if he had already met Grieg, then this note may well be, as Conrad Aiken suggests, a "polite brush-off."[12] But since, as Aiken points out, the note was discovered along with a batch of letters in a fragment of manuscript of *Ultramarine*, Lowry could have received it in England; unfortunately, we will probably never know just what kind of "invitation" he had extended to Grieg or where he was when he made it.

Lowry's letter to Aiken, of course, puts in serious doubt the whole question of whether he ever did sign on board the ship headed for Archangel, unless he made two trips to Norway, for if he arrived on the s.s. *Fagervik*, then he could hardly have come, as Margerie stated, by train from a port in the north. All the evidence suggests that the version in the letter to Aiken is the correct one and that the year of his visit was 1931 rather than 1930. If it were 1930, he would have been lucky to catch Grieg at all, since, according to both Grieg's wife and his brother, he was barely in Oslo that summer. Gerd Ring was an actress and singer when she first met Nordahl in the spring of 1931, though their close relationship didn't begin until 1935, and they were married in London in 1940. In connection with a wartime posting to Iceland in 1942, she had this to say: "He had been in Iceland before. As a contributor to *Tidens Tegn* [a Norwegian newspaper] he had in the summer of 1930 travelled to Tingvellir for its thousand-year anniversary celebrations, and written enthusiastic articles that aroused the Icelanders' delight."[13] Grieg's brother confirms this and gives a closer approximation of relevant dates. "In June [1930]," he recalled, "Nordahl left Barbizon and settled for a short while in Paris ... Not long after he came home. What prompted him to leave Paris was an offer from *Tidens Tegn* to become its foreign correspondent to officially cover the Iceland ceremonies."[14] He goes on to say that (later) in the summer of 1930 he himself had rented Christian Krohg's residence near Kragerø, some distance south of Oslo, "and there Nordahl visited us for a while" before moving on to Bliksund in Sørlandet.

Further evidence of a 1931 date derives from Margerie's statement, referred to earlier, that Malcolm knew of Grieg's residence on Bygdø Allé. Now in fact Grieg did live on that street, but not in the summer or early in the fall of 1930. Gerd Grieg recalls precisely the first time she met him, on an occasion when he was invited to read his poetry at a benefit concert in Oslo, on the evening of 4 May 1931. She and Nordahl had met earlier that day to talk about his poetry, and he had said to her: "Will you help me with my poetry? ... I live at 68 Bygdø Allé, third floor."[15] And Harald Grieg, remembering a long gap in the correspondence between himself and his brother, lasting from Christmas of 1930 to the fall of 1931, says simply that Nordahl wanted to settle in Oslo for a while, particularly since he had "got wind of a small suite of accommodations in Bygdø Allé."[16] Here he stayed, working on his play *Atlanterhavet* (mentioned by Lowry in his letter to Grieg) until the end of June 1931, when he suddenly left to live temporarily in a railway hotel at Eidsvoll, about one hundred kilometres north of Oslo. "Nordahl had a weakness for railway hotels," Harald recalls, but he returned to Oslo when he had finished the first draft of the play to arrange for its production later in the year. "Then Nordahl took it reasonably easy for a while," Harald continues. "Among other things he accompanied me on my annual bookselling tour ... That year the tour went along the coast to Stavanger and back home over Haukeli. I remember we talked a lot about *Atlanterhavet* ... and Nordahl wasn't totally satisfied with it."[17] Looked at in this context, it seems quite probable that Grieg's 17 September note was written in 1931, when he was busy with the revisions of *Atlanterhavet*, and he might well have met Lowry not long before that.

Lowry's mention to Aiken of the novelist Julian Green also allows us, in spite of the danger of equating an author's fictional characters with the author himself, to find internal evidence in his fiction to support the 1931 date. In *Dark as the Grave* Sigbjørn Wilderness, thinking about Green's *The Dark Journey*, remembers the first copy he had bought, "fourteen years ago, not the first edition, but a Tauchnitz, on the first dramatic occasion of his having met Erikson and just after they had parted in the street, in the dark stormy tree-tossed Bygdø Allé in Oslo, in the little bookshop near the huge Biblioteket."[18] Since the action of this novel takes place in 1945, Sigbjørn at any rate was in Oslo in 1931, which clearly suggests that Lowry was as well.

The speculations about whether Lowry met Grieg in a mountain hut must, I think, be written off as more of the fanciful elaborations of this relationship, but there are some clues in both Grieg's and Lowry's stories to direct readers towards such a conclusion. Grieg did from time to time inhabit a mountain cabin of sorts at Ringebu, some two or three hundred kilometres north of Oslo, which he would occupy on his many trips back and forth from Finnmark. He also, according to a letter he sent to Graham Greene, confirmed in Harald Grieg's memoirs, lived for a while in a ski hut in a forest at Asker, just outside of Oslo,[19] but that was in the summer of 1935. Readers might be misled, too, by Lowry's statement to Aiken about that "swellest place," Frognersae-teren, being "up in the mountains": this it certainly is, but in the same way, for example, that West Vancouver's British Properties are up in the mountains, merely a fashionable suburb overlooking the city. A stranger may require a city map to find his/her way there, but hardly the compass and overland navigational skills implied in the James Stern version!

Whether Lowry met Grieg and whether they remained "fast friends," as Margerie Lowry stated, Lowry did apparently learn of his whereabouts from time to time, for he accurately informed the Aikens early in 1940 that Grieg was in Lapland on military service, though the reason he gave – "as punishment for defending Russia in the *Arbeiderbladet*"[21] – cannot really be taken seriously. How he knew of Grieg's posting to Lapland and yet didn't know of his death until six months after it happened is yet another puzzle in this relationship. But that Grieg died on an anniversary of the Lowry's marriage seems to have presented a kind of moral obligation on Lowry's part to preserve or immortalize whatever state of friendship with Grieg he believed had been created.

In this respect, perhaps one can argue that the relationship between these two writers was as much psychological as literary, even though there is no doubt about the formal impact of *The Ship Sails On* on Lowry's early work. In many respects the two men were remarkably similar: both manifested a romantic vision about the world, about their roles as writers, about the necessity of gaining experience in the larger world. From the outset Lowry was determined to be a writer, and that Grieg had similar ambitions is made clear in an episode described in Harald Grieg's book: "In our new home at Hop, Nordahl had his own room, which he had to share with me. It was in these two months [in the fall of 1916] that we two brothers – really for the first time – got very close to each other. And now it was he who read his poetry and I who was the listener – and the judge. Nordahl had singularly a clear and precocious view of his goal: when his teacher of Norwegian in the first intermediate grades asked his students, one by one, what they thought of becoming, he answered without hesitation: 'Poet.'"[22] And like Lowry too, he really had no lasting love for the sea but saw it as a means of gaining experience. "Before he surrendered himself to the full power of the world of books," Harald remembers, "he wanted to live a bit. And without having the remotest thought of wanting to be a sailor, he signed on as a deckhand on a cargo ship bound for Australia."[23] Grieg was then eighteen years old, the same age Lowry was when he shipped aboard the s.s. *Pyrrhus* in 1927.

Both were restless men engaged on their respective endless voyages, and as Sherrill Grace neatly points out, it is only "a minor step from the idea of 'the ship sails on' to 'the voyage that never ends.'"[24] Grieg's numerous wanderings after he returned from Australia – to Oxford, to the Riviera, to Berlin, on a walking tour from Hamburg to Rome, to China, Russia, Estonia, several times to his beloved Finnmark – these are the manifestations of a man obsessed with gaining a totality of experiences. "How marvellous it is to travel, travel, travel," he rejoices to his mother, but not long after he communicates a deep pessimism about his role in the world. "But what in Heaven's name shall man pronounce in our time?" he writes to his brother. "Obviously, that the ship sails on, that the world *is not* ours! That is the disheartening situation ... I do not want to write *A Young Man's Love* again. I want to *will* something, but I don't know what."[25] Like Lowry, Grieg was often impulsive, disorganized, and dependent on others for bailing him out financially from some of his predicaments. Both men, too, were obsessed with finding the right voice and form for the expression of their intense and often inconsistent views of the world.

Grieg was of course the more disciplined and successful of the two: by the time of their supposed meeting he had achieved national and international recognition as a poet, novelist, dramatist, and journalist, and one can understand his hesitation about meeting a relatively unknown person like Lowry. In light of his stature it is impossible to believe the generally accepted supposition that he gave permission for Lowry to transform *The Ship Sails On* into a play – an assignment, by the way, that he does not mention in his letters to his brother. Lowry informed Grieg in 1938 – that is, if he sent the letter – that he had finished this task, yet a 1952 letter from Norman Newton of Winnipeg to Lowry indicates that Newton is doing the play and that he will have it finished before arriving in Vancouver to see Lowry.[26] Newton's comments on the characters of *The Ship Sails On* make it clear that he thoroughly understood Grieg's vision in that novel, and it undoubtedly could be a powerful play. But one can only conclude that this was an exercise Lowry undertook on his own, perhaps to satisfy what he said to Markson was his "earlier passion" for drama; his convoluted explanation to Markson of how this exercise would transform not only author A of *In Ballast* but also author X – "a hell of a plot," indeed, as he conceded – undoubtedly belongs more to the fictional reality of that novel than to the biographical reality of Lowry's own life.

The reality of Lowry's "Norwegianness" also belongs more to imagination than to fact, though the possibility of a Norwegian ancestry on his mother's side has not been completely dismissed. Lowry once told the Norwegian-American Norman Matson, "You know, I'm Norwegian, too," and Matson went on to observe: "I don't know what I mean when I say that I felt he was Norwegian – but I felt we were alike in something."[27] This uncertainty about his nationality constitutes a modulation of Sigbjørn's plight as Lowry formulated it, and as it is cited at the beginning of this paper, but it was sounded first in *Ultramarine*, the most "Norwegian" of his novels. Here, when the Norwegian fireman Nikolai hears Hilliot say he was born in Norway, he replies, "I tink you are very much English all the same ... English or Norwegian all the same,"[28] an observation that is later experientially verified when he selects Hilliot, the "Liverpool-Norwegian," to work with him in the stokehold, thus completing the Norwegian connection Hilliot sought at the beginning of the novel with Andy Bredahl and Norman Leif.

That this "plight" of nationality occupied Lowry for much of his life is evidenced by his later fiction, where the protean protagonist Sigbjørn Wilderness reflects an aspect of this dilemma in the very structure of his name. It is as though a significant identity can be realized by juxtaposing a precise and common Norwegian name against a surname that is at once literal and symbolic, physical and psychological. In that the last syllable of the name Sigbjørn is the Norwegian word for "bear," there is perhaps a natural tendency to link it with the literal wilderness of Eridanus where he lives, though it troubles me to attach, even symbolically, any ursine qualities to either Sigbjørn or Lowry. Within a Norwegian context the name links more readily with the great nineteenth-century writer Bjørnson, whom Grieg profoundly admired, emulating his verse forms and writing in 1932 a poem for the Oslo newspaper *Aftenposten* celebrating the centenary of his birth.[29] Interestingly, too, Bjørnson was the name Lowry gave to Erikson, his fictional counterpart of Grieg, and thus one more coincidence is added to the many others that already link these two writers. Whether all this evidence has been strong enough to verify that Lowry met Grieg in the summer of 1931, or even that he met him at all, Lowry at the very least was consistent in his using the Grieg connection not only to shape his own fiction but also to buttress his sense of his own "Norwegianness."

POSTSCRIPT

A Lowry Letter to Nordahl Grieg

Some three months after presenting the preceding paper at the Malcolm Lowry Symposium, I had the occasion to examine the Nordahl Grieg

Collection at the University of Oslo Library,[30] and I there discovered a letter that in a sense renders all my foregoing arguments superfluous, though it verifies my conclusion. This letter, whose existence to my knowledge has never before been commented on, Lowry wrote at the Hotell Parkheimen, Drammensveien 2 [Oslo], and it bears the clearly inscribed date 8.9.31 [8 September 1931], thus firmly solving the confusion over when Lowry did in fact visit Norway. The question of precisely where and under what circumstances he met Nordahl Grieg is not totally answered here, though there is enough evidence in the letter to allow for some reasonable speculation on these points.

After a cheerful salutation, "Nordahl Grieg, I greet you!" Lowry begins his letter by apologizing for having to write in English, and then proceeds with a somewhat curious passage: "I was actually thinking out a letter to you when I met you in the Red Mill: and now can't be altogether sure about the meeting; it might have been imagination. This is not the letter: but this *is* to say that I hope profoundly – provided I *did* meet you and you *are* in Oslo – that you will find time for us to talk again before your return to the mountains or to Bergen, or to both." In this sentence Lowry first used the word "meet," then crossed it out and inserted "talk."

The word "again" in this sentence suggests that the two had at the very least talked to one another on a previous occasion, possibly in the Red Mill,[31] but that they also met in person at least once is indicated by a number of other sentences in the letter. Speaking of Rupert Brooke, Lowry at one point writes: "In his case, the war came along and that as you very justly pointed out in Bygdø, ..." clear evidence that Lowry did visit him at his Bygdø Allé residence, a meeting verified by a later sentence: "I have long been a friend of Benjamin Hall's,[32] and I am delighted to have met the earthly author of his blood, and very grateful to that author for having been so hospitable to one who was a complete stranger." And that they met in another location (and it could be a continuation of the visit to Bygdø) is suggested by Lowry's last sentence in the letter: "But most of all I shall never forget looking at the Viking Ship and then suddenly we were speaking in whispers – ."

Whether Lowry and Grieg met in the Red Mill is not verifiable, though since it was a popular rendezvous for writers, actors, and artists, it seems likely that they would, and in location it was very close to both Lowry's hotel and Grieg's residence. One wonders if Lowry's confusion on this point derives from his ecstasy at having met Grieg, or from his already well-developed drinking habits. "I hope we meet again," he writes, "before the worm pierce our winding sheet," but Grieg's brief reply, written on 17 September (though no year is given), must surely be seen as his response to this letter, so it is virtually certain that the two did not meet again. Since the Red Mill was in the theatre

Nightscene by the Red Mill, Oslo, 1933. Drawing by Kirsten Kalmer.
Courtesy Rolf Widing, Oslo

district, it is tempting to speculate that that is where the idea was born of Lowry's turning *The Ship Sails On* into a play, but the fact that neither Lowry's letter nor Grieg's reply makes any mention of this assignment leaves the question unanswered.

Lowry devotes most of his letter to expressing his ideas about Rupert Brooke, giving some details about his life that, he informs Grieg, "you may not find elsewhere." In addition, he writes briefly about Donne, Webster, Marston, and Keats, with passing reference to a number of other writers, but it is not my intention here to analyse the substance of these remarks, except to say that Lowry seems intelligently informed about all this. Whether Grieg was impressed by Lowry's knowledge of Brooke we have no way of knowing, though he was undoubtedly interested, for he was at that time in the process of completing a book about six poets, including Brooke, which was published in 1932 as *De Unge Døde* ("The Young Dead"). In the section on Brooke, Grieg mentions one or two items referred to by Lowry (such as Brooke's one-act play *Lithuania*), but he makes no comment on Lowry's major assertion that "most biographers have overlooked [the] metaphysical side of Brooke." Whether Lowry said anything new about Brooke is difficult to say, but it seems likely that Grieg knew more about Brooke than his youthful visitor did, a point that Lowry had virtually conceded: "It is possible that some of all this sounds unnecessarily portentous, possible also damn it all that you know it already or had dismissed it as beside the point."

Though questions about the Lowry-Grieg relationship still need to be answered, this letter provides some of the crucial information that Lowry scholars have long wondered about. In addition it conveys the enthusiasm of a writer just beginning his career, one whose affinity for Grieg and things Norwegian never entirely left him.

NOTES

1 Malcolm Lowry, *Hear us O Lord from heaven thy dwelling place* (New York and Philadelphia: Lippincott 1961), 96.
2 Hallvard Dahlie, "Lowry's Debt to Nordahl Grieg," *Canadian Literature* 64 (Spring 1975): 41–51.
3 Margerie Lowry, "Introductory Note," *Ultramarine* (Philadelphia and New York: Lippincott 1962), 6.
4 Quoted in Douglas Day, *Malcolm Lowry* (New York: Oxford UP 1973), 121. See also *Selected Letters*, 262–3.
5 M.C. Bradbrook, *Malcolm Lowry: His Art and Early Life* (Cambridge: Cambridge University Press 1974), 156, n 14.

6 Day, Malcom Lowry, 122.
7 Russell Lowry, "Preface: Malcolm – A Closer Look," in *The Art of Malcolm Lowry*, ed. Anne Smith (London: Vision Press 1978), 21.
8 Harald Grieg, *Nordahl Min Bror* (Oslo: Gyldendal 1956), 163, my translations throughout.
9 Conrad Aiken Collection, Huntington Library, San Marino, California.
10 Ibid.
11 *Ultramarine*, 19.
12 Joseph Killorin, ed., *Selected Letters of Conrad Aiken* (New Haven and London: Yale UP 1978), 306.
13 Gerd Grieg, *Nordahl Grieg: Slik Jeg Kjente Ham* (Oslo: Gyldendal 1958), 256, my translations throughout.
14 Harald Grieg, *Nordahl Min Bror*, 209–11.
15 Gerd Grieg, *Nordahl Grieg*, 10.
16 Harald Grieg, *Nordahl Min Bror*, 215.
17 Ibid., 217.
18 Malcolm Lowry, *Dark as the Grave Wherein My Friend Is Laid* (New York: World Publishing 1968), 45.
19 Graham Greene, *Ways of Escape* (Toronto: Lester & Orpen Dennys 1980), 13. See also Harald Grieg, *Nordahl Min Bror*, 45.
20 See Stern's reminiscences of Lowry in "Malcolm Lowry: A First Impression," *Encounter* 29, no. 3 (1907): 58–68.
21 Conrad Aiken Collection.
22 Harald Grieg, *Nordahl Min Bror*, 11.
23 Ibid., 13.
24 Sherrill Grace, *The Voyage That Never Ends: Malcolm Lowry's Fiction* (Vancouver: UBC Press 1982), 7.
25 Harald Grieg, *Nordahl Min Bror*, 143, 163.
26 Malcolm Lowry Collection, University of British Columbia Library, Vancouver.
27 Norman Matson, "Second Encounter," *Malcolm Lowry: Psalms and Songs*, ed. Margerie Lowry (New York: New American Library 1975), 97–8.
28 *Ultramarine*, 18.
29 Harald Grieg, *Nordahl Min Bror*, 172, 248.
30 I am grateful to Mr Sverre Flugsrud, Manuscript Librarian of the Royal University Library, Oslo, for his kind assistance in locating this letter. I also thank him for granting permission to quote from this letter.
31 The Red Mill was a popular night spot in Oslo's theatre district between the wars. It was torn down in the late 1930s, as was the Hotell Parkheimen. Grieg's residential apartment at No. 68 Bygdø Allé still stands.
32 Benjamin Hall is the central character of Grieg's *The Ship Sails On* (1924, trans. 1927).

"Nordahl Grieg, I greet you!"*

EDITED BY SHERRILL GRACE

Lowry's letter of 8 September 1931 to Nordahl Grieg[1] is a fascinating document for several reasons. Like most of Lowry's letters, it throws interesting light on the man, illuminating biographical details and more general aspects of his personality. The "facts" it provides about the much-debated Lowry/ Grieg connection, however, confer a special importance on it. Of equal, or even greater value to the literary critic are the innumerable tantalizing sidelights revealed by its veritable collage of literary allusions, the majority of which are quoted from memory. Here, it seems to me, we have the twenty-two-year-old Lowry demonstrating, indeed flaunting, his knowledge of literary history and the capillary links that connect writers and works across continents and historical periods; typically, he adds some rather striking original links of his own.

But if it is the "facts" that are of value to the biographer and the allusions that intrigue the literary critic, then for the editor (for myself at least) it is the text itself that fascinates. This letter highlights Lowry the artist: his passion for literature and language, his obsession with origins and influences, his fear of plagiarism lurking just behind his allusions and turns of phrase, and of course his weaving and interweaving of texts, his dense, complex textuality that several contributors to this volume call postmodern.

For all the above reasons, and particularly because of the relationship between this letter and Hallvard Dahlie's investigations, it seems appropriate to include the annotated transcription in this volume. But this letter also belongs with the edition of *Collected Letters* that I am preparing and thus conforms to the following principles. Inside address, date, and complimentary close have been standardized, but in all other respects (spelling, punctuation, paragraph divisions, etc.) the letter is a faithful transcription of Lowry's holograph text. I am attempting to annotate thoroughly but judiciously in the belief that annotations on the annotations are a curse. The ideal balance is often elusive, however, and the annotations to a letter as complicated as this one could rapidly grow to be twice as long as the letter itself. When necessary, noteworthy features or complications with the copy text are briefly described in separate editorial notes, but some modifications have been made to both annotations and notes to suit the present context.

S.G. 1991

Hotell Parkheimen
Drammensveien 2
[Oslo, Norway]
8 September 1931

Nordahl Grieg, I greet you!
Will you forgive me having to write, throughout, in English? – I was actually thinking out a letter to you when I met you in the Red Mill: and now can't be altogether sure about the meeting, it might have been imagination.[2] This is not the letter: but this *is* to say that I hope profoundly – provided I *did* meet you and you *are* in Oslo – that you will find time for us to talk again before your return to the mountains or to Bergen, or to both.
Still, in case you can't, in case the chief engineer burns me up for more speed, in case of thunderbolt or act of God which may make it impossible for us to meet in Cambridge, herewith the following detail about Rupert Brooke which you may not find elsewhere. (I don't know whether his John Webster and Elizabethan drama is in print in England, or even procurable in Cambridge, & I have no copy.)[3]
The year before the war, in reviewing the new edition of Donne's poems, Rupert Brooke remarked that between 1595 and 1613 "English literature climbed and balanced briefly on the difficult pinnacle of sincerity." "Donne belonged to an age when men were not afraid to mate their intellects to their emotions. Hamlet with his bitter flashes, his humour, his metaphysical inquisitiveness and his passion, continually has the very accent of the secular Donne. To Ophelia he must have been Donne himself – "[4]
I mention this only because it shows, especially in the light of what follows in my letter, that Brooke also had within himself the germs of

a metaphysical inquisitiveness which he had not time to develop, which the war finally killed – & him with it. Most biographers have overlooked this metaphysical side of Brooke, I think – the more terrible and bloody side – in a sense, if I may so put it, the 'skibet gaar videre'[5] side of his nature – that which was, like Webster (in Eliot on Webster)

... much possessed by death
And saw the skull beneath the skin:
And breastless creatures underground
Leaned backward with a lipless grin.

Daffodil bulbs instead of balls
Stared from the sockets of the eyes!
He knew that thought clings round dead limbs
Tightening its lusts and luxuries.[6]

and have been content with him merely as The Great Lover, as the author of[7] such admirable poems indeed, but deceitful biographically as I shall attempt to show, as The Hill: and The Soldier: and The Fish (squamous, omnipotent & kind, but which please God may not get either of us!)[8]

Because, because, for one reason, it was Brooke astonishingly who appreciated more fully than anybody before or since the far reaching importance of John Marston, an Elizabethan misanthrope who revived the old Senecan tragedies of blood on a subtler plane, and with what complicated & triumphant issues God only knows: it was Brooke again who first expressed the historical fact, & with brilliant concision, that Marston more or less invented the *malcontent* character which led, by devious mists and poisons, to Hamlet, to Jacques & to Flamineo: to the clerk in Georg Keiser's "From Morn to Midnight" I might add, and in a different art-form, to Daedalus & Demarest & Swann, not to mention all the ruthless women who foreshadowed Webster's flaming duchess "The Duchess of Malfi": and exhibited a clinical interest in satyriasis and nymphomania – by that I mean, roughly speaking, in the dirt, mud, & blood, of sex, in its eternal and ruthless power rather than its subtleness and goodness – which is like Strindberg and O'Neill.[9]

It was left to Brooke to point out in his "John Webster & Elizabethan drama" that Marston was one of the most sinister, least understood, figures in Elizabethan literature: that more than anyone else he determined the channels in which the great flood of those ten years (1600–1610) was to flow: that he is responsible for that peculiar *macabre* taste, like the taste of copper, that is necessary to, if it is not the cause, of their splendour.[10] While Webster, as Swinburne said, took the last step into the darkness – Well![11] ... I think you will agree with me that this interest in, this trouble taken on behalf of old bloody minded Marston is partially if not definitely indicative of some sort of identity between the two, which Rupert Brooke somehow felt tremendously: in other words I think, to go a step further, not only would Brooke's poetry have become harder, tenser, more complex if he had lived but that it is even possible that later he might have devoted himself, largely, to the drama (he did in fact write one one act play, called, I guess, *Lithuania* which in England has been produced only once and that if I am not mistaken at the Everyman Theatre Hampstead, for a short run);[12] that briefly he was *approaching a Keatsian predicament.*

Certainly, unlike Keats, he had not yet reached the brink of the chasm, that canyon in his genius where he was going to wonder whether or not his work was sufficiently according to an intellectual formula: whether unless he devoted himself more to philosophy and metaphysics his poetry would degenerate into mere sensibility unaccompanied by thought: Certainly not, not yet, and he never lived to wonder *hard* at it but nevertheless in his most uneasy moments without having his temperature altered he was already trembling with the symptoms of that most terrible of all fevers, spiritual ambivalence (I mean split mind, divided mind –) or schizophrenia, – ηβεφρενε,[13] is it?, – call it what you will. Is it not at such times, sir, that one climbs, or attempts to climb Mount Everest? It is at such times that one roller skates to Saigon or Tastizond: or to the South Pole or Arcturus or Popocatapetl.[14] It is at such times that one hops on one foot from Sofia to Jerusalem and dies at the foot of the cross, the weeping cross.[15] At such times one works for ninety-nine years in a Chinese ricefield, sleeping in the mud. Or one goes to sea, or commits suicide; or delicately combines the two ...

In his case the war came along and that as you very justly pointed out in Bygdø, is a sort of artificial Katharsis, a mechanic purgation for such a state of mind: and my brother Stuart (who served in the war with some distinction,) bears you out on that point, although he is not without a nostalgia for fighting any more than we can hope to be entirely without a nostalgia for the sea, however fiercely we hate it! To dream of both is to dream of comradeship, of danger: although perhaps underneath it all is the desire for crucifixion on the basis that misery is creation, and creation is love ... A soldier once said to me that if he had been a war-poet he would have started a poem – 'Not all of us were heroes.' The war was better than 'pushing a pen in the guvnor's office,' he said!

So, was it not natural that he should have celebrated the war: that Brooke should have celebrated it poetically in this sense, that the glory and the pity war distilled was partly a magnificent substitute, – or a ghastly compensation!, – only dimly perceived by him, for the metaphysical danks and darks he would never absorb, *could* never absorb? sheerly in terms of mud and blood was it not going one better than Marston? or to put it all more brutally was not the red sweet wine of youth nobler than all the property red ink of all the Antonios and Mel-lidas and Malcontents and Insatiate Countessas, not to mention Sophon-isbas, on the Elizabethan stage or off it?[16] Was it not better to fall with Icarus than thrive with Smith? fall I mean in that international, unscen-ical, Tragedy of blood which was the great War?

There seems to me no doubt, to give another parallel, that Keats saw in the death of Chatterton the consummation of his own poetic theory so that he was ready for and even delighted by the prospect of his own death;[17] he died *consciously*: so with Brooke the 'Dark Self that Wants to Die' (that's not a bad title for a book, by the way) was always present even when he himself was most happy and vigorous.[18] It is possible that some of all this sounds unnecessarily portentous, possible also damn it all that you knew it all already or had dismissed it as beside the point, and I have wandered rather from the central fact which is simply that Marston should have had to wait for Rupert Brooke, whom one had thought to be sitting safely on the other side of the spectrum, so per-fectly to apprehend him, that that in itself is a remarkable thing, and has seemed to me worthy of your notice if not of course, necessarily, in its ramifications, of your agreement.

In conclusion I must say that I can think of noone more qualified to write a book on Brooke than yourself: or of anyone who could surround his position more skilfully: or of anyone who is just such a literalist of his own imagination as to be able to do it.

Needless to say it is an extraordinary compliment to England and to English literature that you should have thought of doing such a thing. I speak at such length because I feel strongly that there are few people in Cambridge who will talk either sympathetically or knowledgeably about him except as a picture postcard, as a sort of present from Grantchester![19]

It is difficult to account, except vaguely (the counter influence of the grim realist, Sassoon,[20] for instance) for his extraordinary falling off in public favour. The best explanation I can give is your own. As with the *Mignon*, so with literature.[21] New men crawl up into the bunks of those that have left, and so on ad infinitum. They take their leavings, and the ship sails on. And so does the whirligig of taste, to yet another cultural cataclysm! –

Lastly, I have long been a friend of Benjamin Hall's, and I am delighted to have met the earthly author of his blood, and very grateful to that author for having been so hospitable to one who was a complete stranger. But when I remember how often Hall and I have tired the sun with talking and sent him down the sky I do not feel so much of a stranger.

By the way, Marston (whom we were discussing) wrote the line,

Rich happiness that such a son is drowned.[22]

That is good, isn't it?

Well: I hope we may meet again before the worm pierce our winding sheet & before the spider makes a thin curtain for our epitaph.[23]

But most of all I shall never forget looking at the Viking Ship[24] and then suddenly we were speaking in whispers –

Yours affectionately:

Malcolm Lowry

ANNOTATIONS

1 Hallvard Dahlie discovered this letter with the Nordahl Grieg papers at the Royal University Library of Oslo in the summer of 1987, and I would like to thank him personally for his collegiality in sharing it with me. I had the pleasure of examining it myself in August 1990. The letter is reproduced here with the permission of the Lowry Estate and the Royal University Library of Oslo, Department of Manuscripts.

2 For details regarding the Red Mill and the Hotell Parkheimen, neither of which is still standing, see Dahlie's discussion, pp. 39–40. Just when it seems possible to confirm absolutely that the two men met, Lowry seems to cast doubt on the matter. However, Lowry's description of his lost manuscript, *In Ballast to the White Sea*, in his 25 August 1951 letter to David Markson (SL 247–66) shows how profoundly he was influenced by Grieg. Moreover, the overlap in reference and event between this letter and the later one to Markson, together with Dahlie's argument, provide what I find to be convincing evidence that the two men really met.

3 Rupert Brooke (1887–1915) was an English poet who had been an under- graduate at Cambridge and later a Fellow of King's College, Cambridge. After his untimely death something of a myth grew up around him which stressed his romantic good looks, his youth and nobility. Lowry is attempting to convince Grieg, who was writing a book on Brooke in the autumn of 1931 when he and Lowry met, that Brooke was a more com- plex and interesting writer and person than the popular idealization of him allowed. *John Webster & the Elizabethan Drama* was written in 1911–12 as Brooke's dissertation towards his fellowship at King's College, and it was first published in 1916. Brooke was in the vanguard of the twentieth-cen- tury rediscovery of Webster, and his study was well thought of. Clearly,

Lowry knew the book well (see anno. 8) and was aware of T.S. Eliot's later attention to Webster (see anno. 5). Moreover, it is worth remembering that Brooke praised the emotional power of Webster's language, stressed the vitality and darkness of his vision, and defended at length Webster's so-called plagiarism of his sources, because each of these characteristics is typical of Lowry's work. Lowry's admiration for the Elizabethans may well have been shaped and encouraged by Rupert Brooke.

4   Brooke reviewed H.J.C. Grierson's two-volume edition of *Donne's Poetical Works* (Oxford: Clarendon Press 1913) twice: in "John Donne, The Elizabethan," *The Nation* 12, no. 20 (1913): 825–6, and again in "John Donne," *Poetry and Drama* 1, no. 2 (1913): 185–8. Lowry is remembering the first review and is quoting from the fourth paragraph.

5   *Skibet Gaar Videre* is the title of Grieg's 1924 novel, translated in 1927 as *The Ship Sails On*, which had such a profound influence on Lowry.

6   Lowry has quoted verbatim the first two stanzas of T.S. Eliot's 1920 poem "Whispers of Immortality." The first line begins: "Webster was."

7   This four-page letter has been written quite neatly, albeit in Lowry's tiniest script and with sloping lines, and there are relatively few crossings out and interlineations. One substantial deletion of about five and a half lines occurs at this point, but Lowry has repeated and developed these points concerning Brooke in the subsequent paragraph. The only marginalia to this letter are the roman numerals I through IV, placed in the left margin, which divide the text very roughly into four parts. On the versos of pages three and four there are three lines heavily crossed out that begin with "My dear Nordahl" and suggest that Lowry had trouble starting this letter.

8   "The Fish," "The Hill," "The Great Lover," and "The Soldier" are poems written by Brooke, and all four were included in the 1931 Tauchnitz edition of the *Anthology of Modern English Poetry*, which Lowry was reading during this visit to Norway.

8   John Marston (1575?–1634) is largely remembered for *The Malcontent* (1604), *Antonio's Revenge* (1602), *The Insatiate Countess* (1613), and various collaborations. Following Brooke's argument, Lowry goes on to connect Marston's malcontents with Shakespeare's *Hamlet* and Jacques in *As You Like It* and with Flamineo in Webster's *The White Devil*. The addition of Georg Kaiser's bank clerk from his 1917 expressionist play *Von Morgens bis Mitternachts* (*From Morn to Midnight*) to the list of Marston filiations is Lowry's own idea, as are the connections with novels as different as James Joyce's *Portrait of the Artist as a Young Man* (1916) for Daedalus, Conrad Aiken's *Blue Voyage* (1927) for Demarest, and Marcel Proust's *À la recherche du temps perdu* (1913–27) for Swann. Lowry's association of the destructive, sex-obsessed females in the plays of August Strindberg and Eugene O'Neill (who was deeply influenced by Strindberg) with John Webster's

The Duchess of Malfi (1614) is again Lowry's idea, and it shows the extent and thoughtfulness of his reading by this stage in his life.

10 Despite his claim, in the second paragraph of this letter, that he has "no copy" of Brooke's Webster study, he is quoting exact terms and phrases from the book; see *John Webster & the Elizabethan Drama* (New York: Russell & Russell 1967) 67–8.

11 Lowry is quoting Swinburne's remark – "The last step into the darkness remained to be taken by 'the most tragic' of all English poets" – from "John Webster" in *The Age of Shakespeare* (1908); see *The Complete Works of Algernon Charles Swinburne*, ed. Sir Edmund Gosse and Thomas James Wise, vol. 11 (London: William Heineman Ltd. 1926), 293.

12 Rupert Brooke's one-act play *Lithuania*, was first produced at the Chicago Little Theatre on 12 October 1915 and later, at a special matinee, at His Majesty's Theatre in London. It was first published in London by Sidgwick & Jackson, Ltd. in 1935 with a note by John Drinkwater, who had acted in the London production.

13 Lowry has written the Greek approximation for hebe, ἥβε; phren, φρενε) which is a form of schizophrenia occurring in puberty and characterized by hallucinations and emotional disorders.

14 Lowry's list of exotic cities, famous mountains, and the star Arcturus also includes what appears to be an English transliteration of Tashi-Chho-Dzong, the name of the fortress and Buddhist headquarters at Thimphu, the capital of Bhutan.

15 Lowry is using phrases from Conrad Aiken's *Blue Voyage* (New York: Charles Scribner's Sons 1927), 139–40.

16 The characters that Lowry lists all appear in the Marston plays mentioned in ann. 5 with the exception of Sophonisba, the title character of Marston's 1606 tragedy.

17 Thomas Chatterton (1752–70), sometimes described as a poetical genius, poisoned himself at the age of seventeen because of his poverty and despair. Coleridge, Wordsworth, Shelley, and Keats saw Chatterton as a symbol of unfulfilled genius, and Lowry may be thinking of Keats's 1815 sonnet "To Chatterton." John Keats (1795–1821), who also died young, like Chatterton, was one of the poets on whom Grieg was working at this time for his book *De Unge Døde* ("The Young Dead," 1932).

18 Lowry is quoting from a passage in Aiken's *Blue Voyage* (241) where Demarest is lost in a Freudian dream about his parents, who are closely based on Aiken's own mother and father.

19 Brooke is still known today for his nostalgic poem "The Old Vicarage, Grantchester (Café des Westens, Berlin, May 1912)," about the pastoral hamlet of Grantchester outside of Cambridge. Brooke lived in Grantchester at several points during his life.

20 Siegfried Sassoon (1886–1967), who was educated at Cambridge and fought in the First World War, was known for his realistic and satirical war poetry and memoirs.

21 The *Mignon* is the name of the ship on which Benjamin Hall is working in Grieg's novel *The Ship Sails On*.

22 Lowry is referring to John Marston's *Antonio's Revenge*; see the Regents Edition by G.K. Hunter, v.iii.3 (Lincoln: University of Nebraska Press 1965), 78. I would like to thank my colleague, Kate Sirluck, for identifying this line. The line is also used, without citation, by the character Mr Smith in *Blue Voyage* (257, 261).

23 Lowry is paraphrasing the lines of Flamineo, that arch hypocrite and schemer, from John Webster's *The White Devil* (1612), V.vi:

> O men
> That lie upon your death-beds, and are haunted
> With howling wives, ne'er trust them: they'll remarry
> Ere the worm pierce your winding-sheet; ere the spider
> Make a thin curtain for your epitaphs.   (153–7)

See *The Selected Plays of John Webster*, ed. Jonathan Dollimore and Alan Sinfield (Cambridge: Cambridge University Press 1983), 126.

24 Lowry reconstructs this scene with Grieg in chapter 2 of *Ultramarine* (51–2) when he has Dana Hilliot remember walking with his father (whom Lowry models upon Grieg) "after we had dined at Jacques Bagatelle in the Bydgø Allé, that day we saw the Viking Ship."

Lowry and the Aesthetics
of Salvation

DAVID FALK

Like Geoffrey Firmin, Malcolm Lowry was all too aware of the smallest
oscillations of his psyche. Given this hyperconsciousness, the desire for
self-discovery provides neither the impetus for nor the goal of his autobiographical fiction. In an early letter Lowry described himself as the
"chap chosen of God or the devil to elucidate the Law of Series" (SL
49), and his personas often seem enmeshed in patterns of fatality that
lie beyond normal causality and so beyond their control. This lack of
control reflects Lowry's sense of being torn by warring inner factions.
Thus, what generates Lowry's work is the search for self-mastery, the
quest for a sense of self as coherent and healthy, as both sane and saved
– an equivalence at the core of his writing. For this reason he typically
speaks of his fiction as a moral victory (SL 332) in the battle against the
"forces in man which cause him to be terrified of himself" (SL 66) or
as a "psychological triumph of the first order ... a matter of life or
death, or rebirth" (SL 339).

In many ways Lowry begins in a state resembling Lacan's mirror
stage; he feels himself a victim of inner chaos, but sees reflected back
an image of himself as unified and firmly situated against a background.[1] The fear for Lowry is that this specular image is a mirage and
that, as with Garcia Marquez's Macondo – another world of mirrors
and mirages[2] – disillusionment (even if it masquerades as enlightenment)
and disaster lie ahead. The last chapter of Under the Volcano, in which
Geoffrey Firmin moves from confronting his image in the Farolito's
mirror to being enveloped by a world populated by projections of the

disintegrating aspects of himself, is Lowry's most powerful dramatization of this fear.

It is crucial to see that the mirror image functions as a *configuration*, achieves its signifying power through its *structural* qualities. The achievement of future coherence is posited on the basis of the already existing specular structure. Though the child may impute psychological wholeness to the image, he or she does so because of the image's "architectural" unity. Gabriele Schwab aptly describes the mirror image as both "conquest and anticipation,"[3] for it is the acknowledged existence of a coherent physical structure that makes possible the very idea of coming to a balanced, ordered emotional life.

I note the circularity of the argument. It traces one of the "great circle voyages" of Lowry's fiction. For Lowry, a notion of a "design–governing posture" (SL 27) had to be firmly set before he could engage in any successful act of writing. He required a clearly enunciated idea of how what he was working on at the moment fit into an overall structure.[4] For, like the mirror image, it is this structuration that offers a guarantee of successful self-mastery. Without it the writer, faced with the "amorphousness of the thing ... wanders around graveyards thinking it is no go" (SL 28). Thus the various lists of arrangements of the parts of *The Voyage That Never Ends* are not, as some critics have maintained, mere time-wasting or symptoms of writer's block.[5] They document Lowry's need to have before him a sense of the essential armature that would give a definite shape to the different attempts at self-mastery that comprise his canon. It is this foregrounding of structure and structural concerns in Lowry's praxis that I intend to explore.

Under the Volcano, of course, represents Lowry's supreme effort to achieve self-mastery through art. His metaphors for the novel are most often architectural: "a churrigueresque ... cathedral," for instance (SL 61). He conceived *Under the Volcano* as an enclosed space that would contain henceforth everything wayward and self-despairing he had projected into Geoffrey Firmin, turning those impulses from real forces in his life into fictions and allowing him to "close the book" on the worst in himself. Having persisted through the numerous rejections of an early version and the arduous years of rewriting in often difficult circumstances, Lowry had even more reason to see his completion of the novel as the accomplishment of a "mighty ... moral deed" (SL 332).

What he was totally unprepared for was the inability of the novel's publication to secure him a permanent sense of self-mastery and salvation. It is this failure and its consequences that lie at the heart of Lowry's late fiction, functioning everywhere at least as subtext and becoming the explicit theme of *Dark as the Grave Wherein My Friend Is*

Laid, "La Mordida," "Through the Panama," and in a comic version, "Elephant and Colosseum." We can see them at work as well in *Hear us O Lord from heaven thy dwelling place*, where every story ends with an epiphany of salvation, only to have the ensuing story immediately undercut that vision.

Lowry's plans for a "drunken Divine Comedy" rested on a schematically simple pattern of self-transcendence, a ceaseless striving upward. With the failure of *Under the Volcano* either to mark that ascent or to supply momentum for it, Lowry was confronted with a self and a world more complicated in every way than he had imagined. It is a world of protean transformations in both the self and the landscape,[6] a world in which the possibility of coherence, in either sense of the term, becomes highly problematical. Therefore, one of the central ways that the struggle to attain self-mastery is enacted in the late fiction is as a battle between form and formlessness.

Three possible attitudes compete within Lowry's late work. One now sees form as negative, all structure as factitious at best. The second rests on an acceptance of formlessness, though this often presents itself as a celebration of organic growth. Third, there is a vision that recovers the sense of structure as creative that I outlined earlier.

Lowry's most extreme reaction to the failure of *Under the Volcano* to provide him with the psychological/spiritual reward he had anticipated is the poem "After Publication of *Under the Volcano*":

Success is like some horrible disaster
Worse than your house burning, the sounds of ruination
As the roof tree falls following each other faster
While you stand, the helpless witness of your damnation.   (*sp* 78)

Here the strategy of searching for self-mastery through art is shown to be futile as triumph turns into a new version of Lowry's worst trauma in Canada: the burning of his shack on Burrard Inlet. Out of the same bitterly tormenting sense of frustration that the poem bespeaks arises the attitude that all Lowry's attempts at ordering the self are literally self-defeating and that the very idea of structuration is fraudulent.

The quest for a coherent self now seems little different from the "hysterical identifications" Bill Plantagenet was supposed to succumb to in the early plans for *The Last Address*[7] and the protagonist was to grow beyond in *In Ballast to the White Sea*.[8] At best this quest seems merely *aesthetic* and leads away from the sort of moral victory Lowry had envisioned. Every artist-figure in the late work at some point confronts the possibility that in ordering his autobiographical material for artistic ends, he has seriously distorted the reality he set out to tame:

"Ethan [Llewelyn's] method of thinking ... involved a process akin to composition ... preparatory to making a brief on behalf of an accused he proposed to defend. But the actual and frightening and certain knowledge ... that he had been *consciously* ... suppressing and misrepresenting the very events of his life for the sake of making them fit into a bearable pattern, came with the force of a revelation" (*October Ferry* 210).

What Llewelyn and Lowry's other personas have done is, in the words of Harold Rosenberg, to exchange a personality – defined by its wide-ranging possibilities – for an identity, in which the multiplicity of events in a real life is replaced by a "scheme that pivots on a single fact central to the individual's existence and which, controlling his behavior and deciding his fate, becomes his visible definition," so that the identity remains constant, precluding growth or change.[9] As Rosenberg points out, it is this substitution of identities for personalities that lies at the heart of the aesthetics of tragedy, and so the strategy draws us back to Lowry's towering tragic persona, the Consul.

Seeing himself as faced with a choice between the grandeur and dignity of tragedy and a life that is often tawdry and ridiculous, the Consul clings to tragedy, hoping to give his life the qualities of high art: balance, harmony, depth. The irony is that he wishes for the artist's "godlike" control but can only achieve it at the cost of turning himself into a character, forced to act not out of his real desires but in conformity to the demands of the role. In the wake of the failure of *Under the Volcano* as spiritual breakthrough, the Consul seems not only the embodiment of the impulses Lowry needed to master but the deconstructor of Lowry's artistic strategy for achieving that mastery:

> Fame *like a drunkard* consumes the house of the soul
> Exposing that you have worked for only this   (SP 78, italics added)

For from this pessimistic vantage point, it is impossible to see how Lowry's desire for a coherent self that will confer upon him a sense of dignity and self-worth differs from the Consul's desire for self-glorification, or to see why the self-controlled author "Malcolm Lowry," created by the writing of *Under the Volcano* and whose name appears on its dust-jacket, is any more real than the self-doomed character Geoffrey Firmin between its covers.

As a basis for literary production, the idea of negative form leads – in such works as *Dark as the Grave*, "La Mordida," "Through the Panama," and "The Ordeal of Sigbjørn Wilderness" – to Lowry's transcribing his recurring anxiety at "being written" and to the corollary theme of the threat of Wilderness's being reduced to the Consul and his life to a mere replay of *Under the Volcano*. At the extreme, it produces a rejection of art as a creative activity: "the average short story is ... a very bad image of life ... for the reason that no matter how much action there is in it, it is static, a piece of death, fixed."[10]

It is to the idea of organicism that Lowry often turned as a response to negative form. Others, notably Sherrill Grace, have examined the positive implications of this attitude,[11] so I will sketch it only briefly. Lowry here sees the universe and the self as in a continual process of protean growth, so that the writer's task is "at least to give the illusion of ... a state of perpetual metamorphosis" ("Ghostkeeper" 224) and to let an organic form emerge as he follows his material: a "work of art, having been conceived, must grow in the creator's mind, or proceed to perish" (*DAG* 154). Since the Romantics the valorization of organic form has been such an unquestioned assumption that the problems with it tend to go unnoticed. To accept the protean universe as permanent leads to the generation not of fully realized narrative but of *chronicle* – to borrow a valuable term from Hayden White: "The chronicle ... aspires to narrativity but ... is marked by a failure to achieve narrative closure ... It starts out to tell a story but breaks off ... in the chronicler's own present. [It represents the world] *as if* real events appeared to human consciousness in the form of *unfinished* stories."[12]

Such a description might have been written with Lowry's late novels in mind, for Lowry's struggles – in some cases his utter inability – to bring them to satisfactory closure are an obvious manifestation of the chronicler's plight. The difficulty is in fact unresolvable, for the chronicle is not only unfinished – it is *unfinishable*. It is the mode for a world in which form and meaning are striven after but never grasped. As Lowry put it, "The minute an artist begins to try and shape his [autobiographical material] some sort of magic lever is thrown ... producing events ... that show him that this shaping of his is absurd, that nothing is static or can be pinned down, that everything is evolving ... into other meanings, or cancellations of meaning quite beyond his comprehension" ("Ghostkeeper" 223).

This is a world in which always just "beyond [a] barrier lay ... the key to a mystery that would give some meaning to their ways on earth" (*DAG* 43). It is a world where the hope that a form might emerge in the process of writing that would secure for the author a sense of self-mastery turns easily to despair. Lowry's best symbol for this transformation of the celebration of organic growth into anguish at the idea of unending formlessness is the Hotel Cordova in "La Mordida." Like his late novels, the hotel is being built in several sections at once – each unfinished and all seemingly unrelated to the others or to any conceivable blueprint for a unified structure. Rather than suggesting a movement towards self-mastery and grace, the Cordova and its process of ongoing construction evoke an "air of impermanence, and of not making up its mind to be anything whatever, that were almost frightening, and on top of that ... an air ... of ruination."[13]

In the end, then, the idea of organicism is as unsatisfactory as the notion of negative form. Its emblems are a picture of Lowry setting out the manuscripts of *The Voyage That Never Ends* and moving from one to the other, groping his way through a labyrinth of paper (*SL* 344), or an even more painful vision of art, not as salvation but only as "salvage operations":[14] "the author, while working, is like a man continually pushing his way through blinding smoke in an effort to rescue some precious objects from a burning building. How hopeless" (*DAG* 154).

Negative form provides the illusion of self-mastery by the imposition of a closure and a meaning that are a reduction of life to the aesthetics of tragedy. Organicism, with no possibility of closure and the perpetual deferral of meaning, does not allow for self-mastery. The first draws Lowry back into his fictions; the second never lets him out. What both block is the attainment of a vision of graspable sanity/salvation: "life ... must have a happy ending ... our tragic sense was the more frivolous ... given us for aesthetic reasons alone ... beyond tragedy ... if not altogether beyond art [lay] our wildest dreams of optimism."[15] It is to Lowry's efforts to forge an aesthetics of salvation, to render this vision in art, that we must turn. As Hayden White indicates, chronicle is transformed into full narrative when it finds the form of an allegory.[16] It is in the most obviously allegorical of Lowry's late works, "The Bravest Boat," that the possibilities of creative form are dramatized.

At the thematic beginning of the story lies a symbolic victory over the destructive forces in the world – the long-since completed voyage of the protagonist's toy boat. The tale centres on a commemoration of this voyage. However, the quest has not proved a lasting success. The protagonist and the wife he has found because of the boat's journey are under threat of eviction from their British Columbian paradise. Moreover, the ritual retelling is itself in danger of degenerating into a rote exercise, of becoming incapable of embodying satisfactorily the mystery at its core or of allowing the celebrants to re-experience its vision of salvation.

The main action of the story is to turn this double failure in life and in art into triumph. As the couple recount the story of the boat's pilgrimage, they are led to re-enact it in a new version. Passing through a protean landscape in which, for instance, the colour white is transformed without warning from something angelic into something deathly, they are led to a renewed vision of perpetually repeated salvation, as in the zoo a demonic lynx leaps at a squirrel, but misses: "The squirrel's hairbreadth escape – the thousand-to-one chance – that on second thought must take place every day, seemed meaningless. But all at once it did not seem meaningless that they had been there to see it" (HOL 23). The account of the boat's voyage runs through the new epiphany at the zoo. Thus the narrative being related by the couple provides a structure by which their new experience is shaped and its meaning molded. But the new experience also recharges the narrative with felt significance, allowing it to become again a positive operative force in the couple's life.

This creative interaction between past and present is one of the hallmarks of Lowry's aesthetics of salvation. In the worlds of Lowry's tragedy and chronicle, repetitions of the past are signs of the protagonists' succumbing to the worst within themselves, turning their presents into Days of the Dead.[17] In "The Bravest Boat" we see a pattern develop in which the past is rehabilitated and in which "going back is equivalent to going forward" (SL 293).

A paradigm of the way creative form generates a Lowry text is offered in the opening chapter of *Dark as the Grave Wherein My Friend Is Laid*. As Sigbjørn Wilderness descends from Vancouver towards Mexico, he is beset by a need to justify himself, "as if he felt obliged ... to make some excuse or explanation for being on earth at all" (11). This sense of guilt calls up a "ballet" of his fears and failures (13–14), culminating in a feeling of dread that he will be refused entry into the United States, as he had been once before. This fear, with its underlying hint of damnation – the port of entry is the City of the Angels – he overcomes by recalling and then planning to add to a long-forgotten poem he had written about the earlier trauma. The production of the narrative account transforms what was potentially destructive in Wilderness's situation into the basis for artistic creation (turns it to account, if you will) while the finished – or finishable – text allows him to account for himself: he is, in fact, a writer, something he had come to doubt.

The worlds of negative form and organicism force Lowry to choose between order and movement through time. It is only with the forging of a sense of creative form that he can accommodate both principles without fear of dissolution or death: "[these gloomy thoughts] flowed ... like an inlet ... Nonetheless these [abysmal] thoughts made me happy in that, though they were in motion they were in order too: an inlet does not overflow its banks ... nor does it dry up" (HOL 265).

Lowry's basic metaphor for structure now changes from the architectural one he employed for *Under the Volcano*, with its implications of a fixed, confining space, to a musical one. In fact, in *Hear us O Lord from heaven thy dwelling place*, the most fully realized of his late works, the fundamental structural device is musical. Lowry uses the dynamics of the round, with its continual repetitions of the same theme in different voicings, to create a surface impression of wavering hope and short-lived psychological/spiritual triumph. Beneath the surface, however, every new return to the beginning is actually part of an ongoing movement towards a harmonic resolution.[18]

It is in "The Forest Path to the Spring" that the achievement of an unassailable self-mastery is depicted, and it is not happenstance that the protagonist is a jazz musician/composer, for Lowry's early love, jazz, rests on the almost endless opportunities for improvising over a set pattern of chords: *of fleshing out through time in a variety of ways an unchanging underlying structure*. In one more rehabilitation of the past, then, jazz becomes Lowry's ultimate symbol of creative form and of the realization of a personality with manifold dimensions and the possibility for growth without loss of coherence for which creative form enables him to strive.

Lowry's original strategy for self-mastery with *Under the Volcano* entailed an ultimate separation of life and art. Geoffrey Firmin would die; Lowry would be freed to carry on his life. I believe there is a real possibility that, had the strategy succeeded, Lowry would not have written again. We see that danger enacted in "Elephant and Colosseum" by Cosnahan, who has been stopped from writing by the success of his novel and whose plans for his career as an author, having the book "revived" in translation, involve no further creative effort on his part. What the aesthetics of salvation permitted Lowry to envisage was a future as a writer grounded on a dynamic, ongoing interaction between past, present, and future, between life and art, a voyage that never ends: "he seemed to see how life flowed into art: how art gives life a form and meaning and flows on into life, yet life had not stood still ... life transformed by art sought further meaning through art transformed by life" (DAG 43).

NOTES

1 Jacques Lacan, *Écrits: A Selection*, trans. Alan Sheridan (New York: W. W. Norton & Co. 1977), 1–7.
2 Gabriel Garcia Marquez, *One Hundred Years of Solitude*, trans. Gregory Rabassa (New York: Harper & Row 1970), 422.
3 Gabriele Schwab, "Genesis of the Subject, Imaginary Functions, and Poetic Language," *New Literary History* 15, no. 3 (Spring 1984): 457.
4 Thus, I disagree with Ronald Binns, who sees all Lowry's plans for *The Voyage That Never Ends* as afterthoughts, in "Lowry and the Profession: Comfort, Discomfort, Strange Comfort," *Proceedings of the London Conference on Malcolm Lowry 1984*, ed. Gordon Bowker and Paul Tiessen

(London and Waterloo, Ont.: Goldsmith's College, University of London, and *Malcolm Lowry Review* 1985): 69.

5 The liveliest statement of this position is by Dale Edmonds: "all of Lowry's grandiose schemes ... are nothing more than pencil-sharpening, finger-flexing, getting-up-to-get-a-drink-of-water (on-second-thought-make-that-whisky) – in short, the things that a writer who can't write does to keep from writing." "Grace's *The Voyage That Never Ends*: A Review," *Malcolm Lowry Newsletter* 12 (Spring 1983): 4.

6 For an examination of this protean universe, see Sherrill Grace, *The Voyage That Never Ends* (Vancouver: UBC Press 1982), and my article, "Beyond the Volcano: The Religious Vision of Malcolm Lowry's Late Fiction," *Religion and Literature* 16, no. 3 (Autumn 1984). Grace reads the implications of this universe more optimistically than I do.

7 "*The Last Address* ... is, among other things, about a man's hysterical identification with Melville" (SL 24–5).

8 Lowry described the plot of *In Ballast* in a long letter to David Markson; the especially relevant section is SL 261–3.

9 Harold Rosenberg, *The Tradition of the New* (New York: McGraw, Hill Co. 1965), 152. The entire brilliant discussion of personality and identity occurs on 136ff.

10 Malcolm Lowry, "Ghostkeeper," in *Psalms and Songs*, ed. Margerie Lowry (New York: New American Library 1975): 223–4.

11 Grace, *The Voyage*, especially chap. 1. See also Elizabeth Rankin, "Malcolm Lowry's Comic Vision: 'Elephant and Colosseum,'" *Canadian Literature* 101 (Summer 1984): 167–71.

12 Hayden White, "The Value of Narrativity in the Representation of Reality," in *On Narrative*, ed. W.J.T. Mitchell (Chicago: University of Chicago Press 1981), 5.

13 Malcolm Lowry, "La Mordida," University of British Columbia Special Collections, 13:3.

14 This is the Consul's derisive term for people's efforts to keep him from death and doom. See *Under the Volcano* (New York and Scarborough, Ont.: New American Library 1971), 61.

15 *Hear us O Lord from heaven thy dwelling place* (London: Jonathan Cape 1961) 171.

16 *On Narrative*, 21.

17 The compulsion to repeat as a manifestation of the death wish is, of course, at the centre of Freud's "Beyond the Pleasure Principle," *The Standard Edition of the Complete Psychological Works of Sigmund Freud*, vol. XVIII (London: Hogarth Press and the Institute of Psychoanalysis 1955).

18 For a fuller treatment of the way the round functions in *Hear us O Lord*, see Falk, "Beyond the Volcano," and Elsa Linguanti's study of the "micro/macrotext" in this collection.

PART TWO

Under the Volcano

Genus Floridum:
Translating *Under the Volcano*

EDITED BY
CHRISTINE PAGNOULLE[1]

How many translators have stood puzzled, perplexed, dumbfounded, but also spellbound, hopelessly and helplessly fascinated in front of (or entangled in) the linguistic snares of Lowry's overwhelming novel? The number of published translations is impressive and is far from representing the total number of attempted translations. Whether commissioned by some publisher or acting on their own initiative, translators have entered into a passionate relationship with a text that proves at times infuriatingly intractable, largely because of that indomitable branching and flowering of Lowry's prose, the overloaded and churrigueresque quality of a style that so often belongs to what can be defined in rhetorical terms as *genus floridum*.

The present essay considers only translations of *Under the Volcano* into four languages that belong to the Indo-European family: Spanish, Italian, German, and French. It thus leaves out the specific obstacles that arise when moving to altogether different cultural and linguistic spheres such as Japanese or Kiswahili. While only one translation is available in Spanish, by Raûl Ortiz y Ortiz, and one in Italian, by Giorgio Monicelli, Karin Graf's German translation can be compared to the earlier one by Susanna Rademacher, and there are now two published French versions, one by Clarisse Francillon and one by Jacques Darras.[2]

Considering some aspects of these seven versions will serve both to illustrate tenets of translation theories and to highlight characteristics of the language used in the novel. The following points will be examined in turn:

1 some plain mistakes;
2 the demand for consistency and some infringements;
3 distortions due to faulty interpretations or corrections of intentional mistakes;
4 linguistic constraints that force transformations even on the most "literal-minded" translator (with a consideration of the novel's longest sentence);
5 problems raised by the convolutions of Lowry's syntax;
6 some deliberate reductions of the original text in order to spare the reader any unpleasant shock; and
7 the translation of puns, allusions, and metaphors.

It should be clear from this list that the present approach is limited and tentative. No attempt has been made to cover the entire range of translation problems or to illustrate a particular point exhaustively.

Like any masterpiece, *Under the Volcano* offers a clear illustration of both the necessity for and the impossibility of good literary translations. They are necessary, since it is of primary importance that such works be made available to those who cannot read them in the original language, yet they are virtually impossible, since one cannot "make soundsense and sensesound kin again"[3] in exactly the same way in two different languages. A translator is entitled and even expected to clarify an obscure or unnecessarily convoluted scientific paper, to rewrite a loosely articulated detective story or romance. But he or she must not tamper with the connotations, allusions, sound effects, syntactic rhythms, semantic associations, and ramifications of a work in which everything (whether intentionally or not hardly matters) contributes to the multiplicity of potential readings that is the hallmark of literature.

The translator knows that any text is a complex structure made up of interlocking systems, each fulfilling a specific function in relation to the whole. But saying this points to the inevitable limits of translation, for clearly not everything can be retained: translators have to make choices, and they must try to compensate for what has to be jettisoned. The more coherent the text, the more difficult the choices to be made – and the more heart-rending the inevitable shortcomings. There may be cases of phrases that cannot be translated. Usually, however, the impossibility has to be qualified. But as Mounin puts it, translation is "une opération relative dans son succès, variable dans les niveaux de communication qu'elle atteint ... jamais vraiment finie, ce qui signifie en même temps qu'elle n'est jamais inexorablement impossible,"[4] or, to quote from an article on the translation of a short poem by Hugo Claus: "La traduction poétique est un exercice fait de tâtonnements, d'essais, d'évaluations, de corrections, d'hésitations entre les exigences du son et du sens, de constats d'insuffisance, d'essais de compensation."[5]

1. Choice of word and phrase will vary from one translator to another, and this partly accounts for the variety among translations. These variations in turn emphasize the polysemy of the original text and the relativity of any translation. However, before considering deliberately divergent choices (see 4) – that is, choices resulting from different approaches to translation – we shall first briefly examine some inadvertently wrong choices. Misunderstood words or phrases fall into what Rado calls the "philological criterion" in evaluating the value of a translation: misinterpretation of one "logeme" (or logical unit) in the source text.[6]

Instances of such misreadings are numerous in the first French translation. The most famous one is probably the "Grisly Orozco" passage in chapter 7: among other cheering sights in Laruelle's room the Consul glimpses "grisly Orozco charcoal drawings,"[7] "grisly" being spelled with a capital letter as the first word of the sentence; this becomes "des dessins au fusain, par Grisly Orozco" (F 344) instead of "de sinistres fusains d'Orozco." In chapter 10 Clarisse Francillon translates "drinkless in a booth" (292) as "sans un verre dans une baraque" (F 487), whereas the context of the Salón Ofélia clearly suggests a partly enclosed eating accommodation in a place almost as full of recesses as the ominous Farolito in chapter 12. When Yvonne is first seen by Hugh on his return from Mexico City near the beginning of chapter 4, we read that "at a little distance [she] appeared clothed entirely in sunlight" (98); this does not mean "à cette faible distance" (F 178) but rather the opposite: you have to be at some distance to perceive her in this way. The words "quote" and "unquote" in the telegram with which the chapter opens do not mean "coté," "non coté" (F 177), as though referring to stock-market quotations. Many more examples could be given, a fact of which Francillon had become keenly aware.

Jacques Darras, who generally avoids such blatant inaccuracies on the surface level, confuses gutters along the sloping streets with the sewer grates through which water rushes under the street: "he could hear ... the water still rushing down the gutters in the street" (46) becomes "on entendait ... des torrents d'eau s'engouffrer par les caniveaux sous la rue" (D 57). Another among Darras' misreadings occurs when Geoffrey looks at the English tourist who acts as a Good Samaritan to him in chapter 3. He notices the "striped tie, mnemonic of a fountain in a great court" (84), but Darras writes: "cravate à rayures, frappée d'un emblématique jet d'eau au centre d'une cour royale" (D 98), thereby missing the reference to the fountain in the larger of the two courts at Trinity College, Cambridge. At one point in an exceptionally long sentence in chapter 12, Darras misreads again: the clock on the wall points to a time still "too early" because the *cantina* to which the Consul wants to fly is not yet open (350); the clock is *not* fast ("en avance," D 382).

Examples of misreading also crop up in the Italian translation. For example, Monicelli makes Hugh "absentmindedly" phone Laruelle from Parián after the Consul's death (19, M 22) because he has confused "distraughtly" and "distractedly" (and gets the meaning of "distraughtly" wrong). When Laruelle thinks of slimming as a possible "reason some people might have for taking up arms" (21), the Italian translation changes "taking up arms" into "sfidarlo," that is, "challenging him" (M 24). In a subsequent passage the excessive weight of Jacques' tennis racket is blamed on the newspapers – the press (21, M 24) – instead of on the racquet press. The combination of negation and adverbs can also cause trouble: "the house Yvonne hadn't yet entered at all" (73) becomes "quella casa in cui Yvonne non aveva mai messo piede" (M 77), the house in which Yvonne had never set foot, which may raise some questions in the reader's mind about the nature of her married life with Geoffrey.

2. An essential demand in any translation is for inner consistency, and this is of particular importance in a novel as densely woven from echoes as *Under the Volcano*. The song that Geoffrey and Jacques used to sing at Leasowe ought to be left untranslated whenever quoted or alluded to, not only because of the tradition of nonsense verse in English but also because of the "linguistic exchange" context of Jacques' visit to the Taskersons. Yet Monicelli translates Jacques' delightfully Frenchified version ("Oh we allll WALK ze wibberlee wobberlee WALK," 26) one way and Geoffrey's memory of one line in it (223) another.

When Monicelli translates Laruelle's comment "what now at a distance one could almost refer to as the 'case'" (14) as "di quello che ora, a distanza, poteva essere definito un 'processo'" (77) – that is, when he narrows the meaning of "case" (Italian "caso") – he not only unduly assumes the reader's normal interpretative urge; he also disrupts an important semantic field, since the Italian reader has no reason to associate the name of the pub to which Jacques and Geoffrey resort after the Hell Bunker episode ("The Case is Altered," "Il Cambiacaso") with the reconstitution of the Consul's story.

Repetitions are also important for establishing the rhythm of sentences. So, in a long sentence in chapter 12, an almost incantatory statement is repeated twice, word for word: "how alike are the groans of love to those of the dying, how alike, those of love, to those of the dying" (350–1). This is, of course, repetitive, but it is meant to be and should not be shortened, as it is in the Spanish translation (O 386–7), or altered the second time it occurs, as it is in Darras' French (D 382, 384).

The demand for consistency also applies to the various voices in the text and the ways English is distorted to convey them. Some phrases act almost like Wagnerian leitmotifs: they identify a character and a mood. One such little phrase is Dr Vigil's "Virgin for those who have nobody them with." "Nobody go there. Only those who have nobody them with," he tells Laruelle (12), and in chapter 10 the Consul remembers his words when Vigil had taken him to that "compassionate Virgin floating in the gloom": "Nobody come here, only those who have nobody them with" (290). Ortiz y Ortiz has a nice, though not quite perfect echo: "Ninguno va alli. Solo los que no tienen a nadie" and "Nadie viene aqui, solo los que no tienen a nadie" (O 15, 321). (Note the recurring difficulty of suggesting a Spanish-contaminated English in Spanish.) The echo is somewhat flawed in Francillon's translation ("Personne ne va là. Seulement ceux qui n'ont personne à être avec eux" and "Personne ne vient ici, seulement eux qui n'ont personne à être avec," F 41, 485) and deliberately altered in Darras' version ("Personne va là-bas. Uniquement si l'on a personne soi avec," "Personne ne venir ici, seulement ceux qui n'ont personne avec," D 23, 319).

Weber's rambling in chapters 2 and 12 is another touchstone. Admittedly, what he says does not make much sense, but the words he uses in some passages are exactly the same in English and should be the same in the various translations too. Here are two instances. In both chapters he uses the striking phrase "We come through with heels flying" (51 and 364, though the sentence in chapter 12 is in the past tense). Ortiz y Ortiz keeps the same phrase ("con talones alados") with two different verbs ("venimos" and "pasamos," O 59 and 402). Francillon retains the same words: "nous passons à travers avec des talons qui volent" (F 104, 602), which is somewhat quaint in French, but suggestive. In Darras' version the phrase becomes respectively "En deux temps trois mouvements, ça y va!" and "doigts dans le nez que ça y a été!" (D 63 and 397).

The other repeated passage is full of understated violence: "The sun parches the lips and they crack. Oh Christ, it's a shame! The horses all go away kicking in the dust! I wouldn't have it" (52 and 365, with changes in the punctuation). Francillon and Ortiz y Ortiz use the same words for both occurrences, but Darras gives two different versions. In chapter 2 we read "Un soleil qui craquait les lèvres de sècheresse. Non mais quelle honte, vraiment! Voilà-t-y pas que les chevaux se débinent dans la poussière! Pas question de laisser faire ça" (D 63), and in chapter 12: "Un soleil à vous fendre les lèvres. Non mais quelle honte! Voir les chevaux se débiner au grand galop dans la poussière! Pas question de laisser faire ça" (D 398).

The italicized quotation on page 351, "*you cannot drink of it*," echoes the words used by Señora Gregorio at the end of chapter 7 when she means (but does she?) "think of it": "Life changes, you know, you can never drink of it" (231 and 233). In order to retain Lowry's intended ambiguity with the phonetic play on drink/think, translators should use the same words in the two passages, but few seem to have realized this.

Another consistency problem is raised by quotations, which are not always accurate, from external sources. Is the translator to use the "authorized" translation in his language when there is one, or to coin his own? The question arises for the German version of the Sophocles epigraph, in which "Ungeheuer," though closer to the Greek original, does not call up exactly the same mental picture as "wonder," and we know that the positive connotations of this opening quotation were important in Lowry's eyes (SL 88). Is the translator to retain inaccuracies because they may be intentional, as in the Bunyan quotation used as an epigraph or in the repeated quotation from Marvell's pastoral poem (78, 84, and 211)? Is the translator expected to trace the countless literary and philosophical allusions?

3. The translator is of necessity a particularly careful reader, and as a reader he or she will thus have an interpretation of the text to be translated. Yet when actually transposing a text from one language into another, the translator should aim at relaying the voice of the author and should therefore refrain from adding explanations or connections that are absent in the original. An interpretation that adds to or departs from the text to be translated runs a serious risk of being misleading.

On this score Darras is often found wanting. In his letter to Yvonne the Consul writes in a parenthesis, "when I am in bed at that time" – that is, at seven in the morning (45). Darras takes it upon himself to translate "quand je m'y trouve encore" (D 56), thus suggesting that the Consul has an orderly life and usually rises before seven. The long sentence in chapter 2 in which Yvonne lets the gorgeous memories of her arrival in Acapulco overlap and partly cancel her painful present experience begins with the word "ashamed"; in Darras' version it becomes, much more forcefully, "morte de honte" (48, D 59). This stress becomes even more striking later in the same sentence when the words "glanced defensively round the square, really tranquil in the midst of this commotion" (48) become "jeta un bref regard d'appréhension tout autour de la place sans vraiment perdre de sa sérénité au milieu du désordre" (D 60).

Translators may be tempted to correct some of the Consul's mistakes as though they were Lowry's, or even, but this is an aspect we shall come back to later, to rectify what they consider heavy or clumsy in Lowry's own style. Two clear instances of such interference are related to gardens: the Jefe de Jardineros in chapter 12 and the sign "Le gusta este jardín" in chapter 5. Two diverging translations of the Spanish sign are given in the course of the novel. The first is the Consul's interpretation of an over-punctuated notice: "You like this garden? Why is it yours? We evict those who destroy!" (132) The second is Hugh's sober reading of the same sign without superfluous question marks: "Do you like this garden, the notice said, that is yours? See to it that your children do not destroy it!" (235) In the Consul's translation "evite" becomes "evict" instead of "avoid" because of the latent connection between his fate and that of Adam evicted from the Garden of Eden, a myth he is about to refer to in his discussion with Quincey. The Italian translator emends the Consul's faulty translation: "Vi piace questo giardino? E'vostro? Cerchiamo di impedire che lo distruggano!" (M 138). Such a correction makes nonsense of the following sentence: "Simple words, simple and terrible words, words which one took to the very bottom of one's being, words which, perhaps a final judgement on one, were nevertheless unproductive of any emotion whatsoever, unless a kind of colourless cold" (132). Or else it makes the Consul appear even more eccentric than he is. The contrast with Hugh's correct version is completely missed too.

Similarly, while Jefe de Jardineros does not mean "Chief of Gardens" but "Chief of Gardeners," the Consul's mistake in systematically referring to him as the Chief of Gardens is highly significant and to be retained, if only because it links the dénouement more closely with the pervasive garden theme and relates this sinister figure of malevolent power more directly to the Alhambra gardens in Granada, thus with the Consul himself at the moment he assumed a vice-consulship (see 359). Why then demote Sanabria, as Darras does, to the function of Chief Gardener ("Jardinier en Chef")?

4. Choices in translation often follow from a fundamental choice between two diverging approaches to the act of translating: either a complete adherence to the source text, including what can be represented as clumsiness or over-elaboration, or adaptation to the target language, with a measure of polishing when necessary. Antoine Berman insists that translation is an "ethical" act that recognizes and receives the Other as Other.[8] What he calls "traduction hypertextuelle et littérarisante" is the type of translation that (whether intentionally or not) denies the "otherness" of the source text, makes it acceptable to the

norms of the target language, but also, very often, to the cultural norms of the common reader. However, the choice between adherence to the text and adaptation can never be consistent: if we opt for the second alternative we are still somehow bound to the source text; yet if we adopt the first, thus following Berman's recommendation, different linguistic constraints in different languages enforce unavoidable modifications.

Since no two languages, however close, have the same structure, some adjustments are necessary when moving from one to the other; otherwise, stylistic awkwardness arises, which not only points to the translation as translation but also spoils the intended effect. Illustrations of such linguistic constraints will be drawn mainly from a comparison between the English text and the two French versions.

The use of a future tense in a time subclause, which is grammatically ruled out in English, may be an instance of compulsory transformation. When Geoffrey addresses his absent half-brother in chapter 3 he says: "I am sadly afraid that you may indeed ... fall heir, as you grow older and your conscience less robust, to a suffering ... more abominable than any you have caused me" (83). Darras translates: "à mesure que tu vieilliras et que ta conscience perdra de sa robustesse" (D 97); but Francillon retains a present tense, which is not altogether wrong after "à mesure que": "à mesure que tu te fais moins jeune et ta conscience moins coriace" (F 154). Note, incidentally, that in this case Francillon is the one who has tried to retain something of the original rhythm.

Another similarly obvious yet not always compulsory transformation when translating from English into French is the omission of the modal in front of verbs of perception. In the last long paragraph towards the end of chapter 1 we read: "he could hear the rain dripping ..." (46). Francillon's literal (word-for-word) translation "il put entendre" (F 96) is here unacceptable. The French equivalent for "I can see you," the sentence in chapter 10 first spoken by the idiot at the station in the opening nightmare sequence (285, 293, echoed on pages 302–3), is "Je te vois" rather than "Je peux te voir." Another sentence heard first in the opening railway nightmare and echoed in the excusado scene, "You can't escape me," *can* be translated as "Tu ne peux m'échapper," but the threat is more final and ominous with a future tense: "Tu ne m'échapperas pas."

There are at least two cases where Romance languages have to choose between different forms where English has only one. "You" in the singular can be either familiar or deferential. The least that can be expected is consistency, and here Monicelli is found at fault, since he has the Consul address his old childhood friend Jacques Laruelle in the expected familiar "tu" form in the course of the novel but with a formal "voi" when, in chapter 1, Laruelle imagines what he might have thought on lending him the volume of Elizabethan plays: "I know, Jacques, you may never return the book, but suppose I lend it you precisely for that reason" (33).

The other unavoidable choice is between a tense expressing a repeated or continuous action and a tense expressing a punctual one when referring to the past. Both are expressed by the English past tense, though continuity can be stressed by a progressive form and repetition by "would," in which cases there is no translation dilemma. But whenever we come across a past tense the French language has to choose between *imparfait* and *passé simple*. The choice is stylistically important in passages of economical narrative prose like the short description of what is taking place in the arena that interrupts Geoffrey and Yvonne's love dialogue in chapter 9. Ironically enough, Hugh is here an agent of persecution: "Hugh tugged; the bull tugged, was free ... Hugh rode the tiring bull round and round the ring" (279). Should the French translator write "tirait" or "tira," "chevauchait" or "chevaucha" (F 467, D 306)?

Other forms will be avoided on stylistic rather than strictly grammatical grounds. But we are here moving into the quicksands of personal appreciation. Co-ordination with "and" is more frequent in English than in French. Should one therefore try to substitute other syntactic structures? Clearly, this is a case where no rule can be automatically applied. One of the parentheses in the Consul's unsent letter to Yvonne reads "Several mescalitos later and dawn in the Farolito" (45). Francillon translates almost word for word: "Plusieurs mescalitos plus tard, et l'aube au Farolito" (F 94). Darras writes "Au Farolito, à l'aube, plusieurs mescalitos plus tard" (D 56). He not only leaves out the co-ordination; he alters the perspective and thus the bearing of the parenthesis: location is emphasized, which might suggest that the rest of the letter had been written elsewhere; moreover, by severing the close link between "dawn" and "Farolito" he cancels the sense that dawn in this particular cantina is a special experience. In a sentence like "as you grow older and your conscience less robust" (83), it can be argued that retaining the co-ordination preserves the balanced rhythm of the double clause, even though this way of co-ordinating subclauses is less frequent in French than in English.

The translation of -ing forms raises an acute problem in most languages. An equivalent form exists in French, but its use is much less extensive and less common than in English. Claude Simon makes an abundant use of the French present participle, but this is highly unusual and has consequently a definite stylistic effect. The recurring question will thus be: is the French translator to use a *participe présent*, which is the closest he or she can come to the original rhythm but is often disconcerting? Or can alternative translations be used (infinitives, relative clauses, verbs in the *imparfait*, etc.)? Again, there can be no general theoretical answer. Each sentence has to be examined separately to weigh the relative importance of rhythm and adherence to normal linguistic expectations. In a sentence such as "he could hear the rain dripping off the roofs and the water still rushing down the gutters in the streets" (46), present participles are virtually impossible in French; relative clauses ("qui s'égouttait," "qui continuait à dévaler") probably fit in better with the sense of delay pervading the passage than the infinitives used by both Francillon and Darras (F 96, D 57).

Ing forms – gerunds, present participles, or present progressives – make up the framework of the two-and-a-half-page-long sentence in chapter 12 that presents the nightmarish dovetailing of two experiences: the Consul's penetration of a prostitute and the repetition of his daily early morning flights in Oaxaca from a hotel that had become a tomb to the deceptive womb of El Infierno, "that other Farolito" (349–52). Some of these -ing forms perform conventionally as nouns, adjectives, or progressive forms. The syntactic weight of the sentence rests on some others, which form the flexible and extended backbone of a sentence that mimics, through the very absence of any definite shape, a calamitous sense of endless descent and pointless escape. At first these forms are clearly dependent on "horror": "[Maria's body] was disaster, it was the horror of waking up in the morning in Oaxaca," "of trying to find the bottle in the dark ... and failing," "of going down the carpeted stairs." Then gradually they stand (or collapse) on their own: "sinking," "half-whispering," "waiting," "trembling," "carrying," "holding," "letting," "subsiding," "feeling," "drawing," "creeping," "not daring to look," "clutching," "groaning," "rounding," "standing," "talking," "drinking," "telling lies," "lying." Clearly, all those suspended verbs whose implicit subject is the Consul do not have the same status. Some merely describe circumstances secondary to the main actions and have to be read alongside a number of other present participles that have separate subjects: "the vulture sitting in the washbasin," "his feet sinking into heartbreak," "his steps sinking into calamity," "one dim light hovering," "the calendar saying," "the manager's nephew ... waiting up," "the bottle of French wine ... still standing," "the clock ticking forward, with his heart ticking," "the Indian nightwatchman sleeping."

As the sentence unfolds, by a quaint reversal of perspective, the sexual act that is being performed becomes almost an intrusive memory twice referred to in parenthesis: Maria's body is practically forgotten, swept away, as it were, by the wind of hope present in the haunting exclamation "the escape!" until the two nightmare experiences are sharply brought together under the shadow of death: "until the lilac-shaded dawn that should have brought death, and he should have died now too; what have I done?" (352) Here the reader too is shaken by two disruptive elements: the startling use of a first-person singular and of a present perfect. Ideally, translations should retain the haunting and dissolving quality of the syntax. Yet something will necessarily be lost, if only because in English a noun can be determined by the same form of the verb as that of the present participle. So again the translator is faced with difficult choices. In French the most adequate, or least inadequate solution is probably to have a number of infinitives ("l'horreur de s'éveiller," etc.), indicating the protagonist's main actions, and, in this case, still an abnormally high number of present participles.

5. Another limitation proper to the target languages may appear in the translation of long and convoluted sentences. A major advantage of English when it comes to juggling with words, particularly in a complex syntactical environment, is their almost unlimited convertibility: a noun is a verb is an adjective, all according to the context, which makes for some rich ambiguity inevitably lost in other languages. This creative capacity within the language is particularly striking in the case of phrasal verbs where the particle – often a preposition turned adverb – carries the main burden of meaning while the verb itself defines the mode of realization. Another advantage is the capacity English has of embedding within a relative clause another clause, often expressing opinion, which gives the relative pronoun a double function, as in "the drink that I can never believe even in raising to my lips is real" (46). This part of the sentence is perfectly clear and "normal" in English, while other languages will have either to add a conjunction or change the word order: "la bebida de la que nunca puedo creer a un quando la lleva hasta mis labios que sea verdadera" (O 52), or "diesem Getränk, an dessen Wirklichkeit ich nicht einmal glauben kann, wenn ich es zum Mund führe" (G 61).

The exuberant weaving of Lowry's sentences is a major stumbling block in translation. Sentences contorted to the limit of linguistic acceptability are a recurring feature all through the novel. Never, however, are these convolutions gratuitous or, worse, evidence of Lowry's inability to cope with words. Quite the opposite. Syntactic complexity always serves a purpose, though the purpose is always different. Hence the importance of retaining it whenever possible, of reproducing in the target languages syntactical or logical dislocations.

Amid the overwhelming intricacies in Lowry's syntactic forest, some signs are liable to escape the translator, however important they may be for the overall meaning. A negation was missed in Monicelli's translation of the sentence "Can it be you didn't realize I was still here?" (43): "Che tu abbia pensato forse che io mi trovavo ancora qui?" (M 47). Possessive adjectives may lead the translator astray: "I also recognize how close Yvonne and I had already been brought to disaster before your meeting" (82), a sentence in which "your meeting" means the meeting between you and Yvonne, becomes "riconosco quanto Yvonne ed io fossimo già stati portati vicino alla catastrofe prima ancora di incontrarti" (M 87).

Many long, intricate sentences, however, do not offer any particular problem other than the translator's willingness to deal with his own language as Lowry has dealt with English. If Lowry leaves out connective adverbs, he intends the reader to do without those convenient signposts. If he has a number of intervening adjuncts and subclauses between subject and verb, he means the reader to be left suspended in expectation. Word order in Lowry's sentences is almost always deliberate and effective, and is thus to be respected by translators.

For instance, in the first paragraph of chapter 2, after the sentence about the transportation of corpses (48), "Yvonne thought" is deliberately placed at the end. It is thus slightly disturbing to have the phrase transferred to the beginning in the otherwise impeccable Spanish translation (O 55). In the long sentence already quoted in which Yvonne's perception of the present is muffled in memories of her past arrival in Acapulco, Darras places the subject immediately before the verb, whereas the delay left in the original corresponds to the expansion of consciousness taking place in Yvonne's mind.

The long whirling sentences at the end of chapter 11 are all the more effective when they are contrasted with the succession of short periods that tell the almost bare facts of Yvonne's fall from the log. All translators have here felt the importance of the rhythm and have closely followed the movement of the original.

The earlier German translator, Susanna Rademacher, has often, in order to retain the original length of the sentences, syncopated them with dashes that destroy the fluidity of the text, produce an unpleasant picture to the reader's eyes, and distort the narrative perspective, since each part of the sentence thus isolated appears as an authorial comment superimposed upon the character's perception.

Monicelli, by contrast, has been particularly alert to the syntactical distribution of Lowry's prose. Because his prose reflects the modalities of thought behind the work through the stylistic arrangement of the verbal structures, the rhetorical activity is conceptual as well as stylistic.

6. The reductive polishing of the text affects more than the syntax. The German translation by Rademacher often illustrates a deliberate nor-

malization of situations. Where the text says, for instance, "the little girl sat on the orange" (46), she has the child hold the fruit in her hand: "das Mädchen hielt die Orange in der Hand, ohne sie zu essen." Probably failing to understand how a ferris wheel can be seen to turn backwards, she simply leaves out "rückwärts" in the last sentence of chapter 1, thus ignoring the hint in the sentence about the structure of the book. The image in the sentence "Yvonne felt her spirit that had flown to meet this man as if already sticking to the leather" (50), she turns into sound, simple prose: "Yvonnes Seele war der Begegnung mit diesem Mann entgegengeflogen, jetzt wurde sie lahm und schwer."

Another way of betraying the text is to leave out allusions that may be thought offensive. A famous instance of this is the way Susanna Rademacher glosses over the sexual innuendoes in the menu scene (chapter 10). Karin Graf, on the contrary, catches them in her translation. "Cauliflowers or pootootsies" (292) becomes "Blumenköpfchen oder Fischfinger" (348); "onans" becomes "Zippeln," which literally means sausages but is used by children for penis; "pepped petroot" are "gepfefferte Gurke," while "stepped on eggs"/"getretene Eier" are suggestive of sexual violence; "somersaults for the queen" becomes "Bocksprünge auf die Königin," with "Bock" (ram) emblematic of sexual power. Graf's menu continues with "Pimmelsan-Huhnbusen" (combining male and female), "gefülltes Täubchen" (a transparent allusion to pregnancy), "Murmelade aus Feigen und Pfäumchen" (female sex organ), "Omlet sehrpiss" (scatological), "Silberspritz" (ejaculation), and "Scha(u)mwein." Rather than having exaggerated Lowry's bawdy, Graf compensates for those allusions in the menu that inevitably get lost while remaining strictly respectful to the direction in which the innuendoes work.

Raûl Ortiz y Ortiz had an even more difficult job here, since he had to render Cervantes' approximative English into Spanish. Yet he has managed it beautifully. Here are two extracts from the passage in the Spanish version:

¿Le gustan los huevos, señora? Huevos pisados. "Muy sabrosos." ¿Huevos divorciados? Para pescado, rebanadas o filete con chícharos. Vol–au–vent à la reine. Maromas para la reina. ¿O le gustan los huevos difíciles de cocer, disifíles en pan tostado? ¿O una rebanada de hígado del Capitán? ¿O chopita de popo en pipián? ¿O pollo espectral de la casa Pichoncito. ¿O un filete de golfo, con un tartaro frito, le gusta?   (O 323)

¿le gustan los calamadres en su tinta? ¿O atunas? ¿O un exquisito mole? ¿Tal vez un melón de moda para comenzar? ¿Mermelada de higos? ¿Moras con mierdabeja a la Gran Duque? Omelésurpus ¿le gusta? ¿Quiere primero un chin fish? ¿Un buen chin fish? ¿Un pez plateado? ¿Sparkenwein?   (O 324)

7. The different French versions of the *Macbeth* concatenations in chapter 5 can also serve to illustrate translators' options, though here it would be difficult to speak of distortion. Geoffrey's neighbour, Mr Quincey, has repeatedly asked about Laruelle after casually mentioning that Hugh has come back from Mexico City and gone out with Yvonne:

Mr Quincey's words knocked on his consciousness – or someone actually was knocking on a door – fell away, then knocked again, louder. Old De Quincey; the knocking on the gate in Macbeth. Knock, knock, knock: who's there? Cat. Cat who? Catastrophe. Catastrophe who? Catastrophysicist. What, is it you, my little popocat? Just wait an eternity till Jacques and I have finished murdering sleep? Katabasis to cat abysses. Cat hartes atratus.   (140)

Clarisse Francillon's version retains most of the tragic fun and is very close to the words of the original, with a necessary softening of the initial *k* sound:

Les paroles de M. Quincey frappaient à sa conscience – ou quelqu'un frappait à une porte pour de vrai – s'éclipsaient, puis refrappaient, plus fort. Ce vieux de Quincey; les coups à la porte dans Macbeth. Pan pan: qui va là? Chat. Chat qui? Chatastrophe. Chatastrophe qui? Chatastrophysicien. Quoi, c'est toi, mon petit popochatepetl? Attends, rien qu'une éternité, que Jacques et moi ayons fini de tuer le sommeil! Chataracte sur chat à rats. "Chathartes atratus" le Vautour.   (F 244–5)

Darras chooses to retain the *k* sound, but drowns the cat:

Les mots de M. Quincey cognaient contre son cerveau, ou bien était-ce quelqu'un qui frappait réellement à une porte, puis les coups cessèrent, puis ils reprirent plus violemment. Ah ce vieux De Quincey! Les coups contre la porte du château dans *Macbeth*. Tok tok tok. Ki va là? Kat! Katastrophe! Katastrophe Ki? Katastrophysique. Komment! Est-ce toi petit popokat? Attends l'éternité que Jacques et moi ayons fini d'assassiner le sommeil! Katabysmale Katabase. Kat hartes atratus.   (D 156)

Pagnoulle has been carried away by the fun of the game and suggests the following "catty" variations:

Les mots de M. Quincey frappaient à la porte de sa conscience – ou peut-être quelqu'un frappait-il vraiment à une porte – s'estompaient, puis frappaient à nouveau, plus fort. Ce vieux De Quincey; les coups à la porte de Macbeth. Toc, toc, toc; qui va là? Chat. Chat qui? Chagrin. Chagrin comment? Peau de chagrin. Quoi, est-ce toi, mon petit popochat? Attends rien qu'une éternité que Jacques et moi ayons fini d'assassiner le sommeil? Chamades pour chutes abyssales, châtiments en enfer de tourments.

The meaning of a word is not a set, cut-off thing: it comes up with roots, with associations, with how and where the word is commonly used or where it has been used brilliantly and memorably. The meaning of a word is a construction, an assembly of those associations, not only linguistic but also referential, historical, and pragmatic. It is, therefore, important for the translator to trace phrases to their sources.

Let us consider two instances. One is the startling opening of chapter 2: "— — — 'A corpse will be transported by express!'" (48, also 286 and 303) In this case the source is given two and a half pages further on, when we read: "the Consul had resumed ... his study of a blue and red Mexican National Railways time-table" (51). It is thus an official instruction on the transportation of corpses, with the exclamation mark added to express the Consul's comment, and also presumably something of his intonation. Translators must attempt not only to find the right register in their target languages but also to preserve the emotional impact of the words in that particular position. It is important that the chapter should begin with the word "corpse" and that it should be in the singular. But both Clarisse Francillon and Jacques Darras miss the administrative tone.

Immediately after Quincey's reference to the possible repetition of Hugh's betrayal, Geoffrey greets the cat with the following words: "Hullo-hullo-look-who-comes-hullo-my-little-snake-in-the-grass-my-little-anguish-in-herba – " (138). The tragically playful words are all the more difficult to translate as they indirectly refer to another form "in absentia," namely a line from Virgil: "latet anguis in herba." Lowry plays on it so that "latet" produces "little" on the basis of phonological echoes, and "anguis," first translated into "snake," produces "anguish." The Italian has in the first edition "anguish" untranslated and in the revised edition "pena" in its place: "– Oh, là, là, là, guarda chi si vede, là, là, mio bel serpentello nell'erba mia piccola pena in erba – " (M 44). If on one side "pena" takes up the alliterative repetition of the *p* sound, it loses the play between "anguis" and "anguish" and the reference to Virgil's line. The blurring of the connection between the serpent-betrayal theme and the Consul's anguish is regrettable, even though, or perhaps precisely because, it appears in a playful context.

What is the translator to do when allusions refer to texts that are common cultural knowledge to most readers in the source language but are unlikely to call up any association among readers in the target languages? Standard instances are Bunyan or Shakespeare. Cultural discrepancies are perhaps even more arresting in the case of such an allegedly widely read text as the Bible. To take just one example, the words in chapter 7, "I can see the writing on the wall" (222), are spoken in Geoffrey's mind by Laruelle, who is no longer present in the flesh – and wittily echoed two lines further in "the writing was there, all right, if not on the wall. The man had nailed his board to the tree." The echo cannot work in the same obviously allusive way in a language other than English. The average English-speaking reader will not necessarily think of King Belshazzar's feast in the Book of Daniel, but he or she will know at once that "the writing on the wall" means a solemn warning with biblical overtones. Will something then have to be added to the translation? For instance: "mais c'était écrit, pas de doute, même si c'était sur un arbre et pas sur un mur, comme au festin de Belschatsar?"[9]

When Lowry's language is described as "poetical," what is referred to is his often elaborate and extensive use of metaphors. Metaphor is central to all forms of language use and is, at the same time, a trope that reveals important differences among languages. A metaphor is by definition a semantic novelty, and there are few set equivalences across languages. What determines the translatability of a metaphor is the extent to which the cultural experience and semantic associations on which it draws, the analogies on which it is built or that it exploits, are shared by speakers of the particular target languages. Lowry's metaphors can rarely be retained in all their richness and their vividness, but some compensatory effects can often be achieved.

To Yvonne coming back to their house on Calle Nicaragua in chapter 2 the high walls covered with bougainvillea are "massive smouldering banks of bloom" (67), which Monicelli translates as "massicci cespi di piante in boccio" (M 72). This is not as rich metaphorically: "smouldering" has been lost as well as some of the connotations of "banks," but a form of compensation is at work and some phonological effects are reproduced.

More difficult is the following metaphor which starts, as so often happens in Lowry, from a simile: "The miradors cut off, floating above, like lonely rooftrees of the soul" (68) becomes "i miradori in fuori, galleggianti a mezz'altezza, come solitari travi dell'anima" (M 73). The boldness and originality of Lowry's metaphor has not been captured completely, and "travi" is both weak and anomalous. In the case of "a wooling of his pain, contemptible" (74), translated as "un lievissimo filo di dolore, trascurabile" (M 78), the metaphor is not only lost but misunderstood: the translation misses both "wooling" and the contempt caused by the "wooling," that is, by the absence of a properly tragic form of desperation. Yet when the semantic associations are shared in the Italian language because they are the outcome of a common cultural experience, the metaphors are beautifully rendered by Monicelli:

a gathering thunder of immedicable sorrow   (218)
l'addensarsi di un nembo d'immedicabile strazio   (M 226)

their hands but blown fragments of their memories   (72)
le mani se non frammenti esplosi dei loro ricordi   (M 76)

white sculpturing of clouds like billowing concepts in the mind of
Michelangelo   (122)
candide sculture di nuvole come spumeggianti concezioni nella mente di
Michelangelo   (M 128)

Under the Volcano can be seen as a re-vision of the "case" involving the Consul, his wife Yvonne, his half-brother Hugh, half a dozen secondary characters, an overwhelming landscape, and a whole society at a specific point in history, with Laruelle, significantly a film director, setting the wheel in motion in the first chapter. Just as the reconsideration of the story one year later results in an inevitable altering of the case, similarly, with each new reading, "The Case is Altered." How much more then, unavoidably, with each translation? Yet while all translations are to some extent betrayals, they are necessary too. Choices in the translation of a literary text are determined by the specific qualities of the text to be translated. Conversely, as suggested at the beginning of the present essay, a translation can help to bring out those essential stylistic features, sometimes through its very shortcomings.

Under the Volcano is a carefully planned, at times overwritten novel. Clearly, not every sentence in it is equally felicitous. Among the many puns and images (whether similes or metaphors), some can be modified or shifted without the novel's incurring any serious damage. As several critics have pointed out, however, a fairly large number of images are carefully laid out (or planted) throughout the novel to weave significant webs of meaning: trees and crosses and towers, volcanoes, mountains and abysses, wheels and water, dogs, horses and conquerors.[10] Once we start on this path there is no knowing where (or whether) we shall stop. The translator cannot of course disrupt at will these underlying nets of signification; he or she should try to retain all specific connotations so as not to break any of the threads in the elaborate web of echoes. Incidental allusions may not be consciously perceived by the reader; the translator's role is not to explain. But the web should be left intact.

It is also the image of the web that comes to mind if we think of the convoluted, sometimes deliberately "bad" syntax used in some passages. Do translators balk at retaining Faulkner's endless unpunctuated sentences in *Absalom, Absalom!* for instance? Lowry's syntax is closer to the received norm than Faulkner's or Joyce's in some of their writings, although it covers in fact a considerable range. Some of his sentences are models of clipped concision, while whole paragraphs (particularly, but not exclusively in the "Consular" chapters) seem to trip themselves up and trap themselves through sheer accumulation of subclauses and embedded comments. The "normalizing" that occurs in some translations, making the syntax far more straightforward than it is in the original, almost always results in distorted perspectives. It certainly disrupts an essential aspect of the novel. In those intricate passages the reader is invited to enter the maze and look for the way out – that is, for the most plausible interpretation – sometimes without any final certainty that another reading is not equally valid. The reader is meant to be puzzled, if not mystified, is meant to try to uncover the thought-pattern underlying the sentence, just as she or he is meant to try to understand the pattern of the tragedy, without any certain, final explanation ever being reached. In other words, complexity of syntax has a heuristic value.

Beyond a mere accuracy of tone and a scrupulous respect for the sequence in which an argument is developed, rhythm is of final importance and is essential to the poetic quality of the novel. Lowry's own assessment of his text was that "it sings, I believe, considerably – the whole thing – in the mind" (SL 146), and it is a standard that should apply to the translation, which must sing at least a little in the mind. And if it sings, even a little, then the translator is not a traitor but a co-creator with Lowry of the *genus floridum*.

NOTES

1 The material in this essay was edited by Christine Pagnoulle from the various contributions to the translation panel by Pagnoulle, Karin Graf, Elsa Linguanti, and Raûl Ortiz y Ortiz at the 1987 International Lowry Symposium.

2 *Bajo el volcan* (Mexico City: Era 1964; Barcelona: Brugera 1981) was translated by Raûl Ortiz y Ortiz. References are to the Spanish edition and are indicated in the text by "O" followed by the page number. My thanks to Dr Carmen Virgili for providing me with an annotated copy. *Sotto il vulcano* (Milan: Feltrinelli 1961, 1984) was translated by Giorgio Monicelli. References in the text are to the 1984 edition and are indicated in the text by "M" followed by the page number. *Unter dem Vulkan* (Hamburg: Rowohlt 1964) was translated by Susanna Rademacher; a second translation was made by Karin Graf (Hamburg: Rowohlt 1984). Ref-

erences in the text are indicated by "G" followed by the page number. *Au-dessous du volcan* was translated by Stephen Spriel and Clarisse Francillon (Paris: Le club français du livre 1959) and was reissued by Gallimard in 1973. References are to the later edition and are indicated in the text by "F" followed by the page number. *Sous le volcan* was translated by Jacques Darras (Paris: Grasset 1987), and references to this edition are indicated by "D" followed by the page number.

3 James Joyce, *Finnegans Wake* (London: Faber and Faber 1939, 1971), 121.

4 Georges Mounin, *Les Problèmes de la traduction* (Paris: Gallimard 1963, 1980), 278–9.

5 Marnix Vincent, "Claus, Icare et traduction," *Pi Revue de Poésie* 6, no. 2 (June 1987): 85.

6 G. Rado, "Outline of a Systematic Translatology," *Babel* 18 (1978): 187–96.

7 Malcolm Lowry, *Under the Volcano* (Harmondsworth: Penguin 1963), 202. Further page references in the text are to this edition.

8 "L'acte éthique consiste à reconnaître et à recevoir l'Autre en tant qu'Autre," and "la traduction, de par sa visée de fidélité, appartient *origi-nairement* à la dimension éthique. Elle est, dans son essence même, animée du *désir d'ouvrir l'Etranger en tant qu'Etranger à son propre espace de langue.* Cela ne veut nullement dire qu'historiquement, il en ait été souvent ainsi. Au contraire, la visée appropriatrice et annexionniste qui caractérise l'Oc-cident a presque toujours étouffé la vocation éthique de la traduction. La 'logique du même' l'a presque toujours emporté. Il n'empêche que l'acte de traduire relève d'une autre logique, celle de l'éthique. C'est pourquoi, reprenant la belle expression d'un troubadour, nous disons que la traduc-tion est, dans son essence, 'l'auberge du lointain.'" Antoine Berman, "La Traduction et la lettre," *Les Tours de babel* (Mauvezin: Trans-Europ-Repress 1985), 88–9.

9 What any reader raised in a Christian environment would perceive, what-ever the language, is the allusion to the crucifixion in the words "nailed ... to the tree."

10 See, for example, Duncan Hadfield, "*Under the Volcano*'s 'Central' Sym-bols: Trees, Towers and Their Variants," in *Apparently Incongruous Parts: The Worlds of Malcolm Lowry*, ed. Paul Tiessen (Metuchen, NJ: Scarecrow Press 1990), 80–109.

Praxis as Prophylaxis: A Political Reading of *Under the Volcano*

HILDA THOMAS

For nearly four decades readers of *Under the Volcano* have been clambering around in Lowry's barranca. Unsuitably equipped with alpenstock and ventilated snow goggles, the Hotel Fausto's information protruding from one pocket and *The Elementaries of the Cabbala* from the other, they have been hypnotized by Lowry into believing that spelunking and mountain climbing are the same thing, only to discover in the end that the Consul's Hell is nothing but a gigantic jakes, and that the expedition leads not to the top of Mount Himavat but to a sign reading "No Exit." This is not to say that the descent is easy. Nor is it dull. Indeed, Lowry's masterpiece (to alter the metaphor) might be described as a tomb filled with fabulous gems and curios, the walls inscribed with mysterious hieroglyphics that the reader is compelled to decipher. My own early attempts at decoding led me from Prescott and Hugh Thomas to A.E. Waite and Carl Jung; "Thalavethiparothiam" required the reading of all of Frazer's *The Golden Bough,* and the elusive Lee Maitland sent me through everything from Edgar Allan Poe to the history of tennis, to no avail.

Now thanks to Ackerley and Clipper's *Companion to Under the Volcano,* the excavation has been completed, every (or nearly every) last artefact tagged and classified. Still the novel as a whole defies analysis. "The narrative adamantly resists the extraction of a single coherent 'reading' which can account for the book as a totality."[1] Any attempt at a comprehensive reading must wrestle with what Ronald Binns calls its "surplus of signifiers," its "elusive connotations and unbridgeable contradictions" (64). And if they are like me, most critics will recognize in Lowry's armadillo the image of what this contest leads to. One is pulled deeper and deeper into the text, unable to let go even when it becomes all too evident that the "hidden magic" of *Under the Volcano* cannot be captured in this fashion.

In fact, this pulling and tugging could be taken as a figure for "the sterile opposition between the arbitrary interpretations of the symbol on the one hand, and the blank failure to see what it means on the other."[2] In order to go beyond this oscillating movement from symbol to meaning and back again, we are, as Jameson suggests, "required to read these symbolic objects to the second power: not so much directly to decipher in them a one-to-one meaning, as to sense that of which the very fact of symbolism is itself symptomatic" (67). What is needed is a sort of "shifting of gears," a relocating of the text in its historical moment. As an example, Jameson cites Plekanov's discussion of symbolism:

The history of literature shows that man [sic] has always used ... [symbolism or realism] to transcend a particular reality. He employs ... symbols ... when he is unable to grasp the meaning of that particular reality, or when he cannot accept the conclusion to which the development of that reality leads ...; when (to use Hegel's happy expression) he is not able to utter those magic words which bring to life a picture of the future ... And so in art, when an artist leans toward symbolism it is an infallible sign that his thinking – or the thinking of the class which he represents ... – does not dare penetrate the reality which lies before his eyes. (337)

Plekanov's pejorative view of symbolism seems narrow and unhelpful when applied to *Under the Volcano*. But it is an apt description of Lowry's hero. The Consul is one of those figures who haunt the modern novel, "the possessed artist with the ailing soul," the underground man whose motto is "*I am alone and they are everyone.*"[3]

Such figures, victims of the ontological sickness that pervades the twentieth century, are the bearers of Hegel's "unhappy consciousness." They suffer from "a stubborn orientation toward the transcendent, ... an inability to relinquish religious patterns of desire when history has outgrown them" (Girard 158). For Sartre, this "surreptitious wish to resuscitate the transcendent," which arises out of "the unhappiness of man without God," is characteristic of "a bourgeoisie which is partially de-Christianized but which regrets its past faith because it has lost confidence in its rationalist, positivist ideology."[4] Like the Consul, whose failure to complete his proposed book entitled "Secret Knowledge" can be explained away by the title, they are no longer able to take seriously, let alone to answer, "such questions as: Is there any ultimate reality, external, conscious and ever-present etc. etc. that can be realised by any such means that may be acceptable to all creeds and religions and suitable to all climes and countries?"[5] As he stumbles from one mirage to the next in his futile search for self-fulfilment, using artificial means like drugs or alcohol, the alienated hero reaches "a stage of *lucid stupefaction* which constitutes the final romantic pose" (Girard 273). Not only is he unable to quench his own thirst; he is like a "Hindu untouchable [who] contaminates everyone and everything with which he is in contact": "The subject is ashamed of his life and his mind. In despair at not being God, he searches for the sacred in everything which threatens his life, in everything which thwarts his mind. Thus he is always oriented toward what will debase and finally destroy the highest and most noble part of his being" (Girard 56, 282).

The true end of this *via negativa* is "death, death, and death again and death": "the final stupid unprophylactic rejection" (*UV* 350, 348). As Girard notes, its pattern is expressed in imagery "as strict ... as the imagery of vertical transcendency in the writings of the Christian mystics" (285). From animal images it progresses through the world of the mechanical, ending in total negation: "The hero wants to express the pride and suffering of being unique, he thinks he is about to grasp absolute particularity but ends up with a principle of universal application ... The greedy mouth closing on nothingness, the Sisyphean effort perpetually renewed do indeed sum up the history of contemporary individualism" (Girard 260–1).

There is no need to point out how closely *Under the Volcano*, with its images of cleavage, circularity, and unreconciled duality, exemplifies the concept of "deviated transcendence" developed so exhaustively by Girard. Nor is it simply the overdetermination of signifiers, the investing of the object world with mythic power both sacred and demonic, that accounts for the overwhelming sense of desolation that pervades the final chapter of *Under the Volcano*. The very structure of the novel rehearses the transparently ahistorical and undialectical theme of the eternal return, the closed circle that permits no escape from the "poor frozen paradoxes" of an "empty subjectivity" (Sartre 12). Within this circle the binary opposition between light and dark, good and evil, salvation and damnation is endlessly repeated, and human freedom is reduced to the choice of one of two hypostasized absolutes. Thus Laruelle in chapter 1 of *Under the Volcano* describes a mental and physical circle around the Consul's "place where you know" in a vain attempt to square the circle, only to be pulled back, along with the reader, into the vortex of memory and remorse. The effect of this infinitely regressive movement is to confer on the Consul a kind of immortality (the dead are not mortal) and to place his death under the sign of a destiny, thus rendering it immune from judgment. It constitutes an affirmation of death – a valorization of narcissistic delusion and self-destruction.

Here it is necessary to take a step backward *pour mieux sauter*. Can it be that it is precisely this apotheosis of self that appeals to certain readers of *Under the Volcano*? Readers who, unable to find in the dominant ideology any explanation for what Sartre calls the *scandal* of existence, turn instead to the irrational, to the pursuit of pure subjectivity, seeking solace (if only vicariously) in madness, drunkenness, and despair? For such readers Lowry has succeeded all too well in portraying the Consul as "the very shape and motion of the world's doom" (UBC SC 25:17,4). But this is also precisely what Sartre means by the "surreptitious wish to resuscitate the transcendent": "The transcendent, indeed, remains veiled; it is attested only by its absence. One will never go beyond pessimism; one will have a presentiment of reconciliation while remaining at the level of an insurmountable contradiction and a total cleavage" (16). For Sartre this attitude constitutes a flight from reality, a refusal of praxis which "takes refuge in an abstract subjectivity, whose sole aim is to achieve a certain inward *quality*." He assigns it to "a certain European bourgeoisie which wants to justify its privileges by an aristocracy of the soul, to find refuge from its objectivity in an exquisite subjectivity, and to let itself be fascinated by an ineffable present so as not to see its future" (16–17). Any reading of *Under the Volcano* that rests on this view of the Consul betrays its surrender to *mauvaise foi*; it might well replace Lowry's own epigraph from Goethe with the words of Adrian Leverkuhn at the end of Mann's *Dr Faustus*: "instead of shrewdly concerning themselves with what is needful upon earth that it may be better there, and discreetly doing it, ... man playeth the truant and breaketh out in hellish drunkenness; so giveth he his soul thereto and cometh among the carrion."[6] The "hidden magic" of *Under the Volcano* is in this event revealed as the seductive power of *thanatos* – the allure of a defeat so absolute that it precludes any possibility of action. This is, of course, an absurd conclusion. On the evidence of the novel itself, and of Lowry's comments, *Under the Volcano* was intended to convey the message of *hope*. Moreover, the "whole churrigueresque structure" is shot through with irony and self-irony – even self-parody. The very style of the novel (which has an analogue in the tourist folder of chapter 10, where "the constant repetition of churrigueresque 'of an overloaded style'" suggests that the book is "satirizing itself," SL 82) prohibits such a one-dimensional reading.

There can be no disagreement that the Consul is the central force in *Under the Volcano*, the axis around which everything revolves, or that an exclusive focus on the Consul produces a powerful and consistent reading of the text. But removed from the political context in which Lowry took such pains to situate it, the Consul's death has the finality of an "unassimilable catastrophe" (UV 8). The word "dingy" (UV 373), derived from "dungeon" and "dung," originally *dynga*, an underground chamber covered with dung, is precisely the right one to describe his death in the barranca; and here the ravine itself becomes an ultimate image of the failure of discourse, the unbridgeable gap between self and other.

But the Consul has another "self" in Hugh, a fact that is too little examined. The splitting of both narrative point of view and political perspective in *Under the Volcano* permits Lowry to step outside the disintegrating consciousness of the Consul, thus avoiding an exclusive concentration on the figure of the lonely hero cut off from the world of action. While the Consul pursues his blind, circuitous path through hell – a path that leads not (alas!) back to God, but always back into the abyss of the self – Hugh has perhaps "turned and thought, ... turned back and questioned, decided to act" (UV 179). The role of Hugh is frequently trivialized. He is dismissed as the "professional indoor Marxman" (UV 8) of Laruelle's first impression, as a parlour revolutionary whose decision to set out for Spain when the defeat of the Loyalists is a foregone conclusion testifies to his political naïveté and his romanticism. But it should be noted that Lowry refers to chapter 6 of *Under the Volcano* as the "heart of the book," and that of Hugh he writes: "Hugh may be a bit of a fool but he none the less typifies the sort of person who may make or break our future: in fact he is the future in a certain sense" (SL 14–15). A product of the same bourgeois upbringing as the Consul, he has to some extent surpassed the limitations of his class. He has a first-hand knowledge of what it feels like to have "fallen down the spout of the capitalist system" (UV 171), and he has avoided, if largely by chance, the temptations of anti-Semitism and narcissism – which, incidentally, are not unconnected: "the modern holocaust ... represents an insane attempt to assert the hegemony of narcissism identified with a state and a race."[7]

When Hugh first appears in the novel, he is reading a telegram he has sent regarding the anti-Semitic propaganda campaign sponsored by the German legation in Mexico City. He is dressed in the style of a gentleman charro, complete with holster and pistol – a fashion that reminds Yvonne of her Hollywood cowboy leading man, Hoot Gibson (UV 261). He is also carrying a jacket borrowed from his brother, and he slips the telegram into the pocket of this jacket, where it is later, ironically, taken as proof of the Consul's political engagement.

Hugh is not, in fact, a political *engagé*. In setting out for Spain, he is motivated as much by remorse and guilt over his earlier acts of personal betrayal (not the least of which is his betrayal of his brother with

Yvonne) as by political conviction. He is aware that his behaviour is Quixotic (he has straw in his feet, like the "stuffed Quixotes tilting their straw mounts on the house wall," *UV* 68), although he misses the Consul's reference to windmills in chapter 8 (248). But through Hugh's meditations, which occupy a good part of chapters 4, 6, and 8, Lowry accomplishes what Edward Said has accused the modern novelist of failing to do: he "deals directly with the major social and economic facts of ... existence – colonialism and imperialism."[8] Through Hugh, Lowry locates his characters in the world of the Spanish Civil War, which has been described as a battle for the soul of the twentieth century.[9] But in doing so he shows how political conflict is inscribed in the lived experience of individuals as a search for authenticity: "Genuine authenticity is ... not a state ... but rather something precariously wrested from inauthenticity, reclaimed and reconquered from it, and in perpetual danger of collapsing back into the older form ... *mauvaise foi*" (Jameson 276–7).

This anguished struggle always involves the overcoming of regret and remorse, "the form which the illusion of being takes for the middle class" (Jameson 277) in Sartre's view. In the Consul's case the conflict is densely elaborated, invested with mythic and psychoanalytic complexity. In Hugh its import is made explicit:

– How splendid it all might be had I only not betrayed that man last night, ... how good indeed, if only it had not happened though, if only it were not so absolutely necessary to go out and hang oneself –

And here it was again, the temptation, the cowardly, the future-corruptive serpent: trample on it, stupid fool. Be Mexico. Have you not passed through the river? In the name of God be dead.   (*UV* 111)

What must die is the poisonous obsession with past failure and suffering. This is the lesson of Juan Cerillo, which Hugh has yet to act upon:

(... that the past was irrevocably past. And conscience had been given to man to regret it only in so far as that might change the future. For man, every man, Juan seemed to be telling him, even as Mexico, must ceaselessly struggle upward. What was life but a warfare and a stranger's sojourn? Revolution rages too in the tierra caliente of each human soul. No peace but that must pay full toll to hell –) (108)

Lowry offers no simplistic political solutions to the existential questions he explores in *Under the Volcano*. At the end of the novel Hugh has indeed taken a different path, has made a commitment to action. But although he sings of fighting "*para un nueva mundo hacer*" (to make a new world), he is "singing ironically" (*UV* 333–4). There is a further irony in the fact that Hugh survives because he has been rescued by the Consul from an impulsive and probably fatal encounter with the vigilantes by the roadside. This does not prevent him from leaping into the bullring, or indeed from setting out for Spain. The suggestion seems to be that Hugh is only responding to "that absurd necessity he felt for action" (*UV* 275) – that he is equally prepared to risk his life out of pity for a fellow creature, to relieve his boredom, or in a gesture of political adventurism. Moreover, the Consul is killed at least partly because he is wearing the jacket in which Hugh has left the politically incriminating telegram. He is thus mistaken for Hugh and suspected of being a spy, a fact that at once clarifies and further problematizes his role as *pharmakos*. The Consul's substitution for him permits Hugh "providentially" (9) to escape not only from the Mexican police but also from the self-enclosed world of nostalgia and regret into the world of action, of praxis.

In the final version of *Under the Volcano* the political content that was overt in the early drafts has been heavily overlaid by the dense symbolic texture. But the palimpsest is still readable. As with the Tlaxcala tourist brochure, the historic record of oppression and betrayal is not wholly obscured. Ironically, the Consul fails to comprehend the sinister double message of the brochure, or to grasp its relevance to himself. Seated in the private hell of the excusado – a hell of the "Svidrigailov variety" (*UV* 9), "a stone monastic cell" (295), he is like some old monk "proving the existence of the mathematical equivalent of *ignoratio elenchi* with obsolete instruments" (310). Only in the public hell of the Farolito, where he encounters the political reality of fascism, does he discover that his "instruments" – withdrawal from the world, alcohol, escape into "complete glutted oblivion" (354) – are of no more use than the dark glasses he dons, "some fatuous notion of disguise crossing his mind" (362), or the machete with which he tries to ward off his attackers. Hugh's weapons and his disguises may prove to be no more effective than the Consul's. But at least his calendar is set for the future. It is not the future of Yvonne's daydream, which bears all the marks of nostalgia for a lost Eden in which time itself is suspended. Nor is it identified with the facile optimism of a political dogma. (It is not the *Internationale* but the Anarchist hymn *Hijos del Pueblo* that Hugh sings in chapter 11.) Rather, it is the unimaginable future that can come to be only when the ceaseless struggle within the human soul is translated into "an adventure in a human cause" (107).

A good deal more could be said about the way in which Hugh and the Consul represent the alternatives open to the middle-class individual in moments of historical crisis. In fact the Consul suggests such an analysis in his quotation from *War and Peace* (*UV* 309) – one that looks remarkably like Sartre's "progressive-regressive" method. Suffice it to say that Hugh survives to act on the side of the revolution and thus, perhaps, to become in Sartre's terms not a "Thing" but a master of things, a notion that may indeed have been on Lowry's mind (*SL* 80). In Hugh's response to "the look of the poor," Lowry holds out at least some hope for the future, some answer to the existential question posed so sharply by his hero: "What is man to do with his staggering freedom?"[10]

There is undoubtedly as much of Lowry in Hugh as in the Consul – perhaps more. As Conrad Knickerbocker suggests, "Lowry was both men, consumed by his characters."[11] Or it may be more accurate to say that Lowry consumed, absorbed, and refashioned two very different points of view, both drawn from life and both profoundly important to him. The Consul voices the political ideology that was a source of dispute between Lowry and Aiken, a dispute so sharp that Lowry, in an unpublished letter to John Davenport dated 31 August 1937, writes: "At parting I no longer thought of the pro-fascist Conrad as a friend." Aiken, for his part, suggests that while in Mexico "Hambo [Lowry] had drifted pretty far, politically, towards something like communism: he had been through something like a social conversion, and clearly felt a need for some sort of fraternal joining and belonging."[12] This conclusion must be treated with some caution, coming as it does from a man who thought himself daring to have voted once for Debs and twice for his "great liberal cousin" Franklin Roosevelt. In any event the Spenglerian ideas about the "freezing of culture" under fascism, which are repeated by Yvonne in chapter 4 and reiterated by the Consul in chapter 10, clearly belong to Aiken (Aiken 351). Nor is there any doubt that when he began *Under the Volcano*, the politics embraced by Hugh represented for Lowry a genuine affirmation.

It is impossible to believe that Lowry was uninfluenced by Charlotte Haldane's leftist circle, or by his friendship with Juan Fernando Marquez in Mexico, and earlier with John Sommerfield in London. According to Douglas Day, Sommerfield "came to know Lowry at this time [1933] far better than anyone else."[13] He is obviously the model for Hugh's "English friend fighting in Spain" (*UV* 101). Sommerfield did indeed lie with his machine-gun in the library at University City, where he read not De Quincey, but "De Quincey's Lake Poets."[14] With him was another Cambridge revolutionary, John Cornford, who is mentioned by name in the novel. A copy of Sommerfield's *Volunteer in Spain*, in my possession, bears Lowry's signature and the date 10–7–37. On the inside cover there is an unfinished poem (ironically much scribbled over in pencil) in Lowry's hand. It reads as follows:

My two hands broke in two: & they broke me!
Our hands were broken anyway, but the thumbs
Said this: at least we are here with our two
Cool moons unclench those tyrant fathers as you will ... We waited long
    for you to do something good
But though we had no songs we still are spokesmen
& what we wish to speak neither is little or rough (perhaps it is in south-
    eastern port, Davenport,
                                            Samarkand
– & if you are lost, well, Billy-be-damned,
You are at a loss anyway, with wine? – but yet thumbs
                                            Were once fingers
– & we were great ...

This cryptic fragment is no evidence that Lowry shared Sommerfield's political views. But he certainly knew a great deal about the
Spanish Civil War, as Ackerley and Clipper have convincingly demonstrated, and he included in the novel an extraordinary amount of
information that was not then in general circulation and that even now
can be learned only by assiduous research. He knew, for example,
about the *Mar Cantabrico* and Potato Jones, and the CNT (it is this
Anarchist Worker's Federation hymn, *Sons of the People*, that Hugh
sings in chapter 11). He knew the date on which the International
Brigade was withdrawn. He even knew about Canada's own volunteers in Spain, the Mackenzie-Papineau Battalion. He also knew a good
deal about fascism, and he was able to include that knowledge in
Under the Volcano in such a way that the social and political insights
function as a dialectical commentary on the spiritual substance of the
text. That Lowry was never again to achieve this "complex interplay
of subjective and objective forces, inevitable deceptions, self-decep-
tions, error and truth"[15] can perhaps be set down to the fact that
"beginning with the Ebro, none could claim innocence again" (Knickerbocker 32), and that although "Lowry ... spent a good part of those
ten years after *Volcano* looking for Hugh ... it was the Consul and the
Farolito waiting in the shadows" (Knickerbocker 36). Or worse, Vancouver's Niagara Hotel on Pender Street.
    In an unpublished and undated letter to Lowry possibly written in
1948, John Sommerfield writes: "Reading your book I could hear you
speaking and hear myself at the time when we spoke to each other – ,"
adding that "buried under all the things that have happened to us there
are still the people we were." A postscript reads: "No Vin Rosé d'Anjou
left." There is no record of a reply.

It now seems, paradoxically, that only in a world where the eternal return of the dead is not merely recorded but is celebrated – only in the Mexico of the 1930s, a revolutionary society pulling against the fetters of the past, in rebellion "both revolutionary and reactionary at once" (SL 68), and confronted with the decomposition of the "eclectic systemë" – only in that place and at that time could Lowry have found an adequate objective correlative for the disintegration not merely of an individual soul but of a whole era. Lowry's genius lay in his use of the kind of imagery associated with Surrealism – "not, indeed, the images so much as the objects themselves, the mysterious pieces of junk, inexplicable artifacts which seem to bear some hidden message, the lettering that leaps out from a shop window in passing as a miraculous coincidence or a thinly disguised omen, the grade-B melodramas in cheap movie theaters, the store windows of inner passageways, now long since torn down, flora and fauna of the city" (Jameson 103) – objects that permit entry into what André Breton calls the "inexhaustible murmur" of the psyche itself.

This dense and allusive imagery is put in the service of a narrative that at the same time preserves the elements of the realistic novel, with its emphasis on the life of the individual and its "appearance of fate or destiny": *Under the Volcano* "link[s] together in a single figure two incommensurable realities, two independent codes or systems of signs, two heterogeneous and asymmetrical terms: spirit and matter, the data of individual experience and the vaster forms of institutional society, the language of existence and that of history" (Jameson 79, 6–7). Through his protagonist Lowry explores the insurmountable contradictions of the modern world, recognizing that reconciliation is impossible in the present historical circumstances. If *Under the Volcano* is lacking in revolutionary fervour, that is no doubt because beginning with the Ebro, the brotherhood of man could no longer be proclaimed in innocence. (In one typescript of the novel there is a curiously repeated error: the word appears on one page as "brotherhood" and on a subsequent page becomes "brohterhood.") But he also recognized intuitively that "the exclusive refuge in the subject results in … a kind of ahistorical historicity, a mystique of anxiety, death, and individual destiny without any genuine content" (Jameson 56).

Under the Volcano is less an Inferno than a Paradise Lost. It is a meditation on nostalgia, the longing for a vanished plenitude, for "a glimpse of what never was at all, of what never can be since brotherhood was betrayed" (*UV* 107). But "if nostalgia as a political motivation is most frequently associated with Fascism, there is no reason why a nostalgia conscious of itself, a lucid and remorseless dissatisfaction with the present on the grounds of some remembered plenitude" (Jameson 82) cannot serve to illuminate the present. It is just such a lucid and remorseless examination that Lowry achieves in *Under the Volcano*. Therein, for me, lies its hidden magic.

NOTES

1 Ronald Binns, *Malcolm Lowry* (London: Metheuen 1984), 62.

2 Fredric Jameson, *Marxism and Form: Twentieth Century Dialectical Theories of Literature* (Princeton, NJ: Princeton Paperback 1974), 66.

3 René Girard, *Deceit, Desire, and the Novel*, trans. Yvonne Freccero (Baltimore: Johns Hopkins University Press 1976), 260.

4 Jean-Paul Sartre, *Search for a Method*, trans. Hazel E. Barnes (New York: Vintage 1968), 15–16.

5 Malcolm Lowry, *Under the Volcano* (New York: Reynal & Hitchcock 1947), 19, 47, 39; further references cited as *UV* in the text.

6 Thomas Mann, *Dr Faustus*, trans. H.T. Lowe-Porter (New York: Knopf 1948), 500.

7 Stuart Schneiderman, *Jacques Lacan: The Death of an Intellectual Hero* (Harvard: Harvard University Press 1983), 179.

8 Edward Said, *The World, the Text, and the Critic* (Harvard: Harvard University Press 1983), 177.

9 "The Last Great Cause," CBC Television, 29 Dec. 1986.

10 Wilfrid Desan, *The Marxism of Jean-Paul Sartre* (Garden City, NY: Anchor 1966), 9.

11 Conrad Knickerbocker, "Swinging the Paradise Street Blues: Malcolm Lowry in England," *Paris Review* 38 (Summer 1966): 16.

12 Conrad Aiken, *Ushant: An Essay* (London: W.H. Allen 1963), 351.

13 Douglas Day, *Malcolm Lowry: A Biography* (New York: Oxford University Press 1973), 152.

14 John Sommerfield, *Volunteer in Spain* (New York: Knopf 1937), 146.

15 Georg Lukács, *Essays on Thomas Mann*, trans. Stanley Mitchell (New York: Grasset & Dunlop 1965), 114.

Revision and Illusion
in *Under the Volcano*

FREDERICK ASALS

From the first, readers have responded to the impression of fictional richness *Under the Volcano* conveys. Soliciting comments to be used on publication, Albert Erskine drew from James Agee a tribute to the novel's "achievements in intensity," from Lowry's old mentor Conrad Aiken a cagey paean to its language as "a changeable shot-silk sun-shot medium of infinite flexibility," and from Alfred Kazin admiration for the "ability to convey in a single texture the different levels of consciousness."[1] This multi-dimensionality is the product of Lowry's compulsive, dogged, inspired, exhaustive and exhausting revising and rewriting of the novel between 1940 and 1945. The sense of "fullness," of the density of experience conveyed by the text, is not a feature of the 1940 version, the version that made a circuit of the New York publishing houses, finding, *felix culpa*, no takers. But over the next years, as individual chapters or passages went through draft after draft, becoming richer, more complex, they were also in the process of becoming more problematic. It is no paradox that as the text became "fuller," it also took on gaps and uncertainties it had not possessed in its simpler earlier version – gaps and uncertainties that are not of course "in" the text itself but in the world it comes to portray and in our apprehension of that world.

Central to *Under the Volcano* is Lowry's sense of mutability, of the dynamic quality of the phenomenal world, a sense articulated – but hardly rendered – from the start. "Life changes," Señora Gregorio had pointed out in 1940 as in 1947; "You can never drink of it."[2] And Jacques Laruelle early and late had noted that fluidity was a feature of space as

well as time: "How continually, how startingly, the landscape changed!"
(9) The 1940 version, like the final one, goes on at this point to evoke
Mexico as microcosm, suggestive of the Cotswolds, Windermere, New
Hampshire, the Sahara, and so on, but it contains no equivalent of one
small clause in that passage: "if you cared to think so" (10). The tem-
poral-spatial world is not, after all, the only source of mutability, and
arguably the single most important alteration Lowry made after 1940,
the one with the most radical implications for *Under the Volcano* as a
whole, was not the well-known one of character relationships (Yvonne
from daughter to wife, Hugh from friend to half-brother) but the decision to abandon a technique of narrative omniscience for one of alternating central consciousnesses.

Much of the thinness of the 1940 *Volcano* may be attributable to Lowry's attempt to employ a technique that would never be congenial to
him. He would confess to Jonathan Cape that "the author's equipment,
such as it is, is subjective rather than objective, a better equipment, in
short, for a certain kind of poet than a novelist" (SL 59); but the 1940
Volcano attempts to be an "extroverted" novel carried largely through
dialogue and character interaction and mediated by a roving narrator
who flits from mind to mind like a hopped-up honey-bee. The characters here have a great many opinions and deliver them at length and
frequently; they rarely have convincingly rendered fears or desires,
guilts or longings, manifestations of "what used to be called: soul." As
Lowry wrote to Aiken in August 1941 about his revisions, "we decided
that all the characters could not be equally dead and have all the same
look – they had to be distributed in different postures throughout the
morgue anyway – and this has presented some nice problems, most of
them neatly solved, we feel."[3]

Lowry was some four years premature in that feeling, but at least he
was on his way. The switch to a chapter-length central-consciousness
technique was not easily or quickly made, however: early post-1940
drafts often have pencilled notations of lapses in consistency. "Hugh
reflect" (30:9,4) Lowry reminds himself when the Consul's thoughts
persist into chapter 8; "Yvonne's thought" (27:2,11) appears against a
similar passage in 9. But consistency was only the outside of the matter;
once he had accomplished that much, Lowry could begin the far more
arduous process of burrowing his way *into* the sensibilities of his figures,
imagining them from the inside, finding for them a language that would
embody convincingly their sense of the world. "Avoid any Malcolm
stooginess like the plague" (26:18,8) reads one early self-admonition;
"This seems too much like a synopsis" (27:7,4) is justified criticism of
another character's supposed recollections. What Lowry had firmly in
place by the 1940 *Volcano* was a skeleton, a structure of incidents that

would hardly alter through all the revisions that followed, that would hold even when Yvonne's death rather than her sexual ecstasy became the climax of chapter 11 ("how alike are the groans of love to those of the dying"), and would barely tremble when relationships among characters were significantly altered. The fleshing (or refleshing) that ensued was not a mere adding to a "given" base of experience but (to drop the anatomical analogy) more truly a discovery of what that experience *was*, less a stuccoing of symbols – the 1940 *Volcano* is already riddled with allusions – than a gradual confronting of the interior, a movement of the imagination into what Joseph Conrad called "that region of stress and strife" where the artist must discover "the terms of his appeal."

Where the 1940 *Volcano* fails is in its most immediate impact as literary experience: it fails as art. In the years that followed, Lowry's private warning, his own handwriting on the wall, printed like the Consul's garden notice in black capitals, was this admonition:

ABJURE THE PLATITUDE OF STATEMENT. FOR IN ART WHAT IS MERELY STATED IS NOT PRESENTED, WHAT IS NOT PRESENTED IS NOT VIVID, WHAT IS NOT VIVID IS NOT REPRESENTED, AND WHAT IS NOT REPRESENTED IS NOT ART.[4]

Somehow, Lowry saw, he must learn to "represent" without abandoning those ambitions that in the 1940 *Volcano* rarely moved beyond grandiose statement – ersatz descriptions that presented the Consul as "King Lear in full face, Hamlet in profile" (25:19,3), or unearned thematic assertions on the order of "the future can change the past" (25:17,35). Furthermore, Lowry's restricting of time and place seemed designed to evoke "Aristotelian" unities (even the slight deviation that placed Yvonne in Acapulco the previous night for chapter 2 was quickly expunged). Yet *Under the Volcano* was, after all, modern fiction, not classical drama: it had to be vivid, precise, plausible, specific in its rendering of its single day even as it ranged as far as the metaphysical and archetypal. Somehow the grand tradition of Sophocles, Marlowe, and Goethe had to be engaged in a time when the established day-books, those of Joyce and Woolf, had accommodated the trivia of the quotidian, allowing to Bloom his prosings and wanderings and to Clarissa Dalloway her social ditherings. Lowry's movement beyond all his models, classical and modern, creating a plausible and recognizable surface that yet allowed for the intensity and resonance of emotional and intellectual depth, was precisely the accomplishment of these years of revision.

A late section of chapter 5 can serve as an exemplary focus for some of the kinds of changes Lowry's text underwent as he transformed the often pedestrian literalness of the 1940 *Volcano* into the vibrant richness of the published work. In all versions the action (summarized at sufficient distance) shows the same elements. Returning through his garden from the encounter with Mr Quincey and Dr Vigil, the Consul finds Hugh and Yvonne, back from their horseback ride, discussing the bougainvillea on the porch. The three talk, Vigil arrives in answer to the Consul's earlier invitation, and the conversation turns to where to go in the afternoon. Hugh and Yvonne swim, the closer bull-throwing is preferred to the doctor's more distant Guanajuato, and Vigil takes his leave. In the 1940 *Volcano* this section covers some fourteen typewritten pages, approximately 4,200 words, of which the following uncut passage is entirely typical:

"We had an absolutely grand ride," Yvonne said. "Why didn't you tell me you could get horses so near?"

"Sorry, I didn't think of it." He yawned. "Have a drink, Hugh?"

"No, thank you sir."

"You, Yvonne?"

"I'll wait a bit."

The Consul poured himself out a drink from the whiskey bottle which stood, half empty, on the parapet.

"Well, Hugh, I didn't ask what brought you to Quahnahuac [sic]," he said, raising his glass. "Cheerio! I'm always glad to see Yvonne's old friends of course." He leaned against the parapet. "This is better than Algeciras, what?"

"Well –"

"Of course, this is a hell of a climate – so was that by the way – but it's a pretty nice place, don't you think?"

"Why yes indeed."

"What's all this I hear about a bet?"

Hugh told him the story, stammering like a schoolboy about his clothes, blushing.

"So you quit Stanford," the Consul said, and suddenly laughed loudly. But his eyes did not laugh, holding a fixed, stony despair.

"And you see," Hugh added nervously, "I ran into Yvonne here, in Acapulco, and that kind of upset everything. Mexico is awfully interesting, it must be a difficult place to leave."

"Too true," said the Consul. "Unless you get thrown out. But still, after all, what is particularly interesting about it?"

"Oh, I don't know –"

"Of course I don't have to say that the social situation interests you, since that's the fashion. Just as it does Yvonne here, eh Yvonne?"

"I wasn't aware there was one."

"And what about Spain, Hugh? I suppose you're on the side of the loyalists too, that goes without saying –"

"I think every good American is, surely."

"You must have some interesting conversations with your pro-Franco friend, Yvonne."

"I never said I was pro-Franco, Father," Yvonne said heatedly. "It's you that are pro-Franco! I only told Hugh that he's a fool to go and fight for the loyalists, which is what he's thinking of doing, the jackass!"

The Consul laughed again, loudly, with still the same stony expression in his eyes.

"The bougainvillea reminds you of home, doesn't it," he said, after a long silence.

After another silence, the Consul said: "Wasn't it Bougainville who discovered the bougainvillea?"

"Why yes," Hugh nodded. "Now I come to think of it, I believe it was Bougainville."

"Hence the name, bougainvillea," Yvonne said feebly.

"That's right, hence bougainvillea."

The conversation languished.   (25:21,17–20)[5]

So, needless to say, did the novel. "Not text, but texture," Nabokov advised: no summary can convey the kind of "world" created in this early *Volcano* or its distance from that of the work we know. The slackness of this exchange, its awkward silences and *politesse* stretched over the tensions and uneasiness of people who do not know one another well (or alternatively know one another only too well), its desultory qualities and its inanities – the dialogue conveys all too successfully the pointless wanderings of actual "social" conversation as recorded by an almost neutral observer who will not repeat a story he has let us hear earlier or force us to undergo the actual emptiness of the silences but who otherwise feels bound to report precisely what transpired on this less than momentous occasion.

The entire 1940 *Volcano* is controlled by this roving narrator who can enter the minds of the major characters at will but who spends considerable stretches, as here, simply recording dialogue, thereby depending almost entirely on verbal interactions among characters to create resonance. And so the arrival of Vigil, provoking offers of drinks, invitations to swim, exclamations about Guanajuato, and, as a climax, the Consul's lengthy telling of an apocalyptic joke about a parrot and a sinking ship, does little to relieve the banality of the episode. Nothing ruffles the narrative surfaces here, yet the only distinctive passages are found not in the dialogue but in the rare excursions into consciousness: in the Consul's conceit of his soul as a ravaged town and in the parallel reflection given to Hugh, that somehow Guanajuato might have been "the solution to all their problems ... there, and in no other place, might be revealed the star that shone above all their lives" (25:21, 27).

Perhaps it was passages such as these that helped Lowry to make the momentous shift in the next version of the novel from roaming omniscience to alternating centres of consciousness. This shift would not of course deny traditional novelistic dialogue, but it began the subtle process by which the book's centre of gravity moved from exterior to interior – yet, equally important, not to the privileged interior of any single figure. It allowed for both sustained penetration of the minds of individual characters and for the kinds of poetic passages noted above, although Lowry only gradually discovered the full implications of this alteration of technique.

The ensuing version was thus crucial, for in addition to the change in point of view, it contains the realignment of the relationships among the characters: Yvonne becomes the Consul's ex-wife and Hugh his brother (not, in this draft, half-brother) rather than Yvonne's young suitor. Yet there is little real rewriting here: Lowry's primary concern was with cutting and tightening his earlier manuscript rather than adding anything new. Quick to disappear is most of the passage quoted above; what is fitting to characters with only passing acquaintance is redundant once those characters become brothers. At the same time Lowry makes use of the Consul's point of view to exploit the sexual tension that now becomes appropriate. When Yvonne reports on the fine ride she and Hugh have had, he thinks to himself, "So. It was starting already," and a pencil addition is his snide, spoken, "It must have been quite like old times" (26:22,20). Still, the primary note here is excision and compression, and the typescript shrinks from fourteen to ten pages.

The next version, of seventeen manuscript pages, somewhat expands the passage again as Lowry begins tentatively to make use of the inwardness of the Consul's perspective. But the dialogue also expands, and given the situation, there must have seemed no way around the introductions, offerings of drinks, invitations to swim, discussions of geographical distances, and now, because Hugh announces his determination to leave the scene, considerations of the local bus and train schedules. The social minutiae that introduce a sexual subtext or embroider the Consul's reflections (however Lowry might change relationships among characters) must have seemed intractable. How was he to maintain a plausible surface, suggest sexual tension, convey the Consul's increasing inebriation, imply the overtones of the choice between Tomalín and Guanajuato, and allow for metaphorical connections between the Consul and the cosmos? Perhaps the germ of an answer was planted in this draft when on Vigil's departure Geoffrey, who in earlier versions had been left alone on the porch, was made to enter the bathroom, groaning, having an obscure sense that with Vigil his last hope had departed.

However it came to Lowry, the alcoholic blackout that appears in the next draft was an inspired stroke. It was easily plausible. Have we not observed Geoffrey's drinking in chapters 2 and 3, to say nothing of the desperate lurch to the tequila bottle earlier in this chapter, and are we not about to hear Vigil's indiscreet references to the previous night's gargantuan consumption? Thus an apparent realism is appeased, while the social minutiae that had so clogged earlier versions drain away into the holes of Geoffrey's lost hour. This next draft, therefore, shrinks to less than eight typewritten pages, about half the length of the previous one, and most of what has disappeared are those emptily literal exchanges, which, not having registered on the Consul's soaking brain, simply vanish. The focus of action thus shifts from narrative presentation of events on the porch to the Consul's pained attempt to recover those events, only imperfectly successful. Time is folded over here as Geoffrey in the bathroom at (according to his watch) 12:15 – and Lowry uses his anguished groans to remind us repeatedly of the novel's present – tries to recollect the previous, vanished hour.

Lowry would refine and polish this episode until the end – for instance, marginal notes here remind him that "all this should be permeated with guilt" – but introduction of the blackout is the last and perhaps most crucial change this episode underwent. Even in its first and roughest incarnation the blackout passage was given a stylistic distinctness. When this episode was in the hands of the neutral narrator it was everywhere conventional. Even as the Consul's consciousness was given fuller prominence, narrative syntax held: Geoffrey's observations might become looser, but they never lost coherence, while the centrality of dialogue always returned the focus to the present scene as, moment by moment, it unfolded before him. But with the blackout comes the sense of the unimpeded flow of the Consul's mind, which suddenly and without warning begins to undergo skips and gaps, to cast up shadows and fragments – rendered in a prose in which long, fluent (fluid?) sentences sit next to dashes and dots, the jagged punctuation of ellipsis. Syntax and rhythm signify not only that the locus of the novel's actions has shifted to the interior but that that interior is being only very unevenly recovered.

With the movement from more traditional techniques into what might be called "alcoholic realism," the experience on the porch has receded into a past that has become altogether problematic. In this fourth version, much as in the published novel, our episode begins this way: "— — — Why then, should he be sitting in the bathroom? Was he asleep? dead? passed out? Was he in the bathroom now or half an hour ago? Was it night? Where were the others? But now he heard their voices somewhere, Hugh's and Yvonne's, for the doctor had gone of course" (29:17, 20). The final version's single significant modification of this remarkable series of questions is at first to identify Hugh and Yvonne as "some of the others," for the Consul has a sense that "the house had been full of people," a modification that points towards the half-dozen voices that swarm in on him at the chapter's close. But it also, like the questions preceding it, points towards the possibility of a complete sensory disjunction. *Had* "the house ... been full of people?" How could we answer such a question? Presumably it was not, but the text denies us the grounds of certainty: the degree of assurance is that of the individual reader. The Consul's first hesitant query here has elicited not an answer but a proliferation of further questions, all of them disturbing. Apparently a state of consciousness, that condition in which one might pose questions and perceive oneself as sitting in a bathroom, is not incompatible with being simultaneously "asleep," "dead," "passed out."

Given this remarkable state, how much of what follows is, perhaps, dream, vision, hallucination – not, in short, simple memory at all? What indeed under these conditions would "memory" (simple or otherwise) actually mean? All of these ponderables are given a further turn by the devastating temporal question, "Was he in the bathroom now or half an hour ago?" which undermines altogether any assumptions about the status of the novel's world of time and space, since what seems the present setting may be hallucinatory, visionary, a warp of linear time that, even as we read the words, has already occurred half an hour ago and is thus over. But if we *are* reading it "now," as the Consul is experiencing it apparently for the first time "now," then in some sense (what sense precisely?) it cannot in fact be "over." If one can see oneself, by apparent daylight, sitting in a bathroom, how is it meaningful to ask "Was it night?" unless one conceives of oneself as at least potentially detached from one's own experience? And if that is the case, then that experience may have an independent existence, inhabit a realm essentially outside of time altogether, which like a film might be run or rerun before one's eyes at any moment. Indeed, within a few paragraphs the Consul will envisage "the faces of the last hour ... like the figures in an old silent film" where their speech, which of course is soundless, belongs not to themselves but to their audience: "their words mute explosions in the brain." The Consul's questions, in short, breed yet further questions in the reader, who is thereby enabled to view the entire sequence that follows either as the partially clarifying answer to the Consul's confusion or as rendered hopelessly uncertain by the implications of the questions with which it is introduced.

However we read this episode, one thing is clear: Lowry has here rendered one hour of his twelve-hour Day of the Dead 1938 obscure, both the exterior or phenomenal and interior or psychological worlds as experienced in the time around noon becoming equally unavailable to us. There is, in short, a gap, not in the text but in the inner and outer worlds the text had seemed to be committed to portraying, not only in Lowry's earlier drafts but in long stretches of the published *Volcano* itself. Nor is this episode unique. The repetition of the technique in chapter 10 will prove even more disturbing. When the Consul finds himself sitting in the "excusado" of the Salón Ofélia, he wonders, recalling his earlier situation, "Why was he here? Why was he always more or less, here?" (294) But by now his drunkenness has advanced (he has had his first mescals), and it is not altogether clear just when – or indeed whether – he moves from the restaurant proper to the toilet and back again. What seems to happen is that while he sits in the toilet several objects – a bottle containing mescal, a tourist brochure, a bus and train schedule – mysteriously materialize, and from these the Consul appears respectively to drink and read. While he does so, he seems to overhear snatches of Hugh and Yvonne's conversation inside, and *we* experience the counterpointing of the read and the heard. But while he appears to hear them, they oddly cannot hear him. Furthermore, as the scene proceeds, the voices the Consul "hears" are not limited to Hugh's and Yvonne's but come to include echoes and snatches of numerous voices from earlier in the day, including his own. Surely (we may say) these others come from within, spun up deliriously, shards of memory released by drink? But these "voices" look no different on the page from those confidently assigned to Hugh and Yvonne, nor is there any indication that to Geoffrey they sound different. What then is the basis for our discrimination of the "real" from the hallucinatory? The text no longer reliably distinguishes between inner and outer experience. Within a few pages the Consul will be discoursing brilliantly to his companions only to discover at the close of a magnificent peroration "a slight mistake ... The Consul had not uttered a single word. It was all an illusion, a whirling cerebral chaos" (308). Yet it is not a chaos as we have read it; Lowry's *oratoria oblique* has suggested a speech fully as impressive as Geoffrey believes it, and none of the conventions of fiction or print reveals it as unspoken. We are, in other words, as taken in by it as the Consul himself and discover our error precisely when he does, just as, back in chapter 3, his long brotherly speech to Hugh from the stones of the Calle Nicaragua had proved to be a silent address to an illusion – facts discovered by the Consul and the reader simultaneously.

All of these gaps and pseudo-presences are late additions to the *Volcano*, the results of Lowry's full exploration of the implications of his shifting points of view. To Geoffrey himself these accompaniments of his drinking have become so routine that in chapter 3 the appearance of a dead man beside his swimming pool he knows at once for "an hallucination" (91). But deceptions of mind and senses are not peculiar to those who drink, and in this regard as in others Lowry is at pains to show Geoffrey as only the most extreme figure on a continuum. For instance, Yvonne's first chapter, chapter 2, is virtually an anthology of perceptual errors (which are not necessarily "errors" in another sense at all), and it would be easy but tedious to repeat the process of our considerations of chapter 5 to show Lowry's transformation of a conventional and unambiguous early text into the richer but more problematic one he published. Thus, for instance, Yvonne originally did not hear several voices coming from the interior of the Bella Vista bar, did not therefore wrongly conclude that it was "evidently crowded"; although she, like her published incarnation, had just been travelling by sea and air, her consciousness was not overlaid by the sights and sensations of her voyaging; she did not on entering believe for an illusory moment that "the bar was empty" nor think, when she did spot the Consul, that he was "talking apparently to himself," and so on, through all the misapprehensions, false assumptions, erroneous conclusions, second thoughts, reconsiderations, and adjustments that the Yvonne of the published novel undergoes on her initial re-encounter with Quauhnahuac, which only gradually were assigned to her as this chapter went through its many versions.

Perhaps it is enough here to recall a single sequence in the walk home from the Bella Vista to show that Yvonne, stone cold sober in the early morning, is almost as much a source of misapprehension and textual ambiguity as is her alcoholic ex-husband. The print-shop window with its photograph of the split rock was a part of the landscape of the 1940 *Volcano*, but Yvonne's response to this obvious analogy to their own situation grew gradually through Lowry's successive revisions. What began as a brief recognition of the parallel became the extended meditation of the published novel, in which Yvonne so identifies with the rock that she imagines herself as one of the divided halves emotionally carrying on a dialogue with the other half – during all of which, ironically, the actual Geoffrey at her side is apparently speaking to her. We, however, hear only the tag end of what he has been saying because, of course, "Yvonne was not following." But as she becomes aware once more of the scene around her, she observes that "the Consul was beginning to shake again." The text then reads:

"Geoffrey, I'm so thirsty, why don't we stop and have a drink?"
"Geoffrey, let's be reckless this once and get tight together before breakfast!"

Yvonne said neither of these things.   (55)

Yet until that final disclaimer, all the conventions of speech and print –
direct address, indentation, quotation marks – have seemed to indicate
that she *has* said them, and no retrospective correction can quite expunge
them, make them as if they had never existed, even if we remain somewhat uncertain of their status. If Yvonne did not say these things, did
she at least think them? We are left to draw our own conclusions about
the level of narrative authority from which they come.

These unsettling lacunae and ghostly presences, the introduction of
the problematic that stems from Lowry's centring of the novel in the
consciousnesses of the major figures, is furthered by another result of
his revisions, this one closely bound up with his practice of revising by
chapter. While he might stick obsessively at a paragraph or even a
sentence that dissatisfied him, casting and recasting the offender again
and again, sooner or later it was incorporated into the handwritten
chapter, which was then passed on to Margerie for typing. Yet while
he kept in mind and made notes for the novel as a whole, he not only
did not wait until he had completed a full novelistic manuscript before
giving it over for typing; he did not even work in sequence on individual
chapters. Both internal and external evidence suggests that between
1941 and the end of 1944 a complete *Under the Volcano* paradoxically
both did not exist – it was perpetually "in progress," never finished in
a "full" draft, still with revisions to come – and yet "always" existed:
had a finished novel been demanded at gunpoint from Lowry during
those years, he could simply have gathered up the twelve latest versions
of his chapters. When he told Jonathan Cape that his book "can ... be
regarded as a sort of machine: it works, too, believe me, as I have found
out" (SL 66), Lowry clearly had in mind those circular and elliptical
contraptions of chapter 7 – ferris wheel, merry-go-round, *máquina infernal* – from which it is so difficult to alight. But as he also told Cape in
speaking of his years of labour on the book, "Each chapter is a unity
in itself" (SL 65).

However, if each chapter is a semi-independent "block" (SL 65) and
not just a necessary piece of the larger narrative, it may take on a form
of its own. As Lowry revised, the unbroken narrative flow of the 1940
version, which had forded chapter divisions without missing a temporal
step, began to give way to more complex connections – and disconnec-
tions – between the novel's quasi-independent units. This involved more
than imbuing each chapter with the nature of its presiding consciousness; as he revised, Lowry began to experiment with beginning some
chapters *in medias res*, sometimes having the bridging action recalled by
the central consciousness, sometimes omitting it altogether. At one

point, for example, Lowry considered opening chapter 6 with the shaving scene; and chapter 9, which begins with the characters seated in Arena Tomalín, has Yvonne recall the events that directly followed the end of chapter 8, events that in earlier versions had been directly dramatized. The latter example, like Geoffrey's blackouts or Yvonne's impressions of her journey in chapter 2, is part of the novel's movement into the past, an interiorizing of events that presents them not in themselves but as they have, however obliquely, struck the consciousness, as they are recollected, not lived.

But Lowry's purposes in opening, say, chapter 9 in the Arena are also related to those that turned Yvonne's awareness in chapter 2 problematic: the first sentences here present her sense of the "wonderful time" she sees all around her: "how happy everyone was! How merrily Mexico laughed away its tragic history, the past, the underlying death!" (254) It is this simple and "merry" mood of shucking off the burdens of the past that Lowry wants to capture at its height, a euphoria that will allow Yvonne in a moment to dismiss not only their half-hearted and belated efforts to help the dying Indian but that entire incident and her own spontaneous tears as of little consequence. The narcissistic distortions of her mood are ironically suggested in her compact mirror, where "Popocatepetl seemed even more beautiful for being reflected" but "however she moved the mirror she couldn't get poor Ixta in" (256). Closing the "traitorous" mirror and moving to reflect to the outer world a merriment she has sensed there, she "turned to the others, smiling." She finds no answering smiles, however, either in Geoffrey and Hugh or in the spectators generally: "Mexico was not laughing away her tragic history; Mexico was bored. The bull was bored. Everyone was bored, perhaps had been all the time. All that had happened was that Yvonne's drink in the bus had taken effect and was now wearing off" (257). "Perhaps": and so we recognize the indeterminacy not only of the action we have not seen – the narrative moments "between" chapters 8 and 9 that exist only as Yvonne recalls them – but even of that we apparently have attended. Both have been fully coloured by her untrustworthy "high."

The lacunae that developed between chapters in revision range from the possibly insignificant – that between chapters 3 and 4, for instance, the unmeasured lapse between the Consul's falling asleep and Hugh's entering the garden – to the indeterminate, as this between 8 and 9, to the potentially crucial, as that between 10 and 11. With the Consul lurching away from the Salón Ofélia, Lowry has him pause momentarily to look back: "No one had come after him. Was that good? Yes, it was good, he thought, his heart pounding. And since it was so good he would take the path to Parián, to the Farolito" (314–15). Yet why have Hugh and Yvonne not "come after him"? In the 1940 *Volcano* such a question hardly arises. The narrative there remains within the Salón Ofélia as Yvonne, half-hysterical from the Consul's verbal assault, flees to the washroom, leaving Hugh to wait loyally for her return. When the two do finally leave the restaurant at the start of chapter 11, they decide not to search for the Consul anyway, thus leaving the novel open for the simple love-death finale that this version presents.

But as Lowry revised, the situation changed. Yvonne's exit occurs earlier (and is now unexplained – another gap. Is she still heading for the "excusado" para las damas? Quién sabe?), and she and Hugh are both presumably at the table through the Consul's final diatribe and departure.[6] When chapter 11 opens, we hear only that "the Salón Ofélia [is] at last behind them" (316). The point here is not merely the existence of the gap but Lowry's underlining of it through Geoffrey's awareness. And since both his and Yvonne's lives hang in the balance at this juncture, any explanations we may offer will be closely bound up with how we read the novel.

Now, of course, what we perceive as a "gap" in consciousness or in the narrative action of this novel may well be seen as the sign of another dimension, a "hole" in space-time or in the surfaces of the mind that may permit the entrance of the unconcious, the archetypal, or (in every sense) the occult – that which has been occulted or hidden behind the veils of the phenomenal world or the too-sober mind. For example, as Lowry pointed out to Jonathan Cape, part of the blackout passage of chapter 5, which "reads like quite good lunacy," also suggests the Consul's identification with the infant Horus of Egyptian myth (SL 74). It has become commonplace to speak of these "deeper levels" of the *Volcano*, more commonplace indeed than to take its surfaces with full seriousness. This novel, we say rightly, is a work of polysemous complexity, and that (to return to my starting point) is a primary source of its richness. In so saying we distinguish between the vision of the novel and that of any of its characters. But what of its readers, even an imagined "ideal" reader? In repeating the truism of the novel's multi-levelled nature, have we asked whether all of those levels can be activated or apprehended simultaneously?

Although apparent lacunae *may* reveal another and deeper "reality," uncertainty undermines all assurances; it leaves us in the conditional, in the apprehension of "perhaps." How often *Under the Volcano* leaves us, like its characters, precisely there, with what seemed, what might have been, what cannot be determined, with what appears certain on one page, in one chapter, but comes into radical question in the next. In focusing the novel's action through alternating central consciousnesses and in revising his chapters to adhere to these limits and to shape their semi-autonomous form, Lowry dramatized a world in which serial sol-ipsism is the inescapable condition and forced not only the characters, but with them the reader, to suffer it. There are, the novel insists, actualities beyond the flickering perceptions of the characters, beyond even the awareness of the narrator, actualities that they and we will never, to all our costs, know – a shadow world that includes such mat-ters as the missing hours from which the Consul can recover only unsta-ble fragments, the unheard words he spoke to Yvonne as they paused before the photograph of the split rock, the reasons (perhaps unknown even to themselves) for the fatal slowness with which Hugh and Yvonne follow Geoffrey out of the Salón Ofélia, and the battle of the Ebro, which Hugh reminds himself is raging even while he dawdles on the other side of the ocean in Mexico.

That final example, an episode from the Spanish Civil War contem-poraneous with the novel's action, perhaps helps to focus the implica-tions of the others, even though, unlike them, it belongs to the spatial world. To the extent that Hugh is aware of the Ebro, it both distracts him from the Mexican scene of which he is on this day a part and contributes its poisonous guilt to the responses he brings to the present occasion. To be aware of it is thus not to be a full participant in the immediacy of one's experience; to be unaware of it, however, is to be less than fully cognizant of the network of one's relationships. Geoffrey's difficulties in chapter 5 and Yvonne's in chapter 2 arise out of the tem-poral and emotional rather than the spatial, but the effects are similar. Geoffrey's alcoholically "lost" hour produces his desperate attempts to recover it, attempts that can at best have only partial success; and the sober Yvonne finds her early morning present overlain by two other dimensions – the immediate past of her ship and plane journeys, whose sights, sounds, and even rhythms remain a part of her consciousness, and the more distant past of a Quauhnahuac familiar to her from 1936–37, the renewal of acquaintance with which sets off deeper emotional resonances. In both instances, to the extent that the past impinges on the present, it obscures, dilutes, transforms the present moment; yet only pieces of the past are available (and who can say with what dis-tortion?) – fragments of Geoffrey's lost hour, the imperfect recollections Yvonne carries – so that no real sense of the continuity of experience is possible. Yvonne's guilt over her affair with Jacques Laruelle, for example, has caused her to "forget" his unforgettably bizarre house, so that memory and desire have rearranged the landscape of Quauhnahuac for her: "On the occasions imagination had led her with Geoffrey down the Calle Nicaragua lately, never once, poor phantoms, had they been confronted with Jacques' zacuali" (57). The effect here of the emotional on one's apprehension of the spatio-temporal is especially clear.

The paradox of such moments is that the most emotionally resonant events of the present are precisely those that lead away from that present through reverberations set up in memory and anticipation – through the stirrings of imagination. Thus it is Yvonne's heightened emotional state in chapter 2, occasioned by her reunion with Geoffrey, that makes it impossible for her to hold a steady focus on that occasion, for it produces in her vibrations on too many frequencies, as hopes, fears, memories, anticipations, reservations, associations, fantasies, and so on are stirred by her return. The Consul too, in his own way, becomes aware of just this intensity of the present that leads away from it. As one of his voices tells him: "for now of course poor old chap you want horribly to get drunk all over again don't you the whole trouble being as we see it that Yvonne's long-dreamed-of coming but alas put away the anguish my boy there's nothing in it ... has in itself created the most important situation in your life save one namely the far more important situation it in turn creates of your having to have five hundred drinks in order to deal with it" (68–9). *Carpe diem*, mocks the novel – an injunction both imperative and impossible.

For of course, beyond the particular concerns or weaknesses of individual figures is the inexorable movement of time itself that Lowry has built insistently into his book. Running counter to all those wheels and circles, to the repetitive movements of history, the eternal return, to the echoing structures and "trochal form" of the *Volcano*, is the inescapable linear motion of the day, the year, of a human life, and at last of the novel itself. "Momentito," says the Consul repeatedly, sensing that he is "missing the next opportunity, and the next, missing all the opportunities finally, until it was too late" (218); but *Under the Volcano* is a book of too-lateness, and not only for Geoffrey Firmin. Against each of the structures in his novel Lowry painstakingly built its antonym: against the recurring archetype, the unique and fleeting moment, against the circle the line, against the eternal the temporal, against the visionary the ordinary, against the cosmic the local, against the tragic the comic. Nowhere is this more powerful than in his setting against the mythic of the evanescent the moments that constantly disappear behind us like the beautiful butterflies that Yvonne encountered on her entry to Alcapulco, "swooping seaward" to greet her and "endlessly vanishing astern" (44).

I have already briefly suggested the plight the reader faces in the methodology of the *Volcano*, but of course the novel itself is full of analogues of reading; a semiotician's dream, or perhaps nightmare, for so many of these readings are clearly misreadings. That some of these misreadings are Lowry's own, not just those of his characters – the Consul's mistranslation of the garden notice is the best-known of these

– is suggestive for what it may imply about our reading of his own "sign," that is, the novel itself. Perhaps even more telling is the first overt misreading in the *Volcano*, for the text here is literary. Surely Laruelle's encounter with the anthology of Elizabethan plays in chapter 1 presents itself as a paradigm of reading. Opening the book at random, he sees

Then will I headlong fly into the earth:
Earth, gape! it will not harbour me!

When he looks again, he realizes that Marlowe had actually written "run" rather than "fly" and "Oh, no ...," not "Earth, gape." Jacques' error is presumably a result of emotion and flickering light (or is it, he wonders, "some correspondence, maybe, ... between the sub-normal world and the abnormally suspicious?"), yet of course his "mistake," as he realizes at once, is all too appropriate – just as is the Consul's misreading of the garden notice, as Lowry would insist when he retained that other error, and we all read by our own flickering lights.

But Jacques' reading does not end here. Continuing with his *sortes Shakespeareanae*, he casts up "*And what wonders I have done all Germany can witness. Enter Wagner, solus ... Ick sal you wat suggen, Hans. Dis skip, dat comen from Candy, is als vol, by God's sacrement* [sic], *van sugar, almonds, cambrick, end alle dingen, towsand, towsand, ding.*" Stunned by his first reading of Marlowe, Laruelle here simply "Close[s] the book on Dekker's comedy" and tries again, this time coming upon the final speech of *Dr Faustus*, a result that leaves him "shaken." Responsive to the Faust story – he has planned a modern film version – Laruelle finds these first and last passages resonating on a frequency he is already attuned to: he views the Consul as a figure of tragedy in the grand manner. But the passage between (actually the elision of three passages) seems (especially out of original context) to create a parodic declension from the grandiose "*what wonders I have done all Germany can witness*" to the replacement of master by servant ("*Enter Wagner, solus*") to a demotic low comedy that appears to reduce "God's sacrament" to "Candy" and tragic overreaching to clownish greed and gluttony. If Laruelle ignores it, Lowry obviously has not, breaking up the too-neat paradigm of the Faustian analogy, allowing for another and more skeptically ironic perspective to emerge. It is also far from irrelevant that this was a late addition, the deliberate introduction of a discordant note, a countering of the tragic by the comic, which has the effect of freeing the reader from the monolothic tyranny of Laruelle's view.

Yet the situation is even more problematic than this. If Jacques prefers Marlowe to Dekker as the "correct" paradigm, what are we to make of the fact that his misreading is more appropriate than the actual text? Has this the effect of undermining or of emphasizing the Faustian analogy? Or does it somehow accomplish both? What are we to make of the stage direction that introduces Wagner? Does this cast Laruelle in the servant's role to the Faustian Consul? Or is it Geoffrey who does not measure up to the archetype, for whom the claim of "wonders" is preposterously overblown? (But then, weren't Faustus's own achievements, as Marlowe presents them, rather overstated?) And are not both men as we last view them indeed *solus*?

There is, however, still another factor to consider here, one thrown into relief by a knowledge of Lowry's revisions. The initial misreading of the Marlowe text, the substitutions of "fly" and "Earth gape," were apparently Lowry's own misremembering of *Dr Faustus*: at least they so appear in the 1940 *Volcano*, with no acknowledgment of the error (25:17, 21). When the final version gives us both the misreading and its correction, how does this affect our response to the novel that contains such a strategy? Do we become wary of a text that openly confesses its liability to error? Or are we reassured by the correction of the error, invited into a trust of apparent narrative candour? And how is our response, now to Lowry's entire text, now simply to the use of the passage from Marlowe, affected by the novel's insistence that such errors have their own validity? Should, for instance, that italicized passage that Jacques reads in the very next paragraph be treated as Lowry presented it, as if it were a *single* quotation and to be thus understood for the purposes of his own work? Or is it important to hunt down the original contexts here, to see that there are three passages involved, not one, and to determine their individual impacts on *Under the Volcano*?[7]

Whatever answers one gives to such questions – and the possible local readings they suggest are far from exhaustive, as even a glance at appropriate pages of *A Companion to Under the Volcano* shows[8] – clearly there are choices involved. Like Laruelle, we cannot be responsive to all possibilities simultaneously. Whatever the flickering lights cast by our own limitations as readers (of knowledge, personality, responsiveness, memory, attention span), the text itself contains its own ambiguities and uncertainties, created out of the shifts and additions, the changes in technique and structure, and the introduction of conflicting perspectives that were a vital part of the process of revision itself. Inevitably, the *Volcano* we read is as partial, as subject to gaps and illusions, not only as Jacques' reading of the Elizabethan text but as any of the characters' "reading" of the world at a given moment – which is to say, a misreading. It is the cost of that richness of Lowry's text that was probably instrumental in drawing us to it in the first place, a richness not unlike that perceived by Yvonne in the cosmic vision of her final chapter.

As she gazes into the brilliance of the Mexican night, she thinks of the turning earth and its solar system, the sun itself revolving in its galaxy, our galaxy part of "countless unmeasured galaxies, turning, turning, majestically, into infinity, into eternity ... all this, long after she herself was dead, men would still be reading" – "reading" and still asking the same "hopeless eternal question: to what end? What force drives this sublime celestial machinery?" (322) Forty years after publication – and thirty years after Lowry himself is dead – we too are still reading his complex, interpenetrating patterns, which seem to recede beyond our vision, still asking our eternal questions of a novel that, perhaps like the cosmos itself, seems to invite our scrutiny but baffles our search for definitive answers.[9]

NOTES

1 Copies of the comments were enclosed with Erskine's letter to Lowry of January 1947, now in the Lowry Collection at the University of British Columbia Library, box 1, folder 20. Further references to manuscript material in this collection will be indicated parenthetically in the text by three numbers – box, folder, page – according to the revised numbering adopted by the Special Collections Division of the library in 1986.

2 Malcolm Lowry, *Under the Volcano* (Philadelphia and New York: J.B. Lippincott 1965), 229. Further references will be indicated parenthetically in the text.

3 Unpublished letter dated 13 August 1941, in the Conrad Aiken Collection, the Huntington Library, Pasadena, California.

4 Unpaginated manuscript sheet in the William Loftus Templeton Collection in the University of British Columbia Library, box 1, folder 14. In the Cape letter (*SL* 61) Lowry attributes this "dictum" to Henry James, but Lowry is, in fact, quoting Richard P. Blackmur, who uses precisely these words in his introduction (xi) to Henry James's *The Art of the Novel: Critical Prefaces* (New York: Scribner's Sons 1934). I would like to thank Kathy Chung for finding the source of this quotation.

5 Although there is no break in the manuscript, pagination skips from 17 to 19 in this draft. Obvious errors have been silently corrected, but the spelling "Quahnahuac," characteristic of this stage of composition, has been retained. Handwritten corrections to the typescript have been followed, all of which are in Lowry's hand except the single most radical alteration, which is in Margerie's hand: in the typescript, Yvonne's reply to her father's query about her interest in the "social situation" in Mexico had been "Exceedingly."

6 "Presumably" because, although the Consul addresses "them," he actually observes, in the final page and a half of the chapter (313–15), only Cervantes "with scared eyes holding the cockerel."

7 For instance, see Jonathan Arac's "misreading" of the passage, where he takes Lowry's arrangement to be definitive and attributes the speech in "stage-Dutch" to Wagner of Marlowe's play: "The Form of Carnival in *Under the Volcano*," PMLA 92 (1977): 482. Arac is the first to my knowledge to point out the comic importance of this speech.

8 See Chris Ackerley and Lawrence J. Clipper, *A Companion to Under the Volcano* (Vancouver: UBC Press, 1984), 59–60.

9 Only after completing this paper did I read Thomas B. Gilmore's excellent "The Place of Hallucination in *Under the Volcano*," *Contemporary Literature* 23 (1982): 285–305. Gilmore's focus is on Geoffrey as alcoholic, but he observes as I do here that the Consul's hallucinations contribute to indeterminacy in the novel.

The Consul as Communicator:
The Voice under the Volcano

JOAN MULHOLLAND

The analysis of conversational discourse by philosophers, linguists, and rhetoricians that has been performed over the years, from J.L. Austin's *How To Do Things with Words* to Harvey Sacks's lectures on sociology, has produced a series of axioms, propositions, and principles that have been used to illuminate that activity as it occurs both in speech and in the novel, when it is seen as a speech act addressed by the author to the reader.[1] I will suggest here that they can also prove illuminating when applied to the represented form of conversation in the novel. To examine the discourse in this way is to go beyond Lowry's speech acts as addressed to us and seek to understand the voices of his characters as he presented them in their spoken interaction.

If any argument is necessary at this stage to demonstrate the relevance of such an analysis to *Under the Volcano*, it can be found in the literary-critical recognition that Lowry transmuted his cultural and personal experience into art in interesting and idiosyncratic ways. Clearly part of this personal experience was conversation, and it too was transmuted in ways that repay critical attention. While one cannot know the conversations Lowry had in life in anything like the ways one can know the books that he read and the scenes he saw, enough is known of real-life conversational behaviour from the work of socio-linguists for an interpretative reading of the conversations in a novel to be both possible and useful. Also, critics have recognized that *Under the Volcano* is full of talk and that problems of communication are a major issue at the level of domestic action in the book. However, they have underplayed the degree to which the novel is also full of talk about talk, which suggests that Lowry himself was aware of the value of his representations of conversation to an understanding of his book and sought to draw our attention to them.

A study that engages with the speech in the novel allows us to draw together considerations of Lowry's preoccupation with the spoken language in the book and one of its major themes – *no se puede vivir sin amar*. For example, one way in which Lowry develops the struggle that arises when the need for love meets the difficulty of loving is through the conversational interchanges of his main characters, and of the Consul in particular. Among his problems are those that occur when love is present and even strongly felt but cannot or does not issue in acts and expressions of love, that is, when it is not communicated. A further justification for a speech-act approach to the represented conversation comes from the way Lowry moved, in successive manuscript versions of the novel, from using speech for direct exposition to having it provide more oblique manifestations of authorial comment and so to making it figure in the final version as unexplained enactment. By the final draft he had produced speech that mimics actual conversation that is apparently random in occurrence and difficult to decipher. Explanation of the speakers' intentions or motivation must be sought elsewhere in the text, from its symbolism, imagery, the use of literature and history, rather than from the speech itself. So, for example, in the represented conversations between the Consul and Yvonne, Lowry enacts rather than comments on their attempts at engagement and commitment in the communication of their relationship. A study of these interchanges will suggest ways in which their conversational behaviour should be seen as a support to or a variant upon the other elements of the novel.

Three particular aspects of conversational analysis seem useful for the study of this particular text. First, there is the recognition that conversational speech is a series of acts performed by the speaker on the hearer, acts of requesting, asking questions, offering statements, etc., with differing kinds of influence thereby being exerted by the speaker and perceived by the hearer, such that requesting is seen as more of an imposition and the asking of questions as more intrusive than the offering of comment.[2] For example, when readers read a command spoken within the action, they measure its degree of imposition and note from the kind of response it receives from the other characters how this imposition is taken, and move then to deduce something of the characters' relationships. Second, it is generally recognized that interactive speech is a matter of exchange, that utterances are related to one another as speakers take turns to produce them, initiate them, respond to them, and as they are successful or fail, etc.[3] Thus, represented utterances demonstrate character behaviours as they match or fail to match with readers' standards of conversation, so that, for example, the absence of a reply by a character will probably be viewed as meaningful by the reader, even in the absence of direct authorial comment on its meaning. Third, there is the more general recognition that the profile of a particular speaker's contributions throughout a conversation leaves an impression that must be measured along with the circumstances within which it occurs to provide evidence of the relationship of that speaker to others. For example, a character who is a major initiator of speech will be perceived by the reader as a crucial actor, while one whose speech consists mainly of questions rather than statements or commands will be perceived as one whose role is that of a seeker of answers from others, with the kind of searching determinable from the kind of questioning employed. Using these aspects of interactive speech, it is possible to analyse a sample text: the conversation in the second chapter between the Consul and Yvonne in the crucial first moments of their reunion on Yvonne's return to Quauhnahuac. This interaction constitutes our first direct evidence of their behaviour towards one another.

Two of the most valuable sources of meaning in the spoken interaction of the two characters are Lowry's use of addressees and his choice of question, command, or statement as speech acts. With respect to the first, a striking aspect of the Consul's speech acts is that in the early moments of reunion, when our expectations (whether derived from natural speech or from representations in other novels) suggest it should be otherwise, only a relatively small number are addressed to Yvonne. This is true of the very first act of speech by the Consul: "A corpse will be transported by express" (48).[4] It is an act within Yvonne's hearing, but it occurs before she and the Consul begin their face-to-face interaction. The next two, which are addressed by the Consul to the barman, have a similar status. All are said while the Consul is ignorant of Yvonne's presence, but all exist within the reader's sense of interaction between the two characters because both are present to the reader and because Yvonne responds emotionally to the voice as "achingly familiar."

Lowry, then, presents the reader with a source of impact and communication – speech – before either party can use it for connection or engagement, and so, at a strategic moment, the novel demonstrates that speech may be a measure of engagement but is not always a sign of communication. We are here given the first of many examples of speech usage that is not engaged interaction. In fact Lowry describes the first remark as being "lobbed" over the windowsill and the next two as addressed to an unseen hearer, unseen by us and at first unseen by Yvonne: "the bar was empty. Or rather it contained one figure [the Consul]." When she does perceive the hearer, she describes him as indifferent: "the barman ... stood at a little distance ... and didn't have the air of listening" (50). That is, we are given an addressee almost invisible to one character, yet so personally known as to be named "Fernando" by the other. By presenting the first speech acts in this way, Lowry establishes Yvonne's role as that of third party or eavesdropper, or as one excluded from interaction, or as one whose reactions to others are very different from the Consul's. This speech begins the process by which the Consul is registered as one who has many brief, casual encounters, while Yvonne has fewer but more intense and problematic ones. Lowry, then, has vividly enacted something of the difficulties in interaction between the two main characters without providing authorial explanation. Furthermore, he has done so in the mode of conversation, which he thus signals as a crucial proving ground for their interaction, or lack of it.

He does more than this, however; these first speech acts are markedly not being used in interactive exchanges. This is the world of no connection, where people can speak in turns and in the presence of others and yet not be in communication. So we are told of the barman that "he was listening after all. That is, while he mightn't understand what Geoffrey (who was, she noticed, wearing no socks) was talking about, he was waiting, his towelled hands overhauling the glasses ever more slowly, for an opening to say or do something" (*UV* 50–1). Or again: "'*Absolutamente necesario,*' he said, ... But he hadn't attracted the Consul's attention, ... 'A corpse, whether adult or child,' the Consul had resumed, after briefly pausing to laugh at this pantomime, and to agree, with a kind of agony, '*Sí, Fernando, absolutamente necesario*'" (*UV* 51). We are enabled to register the importance of the utterance as action in itself because none of the standard aims of represented speech are being met. We do not perceive this speech, for example, to be formulating a character's ideas, or getting some plot action performed, both of which can be carried forward in the speech without readers needing to register the degree of communication occurring. Its main function is rather to alert us to "turns" in speaking, and the ways in which these can occur without participants really hearing each other.

Certainly the topic dealt with in the speech may be of thematic value, as in the first instance of the corpse and its transport, but it occurs at a moment when its role in interaction forces us to consider it in another light, as constituting neither a topic of joint interest or shared experience, nor one labelled as deliberate avoidance of mutuality. Indeed, this possibility is made less likely because it is a topic begun before the joint-speech behaviour of the Consul and Yvonne and continuing into it. We are left to consider it as an indicator of action in itself. It also has value, within so very structured a novel, as a rendering of one of those moments in real life that are awkward precisely because they lack the organization of literature and are unprepared for. The scene resembles those occasions when a real-life reunion's emotional impact is affected by peripheral elements – for example, when an exchange of greetings is interrupted by a business phone call, or a meeting place is mistaken and so the reunion moments include grumbles about directions.

Even when the Consul becomes aware of Yvonne's longed-for return and they speak with each other, he continues to have spoken interactions with peripheral addressees. He speaks to others, notices and responds to the presence of others, even to the extent of interrupting his speech with Yvonne. She, in contrast, either does not notice others, has minimal spoken contact with them, or seeks to avoid them. While it is true of natural conversation that the context, including the presence of others, will affect the speech activity of a central pair of speakers, it does not usually do so in the representation of speech in novels except in certain recognized ways, such as providing extrinsic topics or constraints or expository matter or previous history and the like, or as indicating some metaphorical or other significance through its content. It is quite conventional, therefore, that the sight of the photograph in the shop window receives mention in speech, and that the passing of Laruelle's house causes an awkwardness in what they say.

But Lowry uses contextual involvement in less orthodox ways. After the first exchange between the Consul and Yvonne there is an intrusion of speech from someone in the bar. This remark, possibly from Weber, although not attributed to him in this chapter, carries little significance in its content, but by its very presence it registers a gap in the speech interaction between the two main characters, thereby making the reader aware of absence in their speech, of silence, of things not uttered. This is to use represented speech not for its content alone but also for its value as action. Another instance occurs when the Consul leaves Yvonne and goes into a shop in the Calle Tierra del Fuego. This part of the scene begins with the Consul: "'– in Tortu,' the Consul was saying, though Yvonne was not following"; it continues with Yvonne's description of the street and its shops, "into one of which the Consul was now, with a '*momentito*,' disappearing" (60). We are told of her feelings – "she waited outside, restless ... A mood of martyrdom stole upon her. She wanted the Consul to see her, when he emerged, waiting there, abandoned and affronted." Then Lowry shows us that she could withdraw in thought from the scene just as the Consul had done in action: "glancing back the way they had come she forgot Geoffrey for an instant" (60). He abandons and she forgets in other ways too, and at other levels of the action. We are then told that the Consul had a good-humoured chat with the shopkeeper, which contrasts with the awkwardness of his talk with Yvonne, which is further illustrated when he returns, repeat-ing, "In Tortu ... " (60), thereby reinforcing the sense that his absence was an interruption of significance because it is left unexplained and without apology.

This juxtaposition of the two conversations further suggests that one of the Consul's problems is the misdirection of communication. Lowry does this by displacing those actions, which should constitute involve-ment of one character with another, from themselves to outsiders. The talk with the shopkeeper, for example, contrasts with a lost opportunity for interaction with Yvonne. Lowry makes use of minor characters not only to introduce other themes, or other aspects of the *no se puede* theme, and to act as universalizing agents in the novel, but also to provide comparison and contrast with the type and kind of speech interaction that occurs between the Consul, Yvonne, and Hugh.

This whole incident is a typical example of the way Lowry intrigu-ingly presents the periphery as a determining feature of the central action while keeping it free of implication in the action. This rhetorical strategy can be construed as a comment on the world of this novel, where actions and people can be contiguous and yet not contingent, and it is another way in which Lowry seeks to present, even in so elaborately structured a novel, the sense of a world beyond its characters' control.[5]

A second, rather different instance of speech interaction with the peripheral context occurs when the Consul offers the following remarks to the scribe: "I am taking the only way out, semicolon. Goodbye, full stop" (58). This is another interruption of his interaction with Yvonne. While it can be read as having thematic significance by pointing forward to the Consul's death and its aftermath, and in so doing joining the many other echoes that bind the events of the novel together, it also sends a message about character and does so, again, more by its mode than its content. It adds to the Consul a dimension of language aware-ness and a capacity for analysis, as shown by his metacomment, through the spoken punctuation marks, not after the event but at the moment when the event is taking place. The Consul is a tragic figure because he knows what he is doing at the moment in which he acts and is yet unable to avoid the effects he is likely to produce. The simultaneity of his awareness and his actions, seen here in language use as well as occurring elsewhere in other ways, makes him a more complex and consistent figure.

Further still, this example shows how speech interaction in the novel is not always or only a way of recording the way main characters affect each other but also a perspective on the way they exist in relation to other people in their lives. In this case the Consul's comment to the scribe is an intrusion into his work; it appears to be a completion, a sharing of his work, and could be a sign of communion (or communion sought). It is as if he knows so well what the scribe will write that he can finish his sentence for him. But there is no evidence that this would be a sensible reading in this case. The Consul's intervention is jocular in tone while being serious in content, and it can be recognized as not in harmony with the scribe's world. It is an instance of wasted communication and of interference, in this case with little effect on the scribe. It does not bring the scribe and his world any further into the novel's main action than this; both remain on the periphery in a typically Lowryan manner. But the verbal intervention does provide a prefiguring of the Consul's other important intervention when he argues with the police moments before his death.

A second source of meaning in speech-act behaviour resides in the nature of the act used. Among the most striking instances in this chapter are the absent acts, the ones the Consul does not offer to Yvonne when they might be expected, and Yvonne's unarticulated responses to him. All that the Consul offers directly to Yvonne, as he registers her reappearance in his life, are the exclamation "Good God" (which Lowry co-ordinates with the physical act of the Consul "he made no move toward her"), a phatic, small-talk question – "Don't you love these early mornings?" and "Have a – [cigarette]," "–" (as he finds he has no cigarettes), and then at last a question about her journey (51–2). All are noticeable for what they do not say. The reader's recognition of their significance in this respect depends not so much on their content, or even on our registration of them as awkward or stressful signs, but on their place in the text, following as they do the letter revealed in chapter 1, from which we know the cost of failed communication: this is what happens when love is expressed too late or cannot be expressed at all. Lowry had written in the Consul's letter: "And why did I not send a telegram or some word immediately? Ah why not, why not, why not? For I suppose you would have come back in due course if I had asked you. But this is what it is to live in hell. I could not, cannot send a telegram" (*UV* 44). Here in chapter 2 we have this torment enacted; this is what such difficulties result in. No further comment is offered, nor is one necessary.

Sometimes, however, the reader's understanding is not so sure. When Lowry represents Yvonne's responses as "–" or when he produces exchanges like "'Remember Oaxaca.' 'Oaxaca?' 'Oaxaca'" (53), such ellipses intrigue or irritate according to one's expectations of what work readers are expected to do as they read. They are paradoxically vivid realizations of absence, leaving Yvonne's attitudes, motives, and even her behaviour in the recorded scene unclear. By giving her replies like "–," Lowry refuses the simplest options of authorial comment, even of the thoroughly conventionalized type that is barely noticeable to the reader, such as "Yvonne said nothing" or "Yvonne had nothing to say." Both of these comments would provide more information than the one Lowry opts for, and one has to assume, since his is the marked or unusual form, that he recognized the value of its difference and omission. There is consistency in the way he retains the phatic and purely practical speech acts that are often given little value in novel-writing and yet takes out those accepted forms that might provide more authorial comment than he wants. That he establishes the meaning of the text in this way appears to support the view that Lowry sought to produce chronicle rather than narration in *Under the Volcano*, making it look like reportage at times, even in the midst of extremely elaborate writing.[6]

During the walk to their home Yvonne begins to show more speech initiative and asks questions, both about fairly trivial aspects of their life together such as the car ("Did you smack up the car again?" [57]) and about more important features ("have you resigned from the service?" [53]). It is noticeable that in her questions she is likelier to use the Consul's name than he is to use hers, and this use of the vocative may reflect her need to call him or to connect with him, or at the least to register him as real. (Lowry has indicated that she finds it unbelievable that she is back in Quauhnahuac.) Opposed to these are two questions offered by the Consul: "Remember Oaxaca?" (53) and "Look, do you remember what Maria used to call it [the little American grocery store]? ... Peegly Weegly" (58). On each occasion he causes her pain, and so damages the relationship. We do not always know what the pain is: in the Oaxaca example Yvonne's thoughts and emotions about the place are recorded for us to share, in the conventional way; but in the Peegly Weegly example we know from Yvonne's response (not said aloud but available to us) "I won't, I won't cry," and from the Consul's reaction "I'm sorry, I never thought," only that pain has been caused but not how or why. In their speech interaction, then, we see Yvonne calling the Consul, and the Consul hurting Yvonne, and have to balance this against the reporting of the off-stage hurting that her actions caused him; the vividness and immediacy of his actions are almost bound to make his the greater blame.

Among the speech acts we offer each other in natural conversation, commands rank among the most impositive. Yet there are two such acts in this chapter which seem perversely to be treated in ways which show them not to impose at all, while yet retaining the power to be important. They are an interesting pair in that they are in almost the same words, "look out," with one instance offered by the Consul and one by Yvonne. The repetition suggests that it may be worth examining them as a pair, since repetition can show agreement or unity, or provide readers with a recognition of disagreement or disunity. In each case the command is addressed to a trivial event – not coming into physical contact with something in the environment. Each is, therefore, an exclamation directed as much to the periphery of their relationship as to the centre of it. Further, they do not indicate depth of relationship, since one can say "Look out" to a lover or to a total stranger, and they are not heeded by the person to whom they are addressed.

The Consul's command is offered in the midst of other speech, and Yvonne's, we are told, might have been better applied to herself, as she is the one who is having physical difficulties at the time. Yet in contrast to this reduction of the power of the commands in their context, they acquire an emphasis through their applicability to the central concerns of the interaction between the Consul and Yvonne. The Consul's "look out" is inserted into a sentence about drinking – "nothing, not even athletics, is allowed to interfere with the business of – look out! ... drinking" (61); Yvonne's is "'Do look where you're going, Geoffrey!' But it was Yvonne who had stumbled" (62). That one command is in the context of his drinking and the other of her stumbling makes plain their thematic relevance in general terms, but it is equally important for our understanding of the novel to recognize that each speaker offers the same type of speech act to the other, but that neither command is of much value in preventing what it seeks to prevent. (In chapter 4 there is a third command to look out, this time offered by Hugh to Yvonne, urging her to avoid a goat [103].)

If we turn from the notion of speech as act to that of speech as exchange, we can see other ways in which Lowry sought to reinforce communication as a central mode for the generation of meaning in the novel. An archetypical speech exchange is a pair of adjacent utterances in which the second is dependent on the first to form a type of interaction between the two speakers. Chapter 2 is full of irregular speech exchanges. I have mentioned utterances spoken by or addressed to unknown second parties (unknown to the reader or to the apparent addressee), to no one in particular, and ones which receive no appropriate responses. In one case, that where the Consul addresses the scribe, it is a third party, Yvonne, who replies. The largest group of exchanges in the chapter, however, is of those that are interrupted by others, or by the first speaker interrupting him- or herself. Some cause the prevention of a reply; some just cause a delay in reply. On many occasions Lowry causes delay by inserting expository material within speech exchanges rather than between them. This gives an unusual power to the exposition, makes it noticeable, offers an interpretation of the world that allows context a very important role in interaction, and produces for the reader a vivid sense of the dislocation of speech caused by the distance between the two speakers, and also (strangely for expository material) produces a sense of immediacy of explanation or comment that can be accepted by the reader as part of the exposition. In this, as in so many other aspects of writing, Lowry shows himself aware of the value of textual placement and structure.

Others of his favourite variants on the speech-exchange pair are to give speech moves as if they are continuations when the reader does not have the first part, as in the Consul's "Yes, it's still there" (62), in reply to only a (possible) look of Yvonne's. Sometimes Lowry gives ellipted or unfinished speech moves, as in Yvonne's "And I'd far rather walk, only –" (57). Often we can guess at an unheard utterance, but not always. In chapter 2 only three of the forty-seven examples of speech exchanges between the Consul and Yvonne are of the standard form; the rest are either interrupted or unsuccessful. It is noticeable, however, that the reader's sense of them as such is not always the same as that of the characters themselves.

Some speech moves have a form that is hard to read but causes no problems for the hearer within the action; at other times, however, the reader hears the speech and only knows it to be problematic after the addressee responds. The nature of the effect of such a variation between characters' reading and readers' reading is unclear, but it must at least reduce readers' certainty of judgment about what is going on in the action and make it seem an unsettling experience to read. Another effect, which arises from the recurrence of such broken or problematic speech exchanges, bears upon the movement of the text and plays its part in establishing a dynamism in speech that counteracts those parts of the novel that present a lack of action in other ways. Thus Lowry is able to create a liveliness on one level of the discourse, although it may be absent on another.[7]

In all, Lowry's use of the mode of speech presentation in the book is as skilful as his other modes of presentation, and it works to present meaning in ways that are consistent with his other techniques. He plots the speech as if well aware of its value as action and of its potential for enrichment of the reading experience, and it is particularly pleasing that he should do so in ways that relate to the naturalistic use of speech and so provide a lively contrast with the literariness of other aspects of the book.

NOTES

1 J.L. Austin, *How To Do Things with Words* (Cambridge: Harvard UP 1962). The late Harvey Sacks's lecture notes, circulated in manuscript form

from 1973, are currently being prepared for publication by Gail Jefferson.

2 John Searle provides a fruitful account of the range of possible speech acts in "A Classification of Illocutionary Acts," *Language in Society* 5, no. 1 (1976): 1–23.

3 G. Sacks, E.A. Schegloff, and G. Jefferson, "A Simplest Systematics for the Organization of Turn-taking in Conversation," *Language* 50 (1974): 696–735, includes an account of speech exchanges.

4 All references are to *Under the Volcano* (Harmondsworth: Penguin 1962) and are included in the text.

5 The related notions of different levels in *Under the Volcano*, and of its central and peripheral aspects, occur frequently in Lowry criticism, from Dale Edmunds' "Under the Volcano: A Reading of the Immediate Level," *Tulane Studies in English* 16 (1968): 63–105, to Duncan Hadfield's "*Under the Volcano*'s 'Central' Symbols: Trees, Towers and Their Variants," in *Apparently Incongruous Parts: The Worlds of Malcolm Lowry*, ed. Paul Tiessen (Metuchen, NJ: Scarecrow Press 1990), 80–109. Hadfield warns that critics should not ignore the ways in which Lowry interlocks the various aspects of the book, a warning I am supporting here in showing how the apparently peripheral actions reflect upon the central ones. For elaboration of the idea of control and freedom, see my paper (as Joan Huddleston) "Noun Modification as an Index of Style in Lowry's *Under the Volcano*," *Language and Style* 10, no. 2 (1977): 73–108.

6 Chronicling may be seen as the attempt to produce an order of narrative understanding different from that resulting from a strong sense of authorial control, say, through the manipulation of symbol and imagery. It seeks to appear more as reportage and usually contains material left ambiguous or unexplained or not drawn into the more organized part of the book.

7 Accounts of the way Lowry manipulates the movement of *Under the Volcano* are given in Terence Wright "*Under the Volcano*: The Static Art of Malcolm Lowry," *Ariel* 4 (1970): 67–76, and in chapter 3 of Sherrill Grace's *The Voyage That Never Ends: Malcolm Lowry's Fiction* (Vancouver: UBC Press 1982).

The *Volcano*
of a Postmodern Lowry

SUE VICE

To consider Malcolm Lowry's *oeuvre* from a postmodern perspective is to discover a new and refreshing model for his work. Critics from Fredric Jameson to Craig Owens and from Edward Said to Jean-François Lyotard have identified elements in postmodern writing of pastiche, self-reference, a schizophrenic attitude to history, the death of the author and of the subject, collage, and allegory.[1] Moreover, the post-modern artefact resists instant consumability (*Under the Volcano* does, after all, literally demand a second reading) in a way that goes beyond the modernist strategy of simply making itself opaquely verbal and removed from the real. The postmodern work, lacking the storyteller's claim to respect and attention, advertises the fact that it is a commodity, not an art object but an artefact. In *Volcano*'s case, this involves the inclusion within the text of pieces of the commodified, market-oriented world of billboards, railway signs, menus, and advertisements, those tangible reminders that our knowledge of the world consists only of the already written, the textual; on the last page the novel has trans-formed itself into a "keep off the grass" sign. The postmodern work is thus an extension of the world rather than an image of it, making clear that there is, as Terry Eagleton says, "no reality which is not itself already image, spectacle, simulacrum, gratuitous fiction ... for art to reflect reality is then for it to do no more than mirror itself."[2]

The central features of postmodernism are represented in Lowry's writing, and the approach indicated by postmodernists is particularly useful in discussing his work as a radically new practice, as becomes clear from the categories under which it is most frequently examined: autobiography, plagiarism, and alcoholism.

Autobiography. Lowry's work has suffered doubly from the classic realist fallacy: it is assumed that the language of the novel offers a clear window not only on to the real world but also on to the real author. In his *Speaking of Chaucer* E. Talbot Donaldson urged that that author be released from the traditional treatment of the poet as if he were "a single Chaucer under the guise of a wide-eyed, jolly, rolypoly little man who ... used to get up early, while the dew was still on the grass, and go look at daisies."[3] The point is, of course, that there is in Chaucer's case no single person uniting the pilgrim, the poet, and the civil servant of contemporary historical records, even though the "three separate entities" may have borne "a close resemblance to one another, and that, indeed, they frequently got together in the same body. But that does not excuse us from keeping them distinct from one another, difficult as their close resemblance makes our task" (Donaldson 1). The very publicity given to Lowry's besetting fears – of being caught out as a literary thief, of existing only as a written subject in someone else's book – has ensured that he has, ironically, been proven right.

Expressions of these doubts are not always equivalent; Lowry's receiving Jonathan Cape's letter accepting *Under the Volcano* for publication from the postman in that very novel is quite distinct from his treatment of this coincidence in *Dark as the Grave*. Personal or historical accounts of this event are necessarily of a quite different order from the novelistic treatment of them. One involves circumstantial biographical evidence, the other a subtle metafictional conceit. Sigbjørn Wilderness in *Dark as the Grave* is not a facile third-person rewriting of Lowry's diary but a "presence" more akin to Jung's "little stone mannikin," which as a young boy Jung kept in his pencil-case and which represented himself not by equivalence but by a species of symbolism. Fictions become metaphors for historical facts, a process that is perhaps clearest in *Under the Volcano*, Lowry's least obviously autobiographical novel.

Autobiography thus exemplifies the realist paradox that more words bring greater verbal opacity, not mimeticism; naïvely transcribing the events of one's life, producing a diary as one's novel, is self-defeating. The central issue of autobiography, the tension between the written and the speaking subject, cannot be treated in this form because minutely detailed description moves steadily *away* from its object. As Jonathan Culler has shown, the most estranging way to describe the familiar action of walking, for example, is to attempt to be exhaustively realistic.[4] Lowry recognized this problem and used other means to solve his need for certain effects. Thus, in an early version of a passage in

Under the Volcano, Yvonne's reaction to the news of Hugh's presence is typical of the striving found in "character novels" to convey psychological realities by over-insistence: "'What,' Yvonne wailed; and stopped in her tracks. The Consul had taken her arm paternally, but her head was buzzing, she felt a strange constriction and a twitching in her temples and she seemed to be floating, rather than walking, sick – this was impossible – outrageous – inconceivable."[5]

This piling up of words in the hope of communicating an emotional state is replaced in the final version by a collection that evades narration by *symbolizing* agitation, through an independent, disinterested voice:

> "He's staying with me."
> – ¡BOX! ARENA TOMALÍN. FRENTE AL JARDIN XICOTANCATL ...
> *Las Manos de Orlac. Con Peter Lorre.*
> "*What!*" Yvonne stopped dead.   (UV 65)

Conflict is shown here by the boxing and suspense-film posters, which also distract the protagonists' attention; the narrator of the earlier version, watching from the outside and presuming to tell the truth about the situation to the reader, has gone, leaving the story to be told indirectly by an assemblage of autonomous words, not by a description.

Although the wish that art might redeem an imperfect life is expressed in Lowry's work – Wilderness claims, for example, that "there is not a drop of mescal I have not turned into pure gold, not a drink I have not made sing" (DAG 223) – there is also a great fear of the collapse of any such distinction. The hope of redeeming one's life by perfecting the work takes on a threatening aspect: "would God close the book on him, as if he were an insect?" (DAG 207). Such a remark derives its meaning precisely from its textuality, its presence in the written form of a novel, not from its correspondence to some unverifiable personal history. Wilderness describes a novel he is writing "about a character who becomes enmeshed in the plot of a novel he has written, as I did in Mexico ... Idea is not new, at least so far as enmeshment is concerned. Goethe ... Pirandello etc. But did these people ever have it happen to *them*?" (HOL 27). This is not simply Lowry-in-disguise straightforwardly recording an idea. *Writing about* the problems of writing has a sophisticated metaphysical twist, and here it culminates in the nightmarish vision Wilderness has of the Panama Canal overseers: out of sight there is probably always another, transcendent viewer spying on the one before, and so on.

In a short story by Julio Cortázar, a man is killed by one of the characters in the novel he is reading.[6] This is a demonstration of the truism that, in fiction, no hierarchy of realism is possible, and Lowry

exploits both the possibility of disjunction between narrator and narrated matter, and their indistinguishability, as a structural metaphor for
his creative difficulties, for the implication of the act of writing in everything that is written. According to Borges, "such inversion suggests
that if the characters in a story can be readers or spectators, then we,
their readers or spectators, can be fictitious."[7] The very processes of
composition and verbal representation are questioned. As Jay Newman
has said, while modernism suspended the referent in favour of the word,
postmodernism problematizes the very activity of reference.[8] Wilderness actively wants to become a paper man; in *Dark as the Grave* he
explains to Primrose the frustration of living in an unwritten book:

> "And besides, *this* is the book."
> "This is what book?"
> "The real book. Now, it's as if everything we do is part of it. I can't write
> it, of course." (*DAG* 102)

This is not merely a poetic rendering of the commonplace that consciousness, perception, and the subject itself are all verbal constructs,
so that life is indeed just another text, formed and learnt by means of
the already written. It also points to the paradox of writing. Of course,
the book *is* written, or Sigbjørn could not say what he does; the more
he insists on his inability to write, the more written he becomes. This
is, in a sense, the structural expression of autobiography; all ephemeral
personal activity is transformed into the permanence of art, a fact recognized by writers from Sterne to Keats.

Expressing this fear of losing the gap between life and art appears,
ironically, to have realized itself. For instance, in a remarkable passage
from Lowry's unpublished manuscript "La Mordida," the writer's
Shandyesque double bind – that each act of writing requires another to
account for it – becomes a truly vicious circle. Primrose tells her husband:

> "But what's the use, you'll forget it unless you write it down."
> "Wasn't I writing it down?" Sigbjørn said, shaking all over and now finding
> the bottle of habanero.
> "Sigbjørn, listen to me. We're living this. You're not writing it."
> "But my god, what earthly point would there be in living it if I didn't write
> it?"[9]

Wilderness already sees himself as textual – and of course he is.

I have suggested that Lowry's response to the problem of verbal
representation was to deploy fragments of our textual world, such as
advertisements, notices, and newspapers, to render his characters' psy-

chological lives. Similarly, his solution to the Wilderness problem of how to present oneself textually was to abandon the viciously circling form of autobiography and to approach the issue more deviously. Examination of the drafts of *Under the Volcano* shows that the events of Lowry's life did not become mimetically transferred to that novel but instead reappear in altered forms, similar to the way in which infant traumata reappear as neuroses in the adult. Undeniably autobiographical origins are not only transformed into unreliable guides to the author's life but also assume the status of symbols rather than facts. The abandonment by Jan Gabrial, Lowry's first wife, of an untenable situation in 1937 comes through in the second draft of *Under the Volcano* as the alteration of the Consul's daughter into his gleefully unfaithful wife and the daughter's young man into the Consul's half-brother; Lowry's angst imposes a new emotion on an existent fictional base. Real events do not appear, but the old ones are altered.

After Lowry's marriage to Margerie Bonner and their move to British Columbia, a further variation on the old theme occurs: the wife is (arguably) unfaithful, but also devoted and long suffering, and her heart is set on a pastoral retreat to salvage their relationship and his liver. It is often the case that the most significant plot-changes in a particular scene involve alteration not in the wording but in the roles of the characters. For example, the Consul's wish for rescue as he spends his final hours in the cantina El Farolito is transferred to *Volcano* almost verbatim from its original draft form: "If Yvonne, as a daughter, who would understand and comfort him had only been at his side now! Even if but to lead him by the hand, drunkenly homeward, through the stonefields as the Indian children led their fathers on Sundays."[10]

In the draft here, the Consul's wish – "as a daughter" – is emphatic: he is merely calling upon filial obligation, hoping his daughter Yvonne will give up her impatience and intolerance. In *Volcano*, however, the Consul is thinking about his *wife*, whom he wants to act like a daughter by adopting a childlike rather than a sexual attitude towards him. Moreover, he has just enjoyed the services of a prostitute, having failed to make love with his wife earlier in the day. The phrasing is not altered, but the changed roles of the dramatis personae make the words speak quite differently to the reader; it is as if the words themselves created the possibility for the new plot. Such radical alteration in the sense of the same sentence in different positions is an image of Lowry's whole *modus scribendi*; he treats his own works as he does those of other writers, grafting together the components of literary sense into a coherent surface.

A similar instance of a loss of innocence occurs in the drafts when Laruelle remarks, "Do you know, I think those two will make a formidable couple";[11] here he is referring to two people who have every

right to be together, and all the Consul can have against such an observation is the ambivalent feelings of a father towards his prospective son-
in-law. In *Volcano*, however, menace is imported into the scene. Now
Laruelle and the Consul are looking at the latter's ex-wife standing with
one of her ex-lovers, the Consul's half-brother. An echo of the earlier
reference in Laruelle's words to Hugh and Yvonne's well-suited good
looks persists in the background here, although now the Consul hears
a painful slight to both himself and the Frenchman (*UV* 216), and "formidable" also carries with it the implication of something powerful and
illicit.[12] This progression of the narrative shows Mikhail Bakhtin's definition of sense as word plus context in action: the words are infinitely
repeatable and have a long and unavoidable history of previous usage,
but each time they are redeployed a unique site of meaning is created.[13]

One of the reasons offered for Lowry's reputation as a writer of
glorified third-person diaries is that he never had time to apply to *October Ferry*, for example, the ten years' hard labour *Under the Volcano*
needed. Although he entertained high hopes of his later works' combining the mythic with the domestic in the near-perfect synthesis that
Volcano achieves, he never managed to transmute the bald facts of his
own history into an objective work of art in his later fiction. However,
his is not the work of an autobiographer but a new kind of writing, in
true death-of-the-author fashion. As several critics have shown, *Volcano*
consists largely of bits and pieces from other writers (the consciousness
of Europe, Margerie Lowry called the novel, adding that the individual
reader was not expected to recognize everything). The author is a maker
of collages, an editor, a character in his or her own fiction rather than
a creator possessed of unusual poetic sensibility. *Volcano* constitutes the
anthology of melancholy that is the substance, or meaning, of the Consul. Voices from all ages and places speak of heartbreak, loss, and
oppression, from the butterfly lost at sea to the *Alas* brand of cigarette,
including the conquest of Mexico, the Fascist conquest of Spain, Negro
spirituals, and the consumption of live shellfish. It is as if Walter Benjamin's wish to "collect and reproduce in quotation the contradictions
of the present without resolution," to purge subjectivity and allow the
self to be a vehicle for the expression of "objective cultural tendencies"
had been realized.[14]

Plagiarism. The logical extension of this practice has been explored in
the infamous concept of grammatology, which amounts to a theory of
writing as citation, and this is manifested in literature most clearly in
the postmodern collage. Intertextuality, the composition of a work out
of the words of others, is simply a procedural fact of using language at
all, as Derrida puts it: "every sign, linguistic or non-linguistic, spoken

or written ... can be *cited*, put between quotation marks."[15] All words possess a history which they carry with them and which spills over into each new context even as they gain new associations: "Each cited element breaks the continuity or linearity of the discourse and leads necessarily to a double reading: that of the fragment perceived in relation to its text of origin; that of the same fragment as incorporated into a new whole, a different totality."[16] An example of this in *Under the Volcano* is the Consul's repetition of the word "strange", starting with the occasion on which the pariah dog follows Geoffrey into his garden; the reader hears in the word each previous context and comes to recognize its multi-voicedness. "Strange" comes to mean not only "how odd" but disruption, estrangement, and a recognition of the symbol- and portent-filled nature of the Consul's world.

The issue of collage as a replacement for autobiographical subjectivity leads into another problem area, that of the "wrongful appropriation or purloining, and publication as one's own, of the ideas, or the expression of the ideas, of another," according to the OED definition. Rather than acting reprehensibly, for example, in his apparently silent adoption of large passages from C.J. Turner's *Barbarous Mexico*, Lowry is foregrounding intertextuality. He is concerned to include details of the fate of the indigenous Mexicans, and clearly the best – or only – way to do so is to rely upon a previously written account for his new written account. The same practice occurs in much postmodern photography – when the photographer wants an image of nature, he or she does not take one but appropriates another's image in order to expose the degree to which nature is always already implicated in a system of cultural values.[17] Quotations are not simply applied to the surface of an existing work; rather, "each grafted text continues to radiate back toward the site of its removal, transforming that too, as it affects the new territory."[18] Intertextuality is not "the investigation of sources and influences as traditionally conceived; it casts its net wider to include anonymous discursive practices, codes whose origins are lost."[19] In Derrida's formulation it is the transposition of one or more systems of signs into another. In this case, Lowry inserts a specimen of historical discourse into his novel, thereby allowing it to signify oppression and injustice as well as fact.

Julia Kristeva claims that intertextuality is "the general discursive space that makes a text intelligible."[20] *Under the Volcano* is thus remarkable for doing what all language-users have to, but with an extra dimension of self-consciousness and what is almost brazenness. Yvonne, for instance, is made up of a series of discourses, including Hollywood movie-speak, domesticated Electra complex, and British Columbian pastoral; she *is* their point of intersection, yet, as has often been pointed out, the result is a surprisingly solid-seeming, verisimilar personage. However, Barthes' observation that "the 'I' that approaches the text is itself already a plurality of other texts,"[21] that every time we say "I love you" we are in fact using a literary quotation, makes our readiness to respond to Yvonne, Geoffrey, and Hugh more intelligible: they are constructed just as we are.[22]

What results in *Under the Volcano* from the fact that, as Kristeva has pointed out, "each text is made up of a mosaic of citations"[23] is a species of multi-voicedness; this polyglossia, as Bakhtin would call it, results when words are taken from the mouths of traditional literature and from dominant discourses such as diplomacy and national history and destabilized by being interleaved with the multiplicity of textual snippets that constitute the bulk of the novel. It is this practice that lays Lowry open to the somewhat over-literal charge of plagiarism. In fact, rather than rifling world literature to fuel a guttering talent, Lowry has performed a Burroughsesque transformation, restoring to the literary some materiality by cutting out words, lines, or paragraphs and reshuffling them; this is the basis of *Volcano*'s carnival, its disruptive ludic force, jumbling up sign and referent, word and object, in a drunken vision that none the less includes a prediction of its own hangover and death. Conrad Aiken's irritation at such appropriation is even given a voice: "Hell, *I* told you that –" (*UV* 312).

If the original is recognizable, and the whole point of the exercise is for it to be recognized, then plagiarism gives way to the games-playing of allusion and citation; such recognizability may depend on internal acknowledgment, as when the Consul overtly connects De Quincey's essay with his thoughts about Macbeth, murder, and knockings at the door (*UV* 140). In fact, a general complaint about Lowry's apparent dishonesty is that, in successive drafts of *Volcano*, he suppressed such overt reference to sources: some of these have been recuperated by critics from Lowry's own manuscripts – somewhat ironically, as Lowry clearly went to some trouble to avoid unnatural-sounding and pedagogic bibliographical statements of origin. For example, there is no translation accompanying the Consul's zipping himself up in *Volcano*: "'Pardon me, *j'adoube*,' he said" (*UV* 137). In parentheses in draft, however, there is a narratorial voice-over: "(though he had in fact used the term customary in chess when touching a piece without meaning to make a move)."[24] Exposition for its own sake has no place in a work that is primarily concerned with other aspects of the appropriated or arcane than mere historical or bibliographical origin.

It is precisely this strategy, the exploitation of what is definitional about language for artistic ends, that fits *Under the Volcano* for Bakhtin's carnival label. The published version of the novel consists of unnarrated, autonomous voices; its varieties of language are left free to subvert and

relativize each other, unsupervised by a master controller. The characters in the work are analogously free, as part of what Bakhtin calls a
"plurality of equal consciousnesses and their worlds, which are combined here in the unity of a given event, while at the same time retaining
their unmergedness."[25]

Alcoholism. There are two parts to *Volcano*'s alcoholic content: the first
is its implications for textual structure, where any attempt at realistic
description becomes quickly self-defeating because the reality of
drunken vision is *unreal*, unnatural, fragmentary, portentous, and confused. These elements also feature in any definition of avant-garde, not
to mention postmodern writing. Lowry takes the opportunity offered
by his alcoholic character to experiment with literary form, recreating
the condition of the alcoholic in the shape of the narrative: chronology
is uncertain; utterances issue from disembodied voices; there are sur-
realist-inspired descriptions of surroundings and events. Alcohol is the
reason and the excuse for it all: the fantastic (hallucinations), the exotic
(verbal games), the narrative trajectory (the Consul's erratic movements), and character (the Consul's jealousy and outspokenness). Alcoholic hallucination becomes a metaphor for the joys and sorrows of
language, for the impossibility of telling, for instance, whether the
insects that afflict the Consul in the bathroom are seen through alcoholic
eyes as overreal and menacing or whether they are entirely imaginary.
Only in a vision or in grammar can such things be true; as Todorov
has said, the fantastic is a symbol of language, which can describe the
non-existent and make the impossible happen.[26] In a sense, language
functions analogously to hallucinogens and alcohol.

The second aspect of alcoholic content in *Volcano* involves the structure of the Consul's alcoholism, which can be analysed in terms of
Freud's essay "Mourning and Melancholia." It is as if alcohol gives
Geoffrey the chance to express pre-existent angst and to acknowledge
his "sourceless sorrow," "his own fruitless selfish ruin, now perhaps
finally self-imposed" (*UV* 346), and his death-wish. He is a melancholic,
mourning although no one has died, and overly preoccupied with self.
He desperately needs the bottle to fill the place left by the lost object
or person he mourns so self-destructively. The lost one's absence is felt
as a betrayal, and the predominant emotions therefore become ambivalent, a mixture of love and hatred: "how he had suffered, suffered,
suffered without her," the Consul thinks, while also experiencing "this
urgent desire to hurt, provoke, at a time when forgiveness alone could
save the day" (*UV* 201).

The lost object is preserved by its incorporation into the melancholic's
ego, so that the conflict between the latter and the loved one becomes
"a cleavage between the critical activity of the ego and the ego as altered

by identification."²⁷ The resulting self-hatred of the subject allows him or her to lavish disappointment and resentment on the self. Thus object loss has been converted into an ego loss. For the Consul the bottle is a transitional object; it stands in for the loved and lost one, and he constantly tries to incorporate it into himself by drinking it, again and again. "I love you," he murmurs to a Johnny Walker bottle, and although he may really be addressing Yvonne, the scotch gets in the way every time. Thus it is not Hugh but the almost erotically detailed vision of the cantina El Puerto del Sol that interposes itself between the Consul and Yvonne when he attempts to make love to her (*UV* 95). Alcohol is a distraction: the Consul is fascinated by the names of the medium that is poisoning him, and in the Terminal Cantina El Bosque he runs through an elegiac celebration of their exotic syllables (*UV* 229). He takes refuge in such lists, circumlocutions, vast and irrelevant speeches, as a means of avoiding the salient point, particularly with Yvonne; he buries real issues under an impenetrable verbal drunkenness. He is afloat on a sea of words as much as one of alcohol; the only way to end the ceaseless movement of signification, the to and fro of rootless signifiers, the constant emptying of bottles and the search for new ones, is death, the end of all meaning. Testimony to the search for the perfect object is the enormous volume of drafts and rewritings, preliminary to the published version of *Volcano*, which Lowry only stopped revising when – as an arbitrary end, a form of death – it was accepted for publication.

The Consul's – and Lowry's – desire for language as signifier, unreferential, a play of different tongues and voices, forms part of his devotion to the bottle, which, like the signifier, becomes reality in itself, occluding meaning. The carnival of intertextuality shows signs of becoming an end in itself, like the movement from glass to glass when the problem drinker's problem becomes the drink itself; but the postmodern revolution, or at least the version of it that appears in Lowry's work, is not merely an apolitical irresponsibility. Drunkenness is, as Lowry pointed out, the perfect expression of contemporary malaise (*SL* 166), and the Consul, like the text in which he appears, is the sum of the discourses of his day, subject to the imposition of power and violence from "the subnormal world itself" and self-annihilating pressures from the "abnormally suspicious delirious one within" (*UV* 355). Drunkenness is a device that accounts for extreme disturbance and defamiliarization, both linguistically and in terms of the plot, and at the same time it constitutes a personal account of drug experience and self-poisoning.

Lowry's work belongs neither to the modernist school of reified, autonomous artwork nor to the glossily packaged high-tech part of postmodern literature, often (mistakenly) taken to be synonymous with the movement as a whole. It preserves all the features postmodernism is credited with: it celebrates not the autonomous modernist work but the provisional, contingent text; it shows in action the death of the subject and of the author; it relies on pastiche and collage; it has a particular relation to the past, using traditional forms in a displaced manner. *Under the Volcano*, for example, includes elements of romantic and existentialist novels, Bildungsromane, and novels of local colour, all edged with irony and exploited principally for their accompanying terminologies and clichés. Any mythology adopted is selected anew; Lowry substitutes Aztec deities, Mexican history, and a whole lore and language of the cantina for the usual high modernist interest in Christian myths and European history.

What distinguishes Lowry from such practitioners of the genre as those architects whose postmodern practice is described as environmentally amoral,[28] or writers such as William Burroughs, is that his art is not heartless. Lowry's art enacts the politics of the carnivalesque and thereby achieves the liberating effect the latter can have upon subjugated languages. As Bakhtin tells us, the "'centralizing' tendencies in the history of Western linguistics and poetics" that underlie the "monologic" novel arise from the "victory of one reigning language (dialect) over the others, the supplanting of languages, their enslavement, the process of illuminating them with the True Word, in the incorporation of barbarians and lower social strata into a unitary language of culture and truth … [and] the content and power of the category of 'unitary language' in linguistic and stylistic thought."[29] The opposite tendencies, however, characterize the dialogic novel, in which foreign and translated voices break free from the narrator. *Under the Volcano* is just such a novel: a collage with a conscience.

NOTES

1 See *Postmodernism*, ICA Documents 4, ed. Lisa Appignanesi (London 1986); *The Anti-Aesthetic: Essays on Postmodern Culture*, ed. Hal Foster (Port Townsend, Wash.: Bay Press 1983); *What is Post-Modernism?* ed. Charles Jencks (London: Academy Editions 1986). For their intertextual interventions I would like to thank Terry Eagleton, Alex George, and John Vice.

2 Terry Eagleton, "Capitalism, Modernism and Postmodernism," in *Against the Grain: Selected Essays* (London: Verso 1986), 133.

3 E. Talbot Donaldson, *Speaking of Chaucer* (London: Athlone Press 1970), 2.

4 Jonathan Culler, *Structuralist Poetics* (London: Routledge & Kegan Paul 1975), 143.

5 Working Notes 26:4, 15–16; these and following references to the drafts make use of the cataloguing system current in January 1986 in the Special Collections Division, University of British Columbia Library. All references to *Under the Volcano* are to the 1963 Penguin edition.

6 Cortázar, "Continuidad de los Parques," in *Final del Juego* (Buenos Aires: Editorial Sudamericana 1965), 9–11.

7 Jorge Borges, *Other Inquisitions, 1937–1952*, trans. R. Stimms (Austin: University of Texas Press 1964), 64.

8 *Postmodernism*, ed. Appignanesi, 44.

9 "La Mordida," 12:21, 141.

10 First novel version B, 23:5, insert 20.

11 Ibid., 22:23, 141.

12 The wording in *Volcano* is slightly but significantly different: "Do you know, I think they make rather a formidable couple," says Laruelle (UV 216). The draft's future tense, predicting a legitimate state of affairs to come, is replaced by a remark about Hugh and Yvonne's present appearance, invoking their formidable past.

13 V.N. Volosinov [M.M. Bakhtin], *Freudianism: A Marxist Critique*, trans. I.R. Titunik (New York: Academic Press 1973), 118.

14 Quoted in Linda Hutcheon, *Narcissistic Narrative: the Metafictional Paradox* (London: Methuen 1984), 95.

15 Jacques Derrida, "Signature Event Context," in *Glyph* 1 (1977): 185.

16 See Gregory Ulmer, "The Object of Post-Criticism," in Foster, ed., *The Anti-Aesthetic*, 107 n 5.

17 See Gregory Ulmer's comments on the work of photographer Sherrie Levine in ibid., 96.

18 From Jacques Derrida's *Disseminations*, quoted by Ulmer, ibid., 90.

19 Jacques Derrida, *Disseminations*, quoted by Jonathan Culler in *On Deconstruction: Theory and Criticism after Structuralism* (London: Routledge & Kegan Paul 1983), 103.

20 Quoted ibid., 105.

21 Quoted ibid., 101.

22 See Jencks's *What Is Postmodernism?* 18, for Umberto Eco's method of getting round this problem: "He [the lover] can say, 'As Barbara Cartland would put it, I love you madly.' ... Neither of the two speakers will feel innocent, both will have accepted the challenge of the past, of the already said, which cannot be eliminated, both will consciously and with pleasure play the game of irony ... But both will have succeeded, once again, in speaking of love."

23 Julia Kristeva, *Semiotikè: Recherches pour une sémanalyse* (Paris: Editions du Seuil 1969), 145; author's translation.

24 Cf Chris Ackerley and Lawrence Clipper, *A Companion to Under the Volcano* (Vancouver: UBC Press 1986), 195–6: the phrase is used "by a player

who wishes to adjust the position of a piece on the board without com-
mitting himself to moving it as the laws of the game normally require
(the open fly here 'verifying' the Consul's failure to make a move towards
Yvonne an hour ago)."

25 Mikhail Bakhtin, *Problems of Dostoevsky's Poetics*, trans. R.W. Rotsel (Ann
   Arbor, Mich.: Ardis 1973), 4.
26 Tzvetan Todorov, *The Fantastic*, trans. Richard Howard (Cleveland 1973).
27 Sigmund Freud, "Mourning and Melancholia," in the Pelican Freud
   Library vol. 11, *On Metapsychology: The Theory of Psychoanalysis*, trans. J.
   Strachey (Harmondsworth: Penguin 1984), 258.
28 Demetri Porphrios, "Architecture and the Postmodern Culture," in *Postmodernism*, ed. Appignanesi, 30.
29 Mikhail Bakhtin, *The Dialogic Imagination*, ed. Michael Holquist, trans.
   Caryl Emerson and Michael Holquist (Austin: University of Austin Press
   1981), 24 and 271.

The Uses of Intertextuality in *Under the Volcano*

D.B. JEWISON

We artists form one of those pathetic human chains which human beings form to pass buckets of water up to a fire, or to bring in a lifeboat. An uninterrupted chain of humans born to explore the inward riches of the solitary life on behalf of the unheeding unforgiving community; manacled together by the same gift.

Lawrence Durrell, *Clea*

Quotation and allusion are the most obvious and self-conscious modes of relating one text to others, but they do not exhaust the full range of intertextual possibilities. Lowry himself draws attention to other relational modes when he comments on the epic form of his novel and describes it as a "kind of opera," "hot music," or "preposterous movie" (*SL* 66), or as an "ideal movie" in "Work in Progress."[1] Discussion of intertextuality in any text is further complicated by considerations of the author/narrator's probable level of intertextual awareness and the reader's own intertextual baggage. What follows is an examination of the intertextual variety of *Under the Volcano*, but I focus primarily upon the allusion and quotation that no reader of the novel can ignore. My aims are to establish a distinction between the ways the author/narrator and protagonist are related to the intertextual element and to suggest how intertextuality has a function in the novel that is independent of the content of the allusions employed and is an addition to the thematic resonance that the allusions create.

Confronted as they are by such a profusion of quotations, parodies, and other forms of allusion, readers of *Under the Volcano* might well feel they have encountered a library with a confusing if not defective catalogue rather than a novel. The density of allusion makes it difficult to keep track of where everything has come from as well as where the text is going. I will first summarize one attempt I made a decade ago to deal in a very general way with the novel's use of allusion, and then suggest a complementary approach through the concept of intertextuality to illustrate the range of Lowry's textual strategies.

In that earlier paper I noted a relationship between *Under the Volcano* and Conrad Aiken's vision of his own work as described through the mask of Demarest in *Blue Voyage*.[2] Demarest says that a writer like himself produces "in the end not so much a unitary work of art as a melancholy *cauchemar* of ghosts and voices, a phantasmagoric world of disordered colors and sounds."[3] Sigbjørn Wilderness presents much the same vision in "Through the Panama" when he quotes Lawrence on *Ulysses*: "the whole is an assembly of apparently incongruous parts slipping past one another."[4] A passage in Lowry's short story "Bulls of the Resurrection," to which my attention had been drawn by Richard Hauer Costa,[5] seemed especially relevant. In this passage a young man named Rydsale relates a dream that his friend suggests was based upon an El Greco painting they have seen. Rysdale replies: "it was like El Greco gone mad. No, I'll tell you what it was like. It was as though a moving picture had been projected onto a Greco instead of onto a screen. There was this fixed, timeless, haunted background, but this was not part of what was going on. This was only the relief against which it could be seen, the means by which it became visible."[6]

Since the main point of the paper was that in chapter 1 of *Under the Volcano* Lowry turns the cinema into Plato's cave, I thought this passage from "Bulls of the Resurrection" was particularly relevant to Lowry's interests and useful in illuminating his vision. The "Bulls" passage describes a cultural backdrop making visible a private vision, all within the context of a dream. The cinema of Rysdale's dream suggests an altered Platonism in which the private dream is invisible without the backdrop of the cultural one to give it substance; reality is dream upon dream. The deliberate intertextual profusion of *Under the Volcano* contributes to the sense of the text as *cauchemar*. The vast array of allusions constitutes that part of the company of "ghosts and voices" that the author/narrator has inherited from his predecessors, but the profession does offer true comfort if the intertextual element validates the private vision and provides a corrective to the solipsism of personal confusion and obsession. The public dream appears to confer authority. "Bulls of the Resurrection" implies that art gives substance and therefore meaning to private realities. In *Under the Volcano* the author/narrator projects his own nightmare on to an intertextual screen made up not of one painting by El Greco but of a very busy cultural collage. His vision thus becomes visible.

The nightmare and vision projected in *Under the Volcano* are both personal and cultural. While the Consul plunges to his death, the world prepares for its descent into war. Both private and public chaos are better understood when seen in relationship to that which is not itself swamped by the flux of the moment. The Consul's destruction is projected, for instance, against the backdrop of Marlowe's *Dr Faustus* and Dante's *Divine Comedy* as well as Plato's "Myth of the Cave." Intertextuality provides the space where reading can take place because of the kind of screen or backdrop it provides. When Jacques Laruelle looks into Sr Bustamente's theatre, which is described with a great number of parallels to Plato's cave, he sees in addition to Plato's shadows on the wall a sign of the moral and political state of the world in 1939. "On the screen, over which clambered an endless procession of torchlit shadows, hung, magically projected upside down, a faint apology for the 'suspended function.'"[7] *Under the Volcano* portrays a man and a world that are both upside-down. The image of the inverted Tree of Life in the cabbala comes to mind. The metaphor I am suggesting as a strategy for reading the novel is that of an intertextual screen that can replace the screen of shadowy images in Sr Bustamente's theatre. The intertextual backdrop alters the projected vision, creating the possibility of meaning and perhaps even of grace where otherwise there would be only the insubstantial images of Plato's cave.

Lowry's method appears to be a version of Eliot's tradition and the individual talent, and, therefore, a way of disturbing traditional narrative structure by forcing the reader away from the immediate narrative line; intertextuality in Lowry's hands is a constant reminder of absence. If *Under the Volcano* strikes the reader as a modernist text with postmodernist tendencies, that is not surprising, considering that Eliot's concept of tradition and the individual talent presages postmodernism. It is not that far from Eliot to Umberto Eco's observation that books talk among themselves,[8] or Foucault's comment that literature begins "where all books are recaptured and consumed."[9] The continuity of modernism and postmodernism on this point is particularly suggested by the fact that, in "Kafka and his Precursors," Jorge Luis Borges specifically refers his reader to Eliot's "Tradition and the Individual Talent" because of its relationship to his own thesis that certain aspects of the work of Robert Browning and other writers could not be perceived until Kafka had made visible what till then had been latent; writers create their own precursors.[10] This is a concept that I think can be usefully applied to *Under the Volcano*. My own reading of Lowry's novel has been altered in recent years by novels that suggest that the Consul is a kind of librarian. Two especially informative texts are *Auto da Fé* and *The Name of the Rose*.

Elias Canetti's deeply disturbing *Auto da Fé* was published originally in German in 1935, thirty-six years before he won the Nobel Prize for literature. It is probably one of the few books Malcolm Lowry did not read. The protagonist is the pre-eminent sinologist Professor Peter Kien, who at first ventures away from his library of twenty-five thousand volumes for only short periods of time. But then he is foolish enough to marry his housekeeper, Therese, who evicts him from the library that is also his home. In order to continue his research, Kien apparently must buy second copies of many of the books now inaccessible to him. "'I urgently require, for a work of scholarship, the following books,' he said, and from a non-existent paper read out a long catalogue ... Despite reading he could spare a watchful side glance for the listening faces ... He delighted in hurling the next title rapidly at the listener, who had as yet not fully recovered from the preceding one. The bewildered expressions amused him. Some asked for 'One moment, please!' Others clutched at their forehead or temples, but he continued to read unperturbed."[11]

Professor Kien takes on the hump-backed dwarf Fischerle as a factotum, and when the two men return to Kien's hotel at the end of the day, the novel moves clearly beyond the conventions of realism and even puts into question the passage just quoted. We are no longer sure Kien needed to buy his books: "To cut short any unwelcome questions [Professor Kien] immediately lifted a packet out of his head and held it out to the little fellow. The latter managed to take it up cleverly in his long arms and said: 'Too many! Where shall I put them down?' 'Many?' shouted Kien, indignantly. That isn't the thousandth part.'... After an hour Fischerle was in the greatest difficulty on account of his hump. Twist and turn as he would he collided with books everywhere. Except for a narrow path from the bed in one room to the bed in the other, everything was evenly covered with books"(176–77). We were told earlier that the professor carried in his head "a library as well provided and as reliable as his actual library" (17). The text has now literalized metaphor.

I will return to *Auto da Fé* after a few comments about Umberto Eco's now famous librarian, Jorge of Burgos in *The Name of the Rose*. The unacknowledged chief librarian and creator of the catalogue in his monastery, Jorge exerts power over the monks by controlling the available concepts of reality. A closure fanatic, Jorge disguises the existence of Aristotle's text on comedy in the catalogue, and he hides himself in his windowless room in the library until William of Baskerville discovers him. (The Consul, we note, substitutes one enclosed space for another throughout the novel.)[12] In her recent book *The Translated World*, Debra Castillo comments on the recurring pattern in literature in which the librarian chooses what she calls the "historical form of the sacred" in order to control a reality that seems too fluid and fatal. Because he chooses form, the librarian creates a dilemma for himself "that forces him to exercise his waning control over reality by excluding all apparent contradictions to the monumental form he has chosen. Eventually, the library becomes the world, as the librarian cannot allow even the smallest hint of life outside to remain. To do so would be to reveal a fatal flaw, to place the entire structure in danger of collapse, of burning down."[13] While the fatal reality for Jorge of Burgos is laughter, for the Consul it is love.

Castillo's formulation of this recurring pattern accurately describes the fates of both Jorge of Burgos and Professor Kien. Jorge dies in the flaming library that he ignites while destroying Aristotle's text. Kien, having repossessed his library, inflicts upon himself the death that the Inquisition reserved for heretics. The novel concludes:

The hall is filled with volume upon volume. He fetches the ladder to help him. Soon he has reached the ceiling. He goes back to his room. The shelves gape at him. In front of the writing desk the carpet is ablaze ... He places the ladder in the middle of the room where it stood before. He climbs up to the sixth step, looks down on the fire and waits.

When the flames reached him at last, he laughed out loud, louder than he had ever laughed in all his life.   (428)

Now to *Under the Volcano*. In *The Voyage That Never Ends*, Sherrill Grace has called chapter 10 the most intensely claustrophobic of the chapters (46). Thomas York has noted it as one of those in which time stops; he finds it "curiously static."[14] Early in the chapter the Consul remembers having in the past waited for Lee Maitland in the self-dramatized role of Baudelaire's angel. This passage precedes the final separation of Geoffrey and Yvonne. The Consul will shortly flee the Salón Ofélia and run off through Dante's dark wood of the senses to El Farolito, where he will be shot by the fascists. But before his flight he "unpacks" a significant part of the library of his mind in such a way as to destroy completely any possibility of love. In the act of unpacking his mind the Consul becomes rather like Professor Kien, with the crucial difference that whereas Kien laughs at others while taking himself seriously, Geoffrey Firmin lacks the self-seriousness that might save him. In this chapter the unpacking begins with the reference to Baudelaire and continues with the Consul's attempt to speak, like Sir Thomas Browne, about Archimedes, Moses, Achilles, Methuselah, Charles V, Pontius Pilate, and Yus Asaf. He fails because in his drunken state the Consul does not utter a word. In this also the text resembles *Auto da Fé* in that the latter too incorporates gaps that are created not by Kien's inebriation but by his madness. The Consul's concern with text when he should be dealing with life occurs at many points prior to this scene, especially, as Chris

Ackerly has noted, when the Consul contemplates his unwritten book instead of making love to Yvonne.[15] Not having managed to become Sir Thomas Browne, the Consul "unpacks" *Othello* at the dinner table, with fatal results. Like Peter Kien he "reads" from a text in his head which he substitutes for the actual condition facing him. And like Peter Kien, he is excessively conscious of the effect he is creating:

"But even if Hugh makes the most of it again it won't be long before he realizes he's only one of the hundred or so other ninney-hammers with gills like codfish and veins like racehorses – prime as goats all of them, hot as monkeys, salt as wolves in pride. No, one will be enough ..."

A glass, fortunately empty, fell to the floor and was smashed.

"As if he plucked up kisses by the roots and then laid his leg over her thigh and sighed. What an uncommon time you two must have had, paddling palms and playing bubbies and titties, all day long under cover of saving me ..." (315)

Of course the mask is layered in ironic associations because some of the crucial words came originally from that arch liar Iago. It is not surprising that the Consul cannot take himself seriously as he renounces love and runs off through the forest.

A character who formulates an experience in terms of a pre-existing text can be thought of as doing one of two things, according to one's metaphysic. The character may be making a choice between existence and text, where existence is ontologically privileged and text is seen as a retreat from reality. Or, if text is seen to be reality, the reader is faced with new questions: How is the character related to the text? Is the text the appropriate one? When the Consul thinks about his unwritten book instead of making love to Yvonne, Lowry seems to be suggesting that the choice to be made is the first one between text and existence. But if I have interpreted correctly the relevance of "Bulls of the Resurrection" to *Under the Volcano*, then pre-existing text is epistemologically necessary and even the basis of ontology. Thus Rysdale says that it is the intertextual backdrop that makes the projected vision visible. In *Under the Volcano* intertextuality can function in a given situation to depict how the Consul retreats from existence into text. But throughout the novel intertextuality is also the basis upon which the text is built; it is conceived of in a way that is analogous to Plato's forms, which are posited as the ontological basis of reality.

According to Castillo, librarians such as Peter Kien die because, seeking to control the library which to them equals the world, they find the enterprise hopeless. The logic for their deaths is founded on the assumption that the library is the world. To control the world they must control the books. The burner of books, as many tyrants have believed, controls the book absolutely. The librarian who has internalized the library therefore burns himself in order not to lose control of the world/library. We know that Lowry was fascinated, as Sherrill Grace has written, with the *process* of writing (4–5, 12). Gordon Bowker also has noted that Lowry was always deconstructing himself. The process of writing was, for him, spiritual growth.[16] For the Consul, the opposite proves true.

While Lowry uses intertextuality, especially in the form of allusion, to create the backdrop against which to project his own vision, he creates at the same time a protagonist whose existence is highly bib-liologic. It would be foolish to impose the pattern of *Auto da Fé* and *The Name of the Rose* rigidly upon *Under the Volcano*, yet Lowry's ending is not entirely dissimilar to Canetti's or Eco's. Having mistaken the direction of his quest up to the last seconds of consciousness, the Consul realizes he is plummeting into hell "through the blazing of ten million burning bodies." (376). He has perhaps not chosen his fiery death in full consciousness like Peter Kien, but like those of Canetti's professor, his choices prove fatal.

The ways that I am suggesting of regarding intertextuality in *Under the Volcano*, as a method used by the author/narrator to provide a validating backdrop and as a device to create a character with a fatal tendency to hide in text, both indicate that, while the specific reference is always thematically precise in *Under the Volcano*, allusions and quotations have a function that operates irrespective of any specific content. As Ruth says in Pinter's *The Homecoming*, "My lips move. Perhaps you should restrict your observations to that."[17]

Where does this leave us in considering the degree to which *Under the Volcano* presages or incorporates elements that we tend now to see as postmodern? Some of the most frequently noted elements and attitudes of postmodernism include the concept of the world as text, ironic rethinking of the past, and a mixture of modes of discourse. The last of these frequently involves a manoeuvre that places realism and fantasy in immediate and sometimes non-hierarchical relation to each other. We have, on the one hand, an Aristotelian/Lockian approach to fiction, based on the assumption that reality can be known through the senses, which leads the writer to create an appearance of specificity in time, place, and character. The qualities of fantasy are, on the other hand, quite different. Borges lists the four aspects of the genre as the contamination of reality by dream, the use of the double, the work within the work, and the journey in time.[18] To these we can add magic, madness, and metamorphosis. In realism the character explains the world, while in fantasy the world tends to explain the character. Lowry's conception of character is consistent with realism, so although some elements of his writing might now strike us as foreshadowing postmodernism, he is a precursor rather than an exponent of it.

While *Under the Volcano* privileges realism, it none the less frequently incorporates elements that suggest the fantastic mode, and the fantastic necessarily weakens, even if it does not overthrow, the privileged status of realism. The setting of the Day of the Dead and allusions to Strauss's "Allerseelen" introduce the ghosts; the Consul's book on necromancy and the extensive use of the cabbala bring to the text the themes of magic and ghosts; the Consul has at least one double in Hugh and probably others in Yvonne and Jacques; his hallucinations obviously contaminate reality. Such elements disturb realism but do not, as in magic realism, overthrow its hierarchy. None the less, if it is correct to suggest that in *Under the Volcano* reality is dream upon dream, we are not dealing with a novel entirely typical of its time. It seems, instead, to be the kind of text to which Umberto Eco draws attention in *Postcript to The Name of the Rose* when he distinguishes between those that fulfil expectations and those that must create their own audience (48–9). Lowry had to begin by creating one reader, his publisher. His letter to Jonathan Cape points out what their reader had missed in a way that draws attention to what Roland Barthes calls the bliss rather than the pleasure of his novel.

One of the ways that Barthes distinguishes between the text of pleasure and the text of bliss is the measure of what happens to the narrative enigma, the "what happens next" element. The narrative enigma is to a considerable extent removed in *Under the Volcano* because we are told in chapter 1 how chapter 12 has already ended. A text of this kind tends to supplant a chronological reading with a synchronic one, a horizontal reading with a vertical one. Perhaps in this case, circular would be the most apt geometric metaphor. The excitement of reading such a text comes not from the "progressive haste" of following and solving the narrative enigma but from the "vertical din" that results from "the layering of significance" through intertextuality.[19] Sherrill Grace has called this an example of Todorov's "vertical … narrative of substitution"(42).

It is in dealing with this aspect of the text that intertextuality, whether it exists in relation to the author/narrator or to the protoganist, is most crucial. In relation to the tradition of realism in fiction, Lowry's plot defamiliarizes the elements of his story despite the fact that his method is not entirely new. The vertical din of intertextuality is therefore crucial to Lowry's re-forming of the novel, creating, as he himself said, the impression that "depth exists."[20] A text such as *Under the Volcano* is so heavily intertextual that reality is not only inherited from other texts but appears clearly to be so, as if in deliberate acknowledgment of Eliot's principle that "no poet, no artist of any art, has complete meaning alone."²¹ The fact that in this fictive world, where reality is dream upon dream, the Consul comes close to acting out the text of the self-destructive librarian creates for the reader a deeper and more disturbing enigma than the narrative one a traditionally horizontal novel would likely have achieved. The dual relationships of author/narrator and protagonist to intertextuality set out the elements of the dilemma. As Castillo comments, while the library represents the basis for spiritual communion, it may also lead to the denial of both spirituality and communion (vii). Unfortunately, the Consul uses text not to carry on a dialogue, not to grow, deconstruct, and construct again, but to die into it, just as he stops time and as a result finds himself in hell.

Under the Volcano both validates the concept of world as text and shows how, if the will is destroyed, the library destroys life. The author/narrator is writing, but the protagonist, because of a lack of will, has succumbed to the fate that Sigbjørn Wilderness will later experience in "Through the Panama"; he has allowed himself to be written. He has become product instead of process. The mask of Othello becomes the Consul's death mask and he dies of guilt.

NOTES

1 See Malcolm Lowry's "Work in Progess" statement (UBC SC 32:1), sent to Harold Matson on 22 November 1951, and Sherrill Grace, *The Voyage that Never Ends: Malcolm Lowry's Fiction* (Vancouver: UBC Press 1982), 39.
2 D.B. Jewison, "The Platonic Heritage in *Under the Volcano*," *Studies in Canadian Literature* 3, no. 1 (Winter 1978): 62–9.
3 Conrad Aiken, *Blue Voyage*, in *The Collected Novels of Conrad Aiken* (New York: Holt Rinehart and Winston 1964).
4 Malcolm Lowry, "Through the Panama," in *Hear us O Lord from heaven thy dwelling place* (New York: Lippincott 1961), 34.
5 Richard Hauer Costa, *Malcolm Lowry* (New York: Twayne 1982), 159–60.
6 Malcolm Lowry, "Bulls of the Resurrection," *Prism International* 5, no. 1 (Summer 1965): 8.
7 Malcolm Lowry, *Under the Volcano* (Harmondsworth: Penguin 1962), 32.
8 Umberto Eco, *Postcript to The Name of the Rose*, trans. William Weaver (New York: Harcourt Brace Jovanovich 1984), 81.
9 Michel Foucault, *Language, Counter-Memory, Practice*, trans. Donald F. Bouchard and Sherry Simon (Ithaca: Cornell University Press 1977), vii. Debra Castillo uses this concept in *The Translated World*; see n13 below.
10 Jorge Luis Borges, "Kafka and Precursors," in *Labyrinths: Selected Stories and Other Writings*, ed. and trans. Donald A. Yates and James E. Irby (New York: New Directions 1964), 201.

11 Elias Canetti, *Auto da Fé*, trans. E. V. Wedgwood (London: Picador 1978), 153.

12 Grace, *The Voyage that Never Ends*, 46.

13 Debra Castillo, *The Translated World* (Tallahassee: Florida State University Press 1984), ix.

14 Thomas York, "Manipulated and Rhapsodic Time," paper presented at New Perspectives on Malcolm Lowry: An International Symposium on the Life and Work of Malcolm Lowry, Vancouver 1987.

15 Chris Ackerley, "The Consul's Book," *Malcolm Lowry Review* 23–24 (Fall 1988–Spring 1989): 78–92.

16 Bowker made this point in his presentation at the 1987 Lowry Symposium, "Constructing and Deconstructing Lowry."

17 Harold Pinter, *The Homecoming* (London: Methuen 1965), 53.

18 In his introduction to *Labyrinths* James E. Irby links the first three of these aspects of fantasy respectively to the nature of the knowledge, the question of the self, and the nature of the world. See Borges, *Labyrinths*, xviii.

19 Roland Barthes, *The Pleasure of the Text*, trans. Richard Miller (New York: Hill and Wang 1975), 12.

20 Malcolm Lowry, "Preface to a Novel," *Canadian Literature* 9 (Spring 1961): 27.

21 T.S. Eliot, "Tradition and the Individual Talent," in *Selected Prose* (Harmondsworth: Penguin 1953), 23.

PART THREE

In the Shadow of the Volcano

The Road to Renewal: *Dark as the Grave* and the Rite of Initiation

CYNTHIA SUGARS

Ye fields of Cambridge, our dear Cambridge, say,
Have ye not seen us walking every day?
Was there a Tree about which did not know
The Love betwixt us two?
Henceforth, ye gentle Trees, for ever fade;
Or your sad branches thicker joyn,
And into darksome shades combine,
Dark as the Grave wherein my Friend is laid.
– Abraham Cowley, "On the Death of Mr William Hervey"

In November of 1945, prior to the publication of *Under the Volcano*, the Lowrys undertook a journey to Mexico, the land of Malcolm's none too angelic past. The many notebooks that Malcolm and Margerie kept in the course of this trip became the basis of another "Mexican" novel, *Dark as the Grave Wherein My Friend Is Laid*.[1] Like Sigbjørn Wilderness in *Dark as the Grave*, Malcolm travelled to Cuernavaca and Oaxaca (which together constitute the Quauhnahuac of *Volcano*) both to revisit the people and places depicted in *Volcano* (Sigbjørn's *The Valley of the Shadow of Death*) and to overcome his obsession with this period of his life. Lowry's friend John Davenport rightly feared that the *Volcano* "would devour its author, unless he would completely cut himself off from it."[2] And in a sense this is what Malcolm (and Sigbjørn) hoped the second trip to Mexico would accomplish – a transcendence of the experiences of the past.

During the course of his journey into the past the novel's depressed, self-absorbed Sigbjørn is initiated into a renewed spiritual and emotional condition. Outlined in *Dark as the Grave*, then, is an initiation rite of sorts, a rite that, according to Mircea Eliade, designates *"the end of a mode of being."*[3] Arnold van Gennep's division of such rites into three stages or "rites of passage" can provide a very useful approach to the novel.[4] According to the English translator of *Rites of Passage*, van Gennep was one of the first thinkers to analyse the ceremonies accompanying an individual's "life crises." The rites of passage occurring at these points in a person's life he divided into three major stages – separation, transition, and incorporation – which were later specifically applied to rites of initiation by the American Jungian analyst Joseph Henderson.[5]

The rite of separation is usually accompanied by acts of embarkation, such as Sigbjørn's leave-taking of Eridanus for the mysterious land of Mexico, and is often represented by a symbolic death and journey into the underworld. It marks the primary stage of initiation in which the individual is temporarily withdrawn from outer actions and experiences a loss of ego-consciousness. Paradoxically, this condition can be regarded as a negative state if the initiate becomes lodged in the stage of separation and ceases to progress forward, thereby leading to the familiar condition of many of Lowry's protagonists, whose withdrawal from the outside world into the stage of separation results in their emotional and spiritual (and in the Consul's case, physical) impotence.

An emergence from this symbolic underworld into the stage of transition results in regeneration and renewed mobility. The "liminal" rites occurring at this stage are "not 'union' ceremonies, properly speaking, but rites of preparation for union, themselves preceded by rites of preparation for the transitional stage" (van Gennep 21). At this point the individual, in his revitalized condition, is capable of entering the final stage of incorporation and being reintegrated into the social group from which he has sprung. This re-entry into society, however, is not a blind reintegration but rather a conscious process of relating to the group while maintaining individual identity. The individual can now devote himself to the task of contributing to the spiritual and cultural life of society (or, in Lowry's terms, the artist is once again able to create) and can finally enter, or re-enter, what Joseph Henderson calls "the spiritual brotherhood of mankind" (66).

Lowry's own understanding of psychic development, based largely upon the works of Dunne, Ortega, Bergson, and Ouspensky, closely parallels the initiation process. He envisaged man's psyche as a microcosmic extension of the universe, existing in a state of continual transformation and development. It was, he believed, of prime importance that man not inhibit this pattern of psychic growth, for in so doing he would stifle his own potential for creativity, development, and regeneration. The individual, then, must continually be integrating his past experiences into his present state of consciousness in order that he not become fixated, as Sigbjørn does, on a particular period of his past and cease to progress. As so many of Lowry's protagonists demonstrate, at such a point of stasis man becomes incapable of functioning productively within his environment and utterly isolated from his fellow human beings in a state closely related to the primary initiatory stage of separation. Becoming increasingly self-absorbed and solipsistic, the individual is rendered immobile and ultimately incapable of living. The alternative is to build up a state of higher consciousness, which is essentially what the initiation process aims to do.

Initiation, then, is simply the process by which the psyche moves from one stage of development to the next. This is not, I must add, a circular pattern per se but rather a form of what Lowry calls "ecdysis" (*DAG* 36), a continual transformation or "shedding of the skin" in the process of discovering a renewed and enlightened state of consciousness. Unlike most mystical systems, however, there is no final goal in this process as Lowry understood it; what is of prime importance is the development itself. The individual consciousness, undergoing constant transformation, can therefore be understood as continually passing through initiatory cycles of separation, transition, and incorporation.

This process of spiritual initiation is metaphorically presented in *Dark as the Grave* in terms of a symbolic passage into and out of the underworld, a process of death and rebirth, in the form of Sigbjørn's southern journey to Mexico. Van Gennep also associated the three rites of passage with cycles of death and rebirth, the period of death representing the phase of separation and resurrection marking the point of incorporation, with a transitional phase coming between the two (92). In the typical layering process by which Lowry creates symbolic meaning, he draws upon various myths and tales associated with cycles of death and rebirth. Coming at specific points in the narrative, these mythical allusions and images clarify Sigbjørn's psychic condition at each stage of his initiation process. These allusions can be roughly divided into three categories corresponding to the three stages of initiation as outlined by van Gennep (see diagram, p. 152). The first, corresponding to the rite of separation, encompasses those myths that involve journeys into the underworld, such as the myth of the Mexican Quetzalcoatl (the Plumed Serpent), Poe's "The Fall of the House of Usher," Dante's *Inferno*, and the Perilous Chapel episode of the grail legend. The second category, relating to the stage of transition, can be divided between those tales that emphasize rebirth and renewal – the legend of Quetzalcoatl and images of crosses – and those that involve the gaining of conscious control over one's development – the Parsifal story (particularly Wagner's version) and Jean Epstein's 1928 film version of "The Fall of the House of Usher." The third category, corresponding to the rite of incorporation, includes those tales concerned with reintegration into society and renewed love for one's fellow humans (sometimes specifically represented by the love between man and woman), such as Keats's "Endymion," Epstein's *Usher*, and Parsifal.

The Sigbjørn that we see at the beginning of *Dark as the Grave* has entered the primary initiatory stage of separation but, in a state of

SEPARATION		TRANSITION	INCORPORATION
	REBIRTH	CONTROL	
Quetzalcoatl	Quetzalcoatl	Parsifal	"Endymion"
Poe's "Usher"	candles	Epstein's "Usher"	Epstein's "Usher"
Inferno			Parsifal
Perilous Chapel			

immobilizing self-absorption and withdrawal, has become lodged at this point and is unable to progress along the stages of transition and incorporation that could lead to his renewal and eventual happiness. Trapped in this stage and wholly obsessed with the horrifying memories of his delirium-filled Mexican past, Sigbjørn has become spiritually paralysed. Not only has his fixation upon the past rendered him incapable of functioning in the present, but he is barely able to consider, let alone look forward to, the future.

The primary sources of Sigbjørn's inability to proceed through the next two stages of initiation are his immobilizing fear and paranoia. From the extreme rear of the plane (and later buses), where he sits in order "to be out of sight" (46), his paranoia reaches ludicrous proportions. In a period of what cannot be more than a few minutes he worries that he may be stopped at customs and refused entry into both the United States and Mexico; that his wife Primrose's Arctic Skunk coat may cause people to think her a Russian spy; that the suspicion incurred in their going to Mexico is superseded only by their having come from Canada (because of its "relative proximity to Russia," 5); that he may be impeached under the "Mann Act, the white slave traffic ruling" (9), when seen with Primrose; and that because of his thirty-nine-year-old wife's youthful appearance, he will be charged with cohabitation with a minor.

In fact, as the journey progresses it becomes "the extension of every anxiety" (47). As soon as he and Primrose have settled into the hotel in Mexico City, he sends her to the liquor store because he cannot "face going through that lobby" (75), and later, in Cuernavaca, he is actually "too frightened to go and get a drink" (120)! Experiencing an increasing reticence to leave the apartment, Sigbjørn suffers anxiety at the prospect of accompanying Primrose on sightseeing trips; not only do these outings involve controlling his drinking for a set period of time, but above all they upset his delicate, though illusory, sense of equilibrium: "there was something in his nature that loathed to break the rhythm; only more than stopping at all did he hate to move on" (98).

This resistance to change and movement is further related to Sigbjørn's fear of relating to others, even on the most mundane of levels. On the plane, for instance, he is unable to converse in a normal manner with a fellow passenger. Not only does he suspect the man's motives, but he also worries, after the "conversation," that he has revealed something that he should not have: "what precisely had this damn fellow drawn out of him! Everything" (10). Like the Consul of his novel, Sigbjørn is an adept only at the "Great Brotherhood of Alcohol," which offers not an affirmation but, as Douglas Day observes, an "avoidance of human or spiritual commitment."[6]

Normally associated with the stage of separation, this condition of self-absorption also renders any sort of genuine communication with his wife impossible. Dwelling on the fears initiated by the trip, he is unable to utter that "something sympathetic" (25) that could make Primrose happy; instead he meets her warmth with "a chill and a shadow" (28). As they sit in the airport bar, Sigbjørn cannot bring himself to celebrate their wedding anniversary because of its associations with his friend Erikson's death. Not allowing himself to love and confide in Primrose, he is re-enacting the very mistake of the Consul in his novel whose refusal of his own wife's love led to his destruction. The lesson of that novel, written on the wall of Laruelle's tower – "*no se puede vivir sin amar*" – has long since been erased from the real wall of the building, now named the Quinta Dolores, in which Sigbjørn and Primrose are staying.

In the hallucinatory masque that plays itself out before Sigbjørn's eyes on the plane is revealed the most debilitating of his fears – the "fear of himself" (13), which is inextricably connected with his fear of the past. It is this fear, or indeed love of the past that Sigbjørn must above all overcome, for not only do all the others stem from it, but it is this one that most hinders his progression forward in the initiation process. Self-destructively drawn to the "old consciousness of fatality" that the past instils in him, he seeks to revive the "cold internal glow" of that "old wine of complete despair" (210).

The fact that the past has not been transformed and overcome by the "sober [and] upright prose" (109) of *The Valley* appears to have taken Sigbjørn by surprise. Writing about the past has not been sufficient. Sigbjørn must physically relive the past and actively steer it in a more positive direction. To do this he must have contact with living people, not fictional characters. As J.A. Wainwright points out, "Sigbjørn will find himself by finding Fernando, not the Consul or Dr Vigil."[7] Although he is terrified at the prospect, he must go to Oaxaca to face both the real Farolito and the "invisible Farolito" of his soul (253), and there, unlike the Consul, he may emerge from his descent renewed and healed.

Before rebirth or renewal can be achieved, however, the initiate must successfully complete the symbolic underworld passage associated with the rite of separation. Often accompanied by acts of departure or embarkation (van Gennep 23), this rite marks the stage in which the initiate undergoes ritual death.

Geoffrey Durrant's discussion of the death/rebirth symbolism in "Through the Panama" is also applicable to the underworld journey in *Dark as the Grave*. The "human spirit" or, in our case, the initiate, "embarks through a port or gate on a southerly voyage ... descends to imprisonment in the Hades of the senses of the extreme south, and then proceeds northwards to the port or gate of the north."[8] While in *Dark as the Grave* the return to the north is implied but not stated, the image of the southward voyage and descent into hell is there in full form. The "gate" that leads to this southern underworld can here be regarded as both the Vancouver and Los Angeles airports, the latter of which gives Sigbjørn a "tremendous sense of *junction*, to north, south, east, and west" (20).

This reference to the four cardinal points can be further related to the significance of the cross in the Voodoo religion, with which Lowry was somewhat familiar, having travelled to Haiti in 1946. The Voudoun cross, representing "the intersection of the horizontal plane, which is this mortal world, by the vertical plane, the metaphysical axis," is an appropriate symbol for Sigbjørn's temporary entrance into the "metaphysical plane," the land of death.[9] And while Sigbjørn may not, as Dr Hippolyte later tells him in Cuernavaca, be possessed by Baron Samedi or Papa Legba, the two Voudoun gods associated respectively with the underworld and crossroads (entrance to the underworld), he has necessarily journeyed past these figures in his progression through the land of death towards rebirth. Furthermore, through its association with the entrance to Dante's Inferno the bar of this airport itself becomes a type of doorway into the underworld, for Sigbjørn equates it with a saloon out of his past that bore above its doorway the inscription "*Through these portals pass the most damned people in the world*" (33). Primrose's anniversary gift to her husband, Julian Green's *The Dark Journey*, is therefore also prophetic (45).

Yet while Mexico becomes the location of Sigbjørn's symbolic death, he does not experience the true initiatory death until he descends into the Valley of Etla towards Oaxaca. It is in Oaxaca, on the Calle de los Muertos, that Sigbjørn first learns of the death of Fernando, who died in the same manner as the Consul of his novel. His visit to the church immediately after receiving the news is particularly significant, for it can easily be related to the Perilous Chapel episode of the grail legends with which Lowry was familiar.[10] The test of the Perilous Chapel "consisted in [the initiate's] being brought into contact with the horrors of physical death" (as Sigbjørn is with the death of Fernando) and, if passed, qualified the individual for initiation.[11]

It is Sigbjørn's physical descent into the tombs of Mitla, however, that represents his final and most explicit underworld experience within the stage of separation. On the most literal level Sigbjørn's remembrance at this point of Poe's tale "The Fall of the House of Usher" is significant, for he, like Madelaine Usher, having entered the tomb alive, is "un enterrado vivo," one of the living dead awaiting resurrection. Moreover, the Zapotecan word for Mitla, "lyoba" or "lyovaana," means "tomb" or "place of rest" (246) and therefore suggests that the place is essentially a Zapotecan cemetery. In fact, many of the Zapotec warriors, in the belief that the underground passage at Mitla terminated after many leagues in an ancestral paradise, begged to be thrown into the chamber while still alive, "sacrificing themselves to the gods, in the hope of resurrection, rebirth" (DAG 250).

The relationship of the Quetzalcoatl myth to the Mitla ruins also associates the site with patterns of death and resurrection, thereby anticipating Sigbjørn's eventual rebirth. Mitla, purported to have been built by the Zapotecans, yet also believed by some to have been constructed by the Aztec god Quetzalcoatl, is also known by the name of "Mictlan," the underworld or Land of the Dead.[12] It is through this Aztec Hades that Quetzalcoatl himself, like Sigbjørn, travelled in an effort to overcome his past failures and sensual desires in order to be reborn.

The association of Mitla/Mictlan with a place of death and resurrection – via the Poe story, the Zapotecan superstition, and the Queltzalcoatl legend – makes it a suitable location for the turning point in Sigbjørn's initiatory journey, for while it is in the tomb that the rite of separation is finally completed, it is also here that Sigbjørn enters the stage of transition.

In the rite of transition Sigbjørn undergoes a spiritual transformation, overcoming the paranoia and self-absorption characteristic of the rite of separation. While it overlaps, as far as the narrative structure is concerned, with the previous stage, the phase of transition can roughly be seen to begin when Sigbjørn first learns of Fernando's death and to end when he emerges from the subterranean tombs at Mitla. He does not, then, undergo a sudden transformation but rather a gradual one, although it does take place within a relatively short period of time.

Lowry uses a number of recurring images and symbols to designate this phase of Sigbjørn's spiritual development. The most significant of these is the cross, a symbol associated with the rebirth-oriented stage of transition, which appears to follow Sigbjørn from the beginning to the end of his journey. This symbol, which in Christian tradition is of course representative of death and resurrection, becomes in Lowry's hands an even more universal and resonant image. As I have already noted, it is connected with the Voudoun cross, which represents the intersection of the physical with the metaphysical plane. The centre of the Voudoun cross marks the point by which the "loa," the spirits of the dead now transformed into gods, enter this world in order to communicate with and advise the living. This centre point, then, marks the "axis both of the physical cycle of generation and the metaphysical cycle of resurrection" (Deren 38). This cross, and for that matter all the crosses in the novel, represents a "way out of the infernal circle into renewed voyaging," a movement through the stage of transition towards rebirth.[13]

Sigbjørn and Primrose's search for the Southern Cross is also relevant, for they are searching in the Mexican sky for the other half of this cross in order to make the unifying potential of the symbol effective. Moreover, while travelling from Vancouver, the present physical realm, to Mexico, the land of the past, Sigbjørn sees below them the shadow of the plane, "the eternal moving cross" (*DAG* 1), following beside them and foreshadowing the ultimate resurrection that is to come. And later, on a short trip to Yuatepec, the cross that is there set atop "the curious hill" (171) appears as a "token of their new life" (172) or, as Ignatius Donnelly describes the cross symbol, "an emblem of ... 'the life to come.'"[14] Even the Calle Humboldt outside the Quinta Dolores appears to Sigbjørn as a "Cross Road Puzzel [sic]" (134), and one, therefore, that he must complete before the stage of transition is finally traversed.[15]

The cruciform tombs at Mitla, through which Sigbjørn must pass in the final stage of his underworld journey, represent his last confrontation with the cross symbol. And it is here for the first time that Sigbjørn is struck by the realization that this symbol bears some particular, though as yet ambiguous, relevance to his own life: "Cruciform tombs. Cruciform tombs – Christ – what was this strange persistence of this symbol? What was the real significance of the cross? Sigbjørn realized he wasn't seeing anything at all, or listening to anything at all. He was going into the Shaftsbury Avenue Pavilion in Charing Cross to see *The Fall of the House of Usher*" (248). The connection between the cross of the cruciform tombs, Christ's crucifixion, and Charing Cross leads Sigbjørn to recall a film of *The Fall of the House of Usher* that he once saw at the Shaftesbury Avenue Pavilion in Charing Cross, thereby leading him both to the answer to his question and to spiritual transformation. Unlike the actual story by Poe, this film concludes with a suggestion of resurrection: "a brilliant cross–shaped tree of stars sprouts from the crumbling house to suggest that horror and evil have given way to faith, beauty, and peace" (Grace 71). This "illumination" of the possibility for transcendence and renewal is given him in "these grotesque terms," as Sigbjørn puts it, precisely "because they [are] terms that he [can] best understand" (*DAG* 248–9). Here the director or creator of the film, like the author of a novel, has altered the original horrifying conclusion of the story to meet his own desire for a positive ending. The theme of Poe's "Usher," "the degradation of the idea of resurrection" (*DAG* 249), has here been consciously reversed by the director, just as Sigbjørn must exercise conscious control over his own fate.

The Mitla ruins, then, while indeed suggestive of Fernando's death, remind Sigbjørn of the "even greater magnificence of being alive" (*DAG* 246). And later, approaching the last remaining temptation of his past, the dreaded Farolito, Sigbjørn muses upon the miracle of being able to descend the stairs of the Hotel La Luna as "a relatively hopeful happy man" (251), which he had so often "descended dead" in the past. Indeed, the Farolito, which had seemed insurmountable, has now, says Sigbjørn, become "associated with freedom" (252). Now he can travel to the Farolito in the middle of the night without the fear of succumbing to its temptations, for its claims on him have been severed some time before he ever reaches the place. Thus Sigbjørn has risen, phoenix-like, or Quetzalcoatl-like, from the "charred ruin" of his past (92). Now able to direct the development of his own consciousness, and not merely that of his characters, he is prepared to enter the next and final stage of initiation: incorporation.

In the rite of incorporation Sigbjørn is reintegrated into the society from which he had been separated at the outset of his journey. Having gained control over his own life in the stage of transition, he is now prepared to accept the simple truth that the Consul in *Volcano* was unable to acknowledge: that he must love God, his wife, and his fellow human beings if he is going to survive.

The "reunion" of Sigbjørn and his wife at the end of the journey, like that of the shearwaters they had seen at the outset of their trip, is perhaps the most striking feature of this incorporation rite. Despite the frightening discovery of Fernando's death, Lowry says in one draft for *Dark as the Grave*, "Wilderness and his wife have drawn closer together" (32:1, 20). Lowry's reference to Keats's "Endymion" at the beginning of chapter 6 foreshadows the approaching union. In the poem Endymion, who was visited in a dream by Diana, pines for the goddess and, like Sigbjørn, embarks on a journey through the underworld in search of her. The occurrence of a lunar eclipse on the first night of the Wildernesses' arrival in Cuernavaca, immediately preceding the Endymion reference, is thus suggestive of Sigbjørn's separation from his own moon goddess, Primrose. However, Sigbjørn's awakening in chapter 6, like Endymion's final awakening at the end of Keats's poem, with the "*moon-light* of a month later streaming in upon him" (emphasis added, DAG 113), anticipates the reunion of the lovers at the end of Sigbjørn's initiation process. The name of the hotel in Oaxaca, the Hotel La Luna, is also a positive sign, for it suggests that Sigbjørn is, at this point in his journey, closer to reaching his Diana than he had previously been. Furthermore, the Mitla temple in which Sigbjørn's initiation is concluded is, according to Ignatius Donnelly, known also as "the City of the Moon" (262).

The significance of this bond between man and woman is best revealed in Epstein's *The Fall of the House of Usher*. Not only did Epstein choose to have the tale conclude on a positive note of hope and resurrection, but he also altered the characters of Poe's story, making Madelaine Roderick's wife instead of his sister. Better yet, the resurrected Madelaine does not, as in Poe's story, collapse in violent "death-agonies" on top of her brother; instead, with the aid of a guiding doctor like Fernando, she is reunited with her husband: "in the film, when the entombed was Usher's wife and not his sister, she came back in time, as it were with the doctor's help, to save him: they went out into the thunderstorm, but into new life" (DAG 249). Similarly do the united Wildernesses make their exit from Mexico after the rite of incorporation has been completed, departing not into a thunderstorm but into glorious sunshine in the Oaxaca mountains.

This new potential for compassion and understanding is not restricted to Sigbjørn's relationship with Primrose but also extends to his relationship with the whole of mankind and nature. Having gained acceptance of himself and control over his destiny in the preceding initiatory stage, he at this point experiences a "renewed belief in humanity" as a whole (DAG 235). When he and Primrose are welcomed and picked up by a group of tourists on the way to Monte Albán, for instance, Sigbjørn identifies with the group; "Buen amigos," he calls them. Later he is united with the Mexicans in the Banco Ejidal in mourning Fernando's death: "Everyone was crying in the bank" (241). Afterwards he goes to the chapel to pray, not only for Fernando but for all of humanity, from the drunk in the little Oaxaca church to his shadow self, Stanford. At the very end of the novel, then, experiencing a "reversal of the persecution motive" (225), Sigbjørn is able, as he has not done since leaving Vancouver, to sit at the front of the bus, thereby exhibiting a renewed trust both in himself and in the other members of society.

It is with his reintegration into nature, however, that Sigbjørn finally completes the rite of incorporation. In the Mitla tombs he experiences a vague feeling of being related to the landscape, but he is unable to pinpoint whence the sensation proceeds. Yet afterwards he finds that the land has acquired an entirely different aspect; it too appears to have been reborn. The regeneration of the land legitimately reminds Sigbjørn of Parsifal's flowers, which had bloomed in his absence, for these flowers too, which appear in the meadow surrounding the grail castle on Parsifal's second visit, represent the new and enlightened spiritual condition of the knight himself.[16]

It is in this regeneration of the countryside that Fernando, as Sigbjørn's guide, performs his final role in the initiation process, for it is he, Fernando, who is reborn in the land. Not only has the old site of the Banco Ejidal (where Fernando worked) been transformed into a rose garden in "glorious bloom" (*DAG* 245), but the entire surrounding countryside of Oaxaca, through the reforms of Fernando and the Banco Ejidal, is now fertile, lush, and alive.[17] Like Osiris or even Quetzalcoatl (who was considered – among other things – the god of agriculture), Fernando has been resurrected through the land: "It was Fernando he saw in all this peace" (226).

Having transcended his past within the stage of separation, regained control over his life in the phase of transition, and become reunited with human society and nature in the final stage of incorporation, Sigbjørn emerges from the rite of initiation prepared to confront and live life with an open and newly evolving mind. In terms of Lowry's theory of psychic development, the initiation process has cured Sigbjørn of his initial spiritual paralysis and enabled him to set his consciousness in motion once again. If, as Lowry notes in the manuscript of the novel, the "true theme" of *Dark as the Grave* "is the struggle between life and death" (8:3, 17), one can definitely say that it is life that triumphs. In fact the novel concludes with a miraculous affirmation and celebration of life, for Sigbjørn leaves Mexico with the ability to appreciate the pure joy of being alive once again.

One can therefore imagine, with good reason, that on his return to Canada Sigbjørn was able to say to his friends precisely what he had hoped to be able to say (but never could) to his old Mexican acquaintances: "I have succeeded, I have transformed, single-handed, my life-in-death into life ... I have come back to show you that not an hour, not a moment of my drunkenness, my continual death, was not worth it: there is ... not a drop of mescal that I have not turned into pure gold, not a drink I have not made sing" (*DAG* 211).

NOTES

1 Malcolm Lowry, *Dark as the Grave Wherein My Friend Is Laid*, ed. Douglas Day and Margerie Lowry (Toronto: General Publishing 1968).

2 See Victor Doyen, "Fighting the Albatross of Self: A Genetic Study of the Literary Work of Malcolm Lowry," PhD Katholieke Universiteit Leuven 1973, 100.

3 See Eliade, *Rites and Symbols of Initiation*, trans. Willard R. Trask (New York: Harper & Row 1958), xiii. I realize, of course, that because this study is largely dependent upon narrative sequence, the possible "corrupt-ness" of the posthumously published text of *Dark as the Grave* should be taken into consideration. A quick examination of the manuscripts in the UBC collection suggests that the basic sequence of events in the text remains essentially unaltered, although the earliest draft of *Dark as the Grave* begins with the protagonist (then called Martin Trumbaugh) already in Mexico. However, this would make little difference to my study, for in that draft the protagonist still initially suffers from a withdrawn, paranoid condition characteristic of the separation phase of initiation, and there are notes concerning his gradual spiritual improvement in the chapters that follow. Moreover, should, as Sherrill Grace suggests, chapters 1 to 5 rep-resent "a dream containing a retrospect of Sigbjørn's life" (65), not only would the sequence of initiatory stages remain unaltered but, on the con-trary, the dream state would represent a further submersion of the protag-onist into the stage of separation. However, it would require an extensive examination of the manuscripts to be truly decisive on this matter; I have therefore chosen to concentrate on the published text alone.

4 See *The Rites of Passage*, trans. Monika Vizedom and Gabrielle Caffee (Chi-cago: University of Chicago Press 1960). All further references to Van Gen-nep are to this translation of his book. In fact Lowry himself thought of his cycle of works, "The Voyage That Never Ends" (of which *Dark as the Grave* was a part), in these very terms: "The Voyage of course is life itself ... an ordeal, a going through the hoop, an initiation" (32:1, 3).

5 See Joseph L. Henderson and Maud Oakes, *The Wisdom of Serpent: The Myths of Death, Rebirth and Resurrection* (New York: George Braziller 1963). Henderson actually distinguishes between two types of initiatory experi-ences: the more common type, that of "engagement," is associated with the individual's entrance into "the spiritual brotherhood of mankind"; the other type, "disengagement," is a shamanistic process comparable to Jung's theory of individuation which aims for release from rather than incorporation into the group (66–9). It is the former type that I am here considering in terms of *Dark as the Grave*. All further references to *The Wisdom of the Serpent* are cited as Henderson and followed by the page number.

6 *Malcolm Lowry: A Biography* (New York: Dell Publishing 1975), 324.

7 See J. A. Wainwright, "The Book 'Being Written': Art and Life in *Dark as the Grave Wherein My Friend Is Laid*," *Dalhousie Review* 59 (1979–80): 95–6.

8 "Death in Life: Neo-Platonic Elements in 'Through the Panama,'" *Malcolm Lowry: The Man and His Work*, ed. George Woodcock (Vancouver: UBC Press 1971), 44.

9 See Maya Deren, *Divine Horsemen: The Living Gods of Haiti* (London: Thames and Hudson 1953), 35. All further references are included in the text.

10 Lowry himself equates this church with the Perilous Chapel in his "Work in Progress" proposal (32:1, 22). Moreover, one of the unpublished chapters of *October Ferry to Gabriola* is entitled "The Perilous Chapel."

11 See Jessie L. Weston, *The Quest of the Holy Grail* (London: G. Bell & Sons 1913), 90.

12 See Lewis Spence, *Arcane Secrets and Occult Lore of Mexico and Mayan Central America* (Detroit: Blaise Ethridge Books 1973), 49 & 110. According to Irene Nicholson in "Mexican and Central American Mythology," *Mythology of the Americas* (London: Hamlyn 1970), 213, one version of the myth relates that Quetzalcoatl was tricked by his enemy Tezxatlipoca into drinking a potent alcoholic concoction. In the drunken state that ensued Quetzalcoatl had incestuous relations with his sister, and in extreme shame and horror he fled the land, heading for the Atlantic seacoast. There he built a funeral pyre and, like the phoenix (another legend Lowry was fond of), threw himself into the flames. However, although his ashes rose to the heavens in the form of a flock of birds, Quetzalcoatl himself had first to journey through Mictlan for eight days before he was resurrected and transformed into the morning star (Nicholson 219). See also Lewis Spence, *The Myths of Mexico and Peru* (London: George G. Harrap & Co. 1917), 80.

13 See Sherrill Grace, *The Voyage That Never Ends* (Vancouver: UBC Press 1982), 73. Interestingly, Quetzalcoatl, whom I have already associated with Sigbjørn, is also connected with the four cardinal points, for he "wears the insignia of the cross": Spence, *The Myths of Mexico and Peru*, 80.

14 Lowry was familiar with Donnelly's *Atlantis: The Ante-diluvian World* (London: Sidgwick & Jackson 1970), 262. See, for instance, Chris Ackerley and L.J. Clipper, *A Companion to "Under the Volcano"* (Vancouver: UBC Press 1984), 18, 132.

15 The Spanish *quinta* can signify either a country house or the ordinal number "fifth." Thus the name Quinta Dolores suggests the fifth of Mary's seven sorrows (*dolores*), which is the one specifically emblematic of the Crucifixion.

16 The flowers that have bloomed in Parsifal's absence are, I believe, the flowers that appear in the set of the third act of Wagner's *Parsifal*. In the translation by H.L. and F. Corder (New York: Fred Rullman Inc. n.d.) the set for the first act of the opera is described as "a Forest, shadowy and

impressive ... Rock-strewn grounds" (5). In striking contrast, the third act, in which Parsifal returns to the grail castle for the second time, opens with a "pleasant spring landscape, with flowery meadows rising towards the back" (33). The visual effect of these strikingly different openings must be quite remarkable on stage. Furthermore, Parsifal's words to Gurnemanz shortly after he enters in the third act – "All's altered here, meseemeth" (35) – also suggest the parallel between the renewal of the landscape and that of Parsifal's spiritual condition.

17 "The Banco Ejidal was an agrarian land bank set up by Cárdenas to restore the quality of farmland and to return it to the peasants. Ejidal riders [of which Fernando was one] were Cárdenas supporters who carried necessary funds to outlying villages." Grace, *Voyage*, 136.

From Innocent Story to Charon's Boat: Reading the "October Ferry" Manuscripts

> Here the challenge seemed – and seems – ultimate, a matter of life or
> death, or rebirth as it were, for its author, not to say sanity or otherwise:
> ... my love for this place and my fear of losing it, nay actual terror, has
> begun to exceed all bounds.   (SL 339)

"October Ferry to Gabriola" is a unique literary document. Lowry
rewrote it over a decade; during the last five years of his life this work
became an obsession and his only literary occupation. A simple short
story about the search for a new home on a nearby island grew into a
spiritual quest for a new Eden and led the protagonist and its author on
a sea voyage through the uncharted regions of the subconscious. The
symbolic conclusion, the hopeful arrival at "the dreamed-of place," was
fixed by the structure of the original story. But its theme of psychological acceptance became increasingly difficult for Lowry, who was threatened with eviction from Dollarton and found himself unwilling to give
up his fictional Eridanus. By lifting his protagonist's suffering to a
religious level, Lowry turned the journey into a search for moral and
spiritual rebirth. In order to find happiness in the future, his fictional
character had to renounce the only place where he had been happy.

The "October Ferry" section of the Lowry Collection fills six boxes,
with a total of 145 folders containing about 4,000 pages, half of them
working notes in a complete mix of reshuffled hand- and typewritten
drafts.[1] A folder may contain one batch of text with a continuous foliation, or forty pages with different drafts from various passages and
with page numbers that could be 115H or B5 or "G after Z." If a folder
contains a batch with continuous foliation, that does not necessarily
prove that the pages belong to the same draft. In a few cases fragments
from alternative typescripts with almost the same foliation got mixed
up and led to thought gaps and overlappings in the posthumous edition
(see Table 1).

Table 1
Sample of MS Reconstruction: Version 4

A. Holograph draft

The holograph draft of version 4 is scattered among the pages of 14 different folders, and should be read in the following sequence:

Part 1

UBC	22:6	1–6
UBC	22:2	A–C
UBC	20:24	A–E
UBC	20:25	F–V
UBC	17:8	A–N
UBC	17:7	A–I
UBC	21:19	A–O
UBC	17:9	C–Y
UBC	17:10	Z
UBC	17:10	1–19
UBC	21:10	20–41

Part 2

UBC	18:2	4–8
UBC	18:3	9–19
UBC	18:4	20–32
UBC	11:5	A–Z1
UBC	18:3	A–J
UBC	16:21	K
UBC	21:16	A–O

B. Typescript (TS 4)

The typescript of the fourth version is a working copy on brown paper with separate foliations for part 1 and part 2. The text is reconstructed from the following folders:

Part 1

UBC	20:13	1–7
UBC	20:30	8–10
UBC	20:19	11–16
UBC	19:18	17–24 (old inventory)
UBC	16:15	25–30
UBC	20:7	31–38
UBC	20:8	39–56
UBC	20:9	57–64
UBC	16:19	65–67
UBC	20:10	68–86
UBC	20:11	87–103
UBC	20:12	104–118

Part 2

UBC	20:5	1–13
UBC	20:6	14–24
UBC	16:21	25–79

In this genetic study of the manuscripts the numerous holograph drafts and restarts formed the indispensible missing links, necessary to determine the chronology of the typewritten fragments. These hand-written pages, however, were also the most difficult to situate in the sequence of versions, not only because of the inserts and marginal notes that often clog the running text, but also because Lowry would rewrite a passage several times before tackling the next. He would start with a particular key line (for example, "Inside the Ocean Spray, on the almost empty Ladies and Escorts side," or "'Gabriola?' the man repeated," or "Yet that he should have a hangover at all was the real trouble"). Then he would rewrite this passage until he reached a specific closing key sentence (for example, "Adam where art thou?" or "And now it has clasped the wheel forever," or "Death Camas and the Destroying Angel"). This technique, whereby a one-page passage, after a number of restarts, could grow into a chapter, necessarily led to overlapping foliations, especially since Lowry usually started with new page num-bers. It also led to conflicting dates within the text itself when an insert in the middle of the story used a new chronology that had not yet been incorporated in earlier sections, and vice versa. (Lowry wrote in the margin of his working notes, "WHEN was Tommy born?" And in the posthumous edition the son is still born two years before his – natural – parents first meet.)

In order to reconstruct the different versions, first the relative chro-nology of various drafts of a single passage had to be established, on the basis of internal evidence, such as the incorporation of inserts in one draft into the body of the text of a subsequent draft, or external evi-dence, such as the paper used, the text appearing on versos of type-scripts, references in letters to the length or motifs of the story at a certain stage, inclusion of newspapers items that can be dated, and Mal-colm's or Margerie's comments – with page references – after comple-tion of a draft.

At this point it became possible to try to link one particular draft of passage A with the corresponding draft of passage B, and thus to obtain a complete picture of one version as a whole, and then to study the development from one version to the next. A reader of the manuscripts who is familiar with later implications and connotations of a particular element or incident may assume unconsciously – and incorrectly – that these motifs are already present in earlier drafts, especially as long as he or she is still working on unrelated fragments. To avoid inreading, the real interpretation of the development of the themes can only start after the material reconstruction of the different versions is complete.

Several factors prove a help in this reconstruction. Lowry rejected previous drafts, but he did not throw them away. Almost any intermediate draft can be found somewhere, if not among the working notes of this story then on versos of another one, because Margerie used the clear versos of rejected or superseded pages of stories and letters to type intermediate working copies. This tells us *after* which date or story draft a certain typescript was made. Another helpful hint is that, with each of his novels, Lowry almost always added text; he rarely cut. The main difference between *October Ferry to Gabriola* and *Under the Volcano* is that the latter grew into a masterpiece while Lowry was looking at the Consul's experience from the safe distance of Dollarton. With *October Ferry* he was too close to the experience. Here he was not only the writer but also a passenger.

The "October Ferry" manuscripts in the Lowry Collection document every stage in the growth and evolution of this work, and thus provide a unique insight into the creative process of Lowry's mind. My aim in this study has been to follow this creative process through the various drafts of the story and to link it to Lowry's own experience. The present discussion will concentrate on the six versions that were written in Dollarton and led up to the posthumous edition. The holograph additions written in England (see Appendix II) are sketched in brief outline and will need further investigation.

I. FIRST VERSION: GABRIOLA, THE DREAMED-OF PLACE

In the fall of 1946 Lowry had completed the final revisions to *Under the Volcano* by means of extensive correspondence with his editor Albert Erskine, and he was invited to New York for the February publication of the novel. His wife, Margerie, had received money for two recently published mystery novels; therefore, the Lowrys could afford to travel to the East, via Haiti, and avoid a cold winter on the beach at Dollarton in their squatters' shack without inside walls or insulation.[2]

Before they left, however, they took a ferry trip to Gabriola to see whether this small and quiet Gulf island of three hundred permanent inhabitants could offer an alternative to Dollarton, from which they might be evicted. In 1945, when he had rebuilt his burned house, Lowry wrote to his old friend Conrad Aiken: "the phoenix clapped its wings" and "paradise [has] been regained" (SL 47).[3] But the victory was soon threatened by city plans to turn this squatters' area into "autocamps for the better class" (SL 50). In June of 1946 Lowry had already written to Margerie's mother that "civilisation, so called, is closing in upon us a little too much for our liking." He added, jokingly, "I think we might buy an island: live half each year on it and work, and travel the other half" (SL 90).

The Lowrys knew about Gabriola Island because Angela Smith, the daughter of their former landlord, had moved there after her marriage to Alfred McKee. After spending a day in Victoria they took a bus to Nanaimo the next morning (8 October), travelling along the scenic road that overlooks the Gulf islands. The local ferry took them to Gabriola, where they stayed for half a week at the Anderson Lodge, took long walks, visited with the McKees, and discussed the possibility of moving to the island.[4]

As was their custom, the Lowrys used a small notebook during the trip. This document contains descriptions, memos and impressions registered while travelling. In Malcolm's hand we find descriptions of the view through the beer parlour window, while they are waiting for the ferry: "little white house on piles gleaming in the distance, on Newcastle Island, against the burning bronze burnt gold ⟨maples⟩ russet – of autumn – white fishing boat sliding across fragrant dark green of pines & faded sage green of the alders, birches that haven't turned gold. blue, blue, deep blue: telegraph wires outside the window intersecting the scene in foreground" (20:34, 2)[5] Lowry was particularly fascinated by the light: "wonderful sense of sunlight & fresh sea wind, feel it even in the beer parlour ... incredible freshness & brilliance of scene" (20:34, 3–4). Later, on the ferry, he sketched the sunset over Nanaimo and the last rays of sunlight still touching Gabriola when the dock came nearer.

On the boat he copied texts from signs and notices: "Trenthum Convalescent Home, Gabriola Island, BC. Mrs R Hulme R.N. (the R.N. was a bit forbidding) ... trespassers using this deck do so at their own risk. Higgs Gabriola Ferry Ltd." He noted that "no signatures were affixed" to a petition by the British Columbia Power company "for the installation of electric light power" on Gabriola Island. At this point Lowry was already consciously collecting material for a story. In between fragments of recorded dialogue we find short memos: "Pretty hard getting the cars on board: describe the iron ramp let down, the first car, the truck, – the ship had to move away from the wharf ... [A] black woman with a mouth full of blood – her tender husband – the boat turns back" (20:34 [9–10]).

Malcolm's notes are interrupted by a longer description, in Margerie's hand, of their walk on the first evening, a passage that will be used in later versions of Eridanus:

the night very still, the sea calm + quiet so that one almost didn't notice it as one walked along the shore ... smelled sharp pungent smoke + then saw burning tree terrifying mysterious flaming phallus in forest, a great cedar burning its full height sparks drifting lazily upwards burning burning against dark silver moonlight + black trees. We stop + follow path. many small fires smouldering among dead leaves & stumps + I am frightened + try to raise help from nearby house – then met man coming along road ... who says people who own land simply burning tree to get rid of it. But later the wind rises ... + now the burning tree is flaming in the rising wind – sparks blowing, spouting rising + spiralling ... + now the small fires that had been only glowing are flaring + blazing like red lightning among the black trees   (20:34 [18–20]; cf *October Ferry* 331)

At the end of this notebook we already find a first outline for a short story, which is based on the actual experience:

(a) – the bus coming in – flashbacks to museum
(b) – Arrival in Nanaimo ... – conversation at ticket window re impossibility of getting to Gabriola Island ... We separate – she volunteers to go + find Higgs Ferry Co – while I go into the pub ...
(c) – the wonderful scene in the pub – punctuated by her going out to telephone the lodge man ...

After the publication of *Under the Volcano* in February 1947, the Lowrys returned to their life on the beach in Dollarton, but the success of this novel also brought unwanted attention to their housing situation. Under the five-column headline – "WEALTHY SQUATTERS FIND RENT-FREE BEACH HAVEN" – the *Vancouver Sun* proclaimed in an illustrated article of 1 August 1947: "a successful novelist who could write a cheque for thousands is 'king' of the beach squatters of Royal Row at Dollarton ... Like hundreds of others in the Vancouver area, Malcolm Lowry occupies a tax-free house built on piling below the high tide mark." While law-abiding, tax-paying Vancouver citizens engaged in a new campaign to turn the beach into a city park and the threat of eviction once more grew imminent, Malcolm and Margerie worked on a story about the search for a new house; their trip to Gabriola provided the inspiration and the material.

On 11 September 1947 Margerie wrote to Malcolm's literary agent, Hal Matson: "About Monday ... I'll finish typing a short story Malc and I have written in collaboration ... entitled "October Ferry to Gabriola." She asked Matson to send it to *Harper's Bazaar*, who had requested an article from Lowry about British Columbia.[6] The story, which is set in October 1946, consists of two parts of equal length: the first follows the outline of the notebook, with reflections during the bus ride, the arrival in Nanaimo, and the scene in the pub. The second part describes the actual ferry trip, and it ends when the ship approaches the Gabriola dock. Since this story already contains the complete outer action and framework of the later novel, and serves as the basis for this genetic study, a detailed description of this first version is indispensable.

Part I

From the very beginning of the story an atmosphere of hope and happiness pervades the text:

Gold and blue, the October morning glittered and flashed through the Islander Limited, the swift bus to Nanaimo. To the left were the forests and mountains of Vancouver Island, to the right the sea.

In the forest skirting the highway, the deep gold of soft maples, flecked by the autumn scarlet of vine-leaved maples, travelled along with them, the fallen leaves making even the ground glow and burn with light ... Ethan and Jacqueline Llewelyn sat at the back of the Limited, arm in arm, silent, and too full of hope and excitement to talk.   (1)

The protagonists, Ethan and Jacqueline Llewelyn, are on their way to Gabriola Island, where they hope to buy either a house or a building lot. In the bus that takes them to Nanaimo she "already saw the skipper's house as theirs, as their new home." The text moves from her dreams of a flower and vegetable garden to Ethan's thoughts about the flowers he saw yesterday in the Botanical Museum: "Wake robin, sea rocket and ocean spray: he was fascinated by these names and had learned them by heart. Veiled stinkhorn, death camas and the destroying angel" (2).[7]

Near Nanaimo the bus draws up at a grade crossing to let a log train pass, while the passengers comment on the bad quality of the lumber: "It's nothing but knots" (3). This leads to Ethan's thoughts about the new house he would like to build with good lumber: "Yes, if he felled the timber this month, and had it all cut and stacked by the end of November, he could build next Spring" (5). But as they enter Nanaimo he sees new houses left unfinished and damaged by the delay, and he is aware of the advantages of buying the old skipper's house, which they could occupy immediately.

After some confusion at the dock they are directed to the Higgs Ferry Company "just behind the bastion." For Ethan this uncertainty, rather than being a disappointment, creates a "holiday feeling, as though he were on leave again."[8] Jacqueline, however, is anxious to reach Gabriola as soon as possible and goes off to find the ferry office and to inquire about the schedule. Meanwhile, Ethan waits in a pub and is impressed by the wonderful view from the big window in the Men's Bar. He lights a pipe and considers once more the pros and cons of building his own house or buying the skipper's place. When Jacqueline returns, he moves to the Ladies and Escorts section of the beer parlour, where another big window displays a similar beautiful panorama.[9] She is excited because there is a hotel in Gabriola, and there will be a ferry at 5 p.m. From a phone booth near the clattering kitchen they can finally reach the caretaker of the Anderson lodge, who is alone but promises to put them up for the night.

Part II

At a quarter to five they go down to the ramp, look around the nameless ferry, and notice various signs and posters. The building motif returns in the description of the ferry, "a sort of ps[eu]do-poop, just the [s]keleton, like a roof in progress of building with planks set at random for the workers to move around on" (17).[10] After a while the other passengers arrive; the boat starts moving, but stops again at the main wharf to take three vehicles on board. Finally the ferry is gone, and while Vancouver Island recedes, Ethan and Jacqueline admire the magnificent scene: "Nanaimo lay in the indigo shadow of the mountains behind it … with the last sunset fire lingering on their murderous peaks" (21).

Because a woman in black is coughing blood, the ferry starts the return trip to Nanaimo, but a doctor among the passengers can help her, and the ship continues on towards Gabriola. Jacqueline and Ethan have different reactions to this "return" of the ferry. She has "a sudden absurd vision of a shipwreck" and takes the incident as "a warning" (24). To Ethan it evokes reminiscences of his first sea voyage as a boy, when he had already boarded the ship and then had to return to Liverpool for his papers. Through this incident "his original impulse to go" had been drained already of "all its romance and adventure, and nothing remained but the cold danger, the platitudinous reality" (24).[11]

One of the passengers, an "old-timer," tells him that the captain's "dump" is for sale because a previous summer occupant "had shot his wife and then himself," and he advises Ethan not to buy it. The "place is full of termites anyhow." These remarks mean that he can no longer choose between buying a house and building one (26).

This disappointment is forgotten, however, when they approach Gabriola in the fading twilight and the ferry siren utters its "deep, protracted chord of mournful triumph." The lighthouse that they pass "could be someone's dream of home." The eager anticipation of the Llewelyns is reflected in the mysterious setting: "Gabriola … Ah, how wild and lonely and forbidding it looked! Not a light glimmered, not a house shone through the trees, there was nothing but the cliffs, so high the trees on top seemed dwarfed, the cliffs, and the uproar of the black sea at their base" (27). In the final paragraph of the story the pastoral images, the voices, and the swinging lanterns extend a symbolic welcome to them: "[They] distinguished the outlines of a sheltered valley that sloped down to the silent, calm harbour. Deep in the dark forest behind was the glow of a fire with red sparks ascending like a fiery fountain: someone burning tree stumps to clear his land. The sound of lowing cattle was borne to them and they could see a lantern swinging along close to the ground. A voice called out, clear, across the water. And now they saw the dock, with silhouetted figures moving against a few lights that gleamed in the dusk" (28).

Margerie's notebook description of a blazing tree as a "terrifying mysterious flaming phallus" and a "red lightning" has become a beautiful "fiery fountain" caused by the controlled burning of tree *stumps*. Apparently there was no room for that frightening image in the peaceful ending of this short story. (In later versions the description is picked up again, but in revised form.) The story has an open ending; no final decision has been made about Gabriola, but the charm of the setting in the last paragraphs suggests that this could indeed be "the right place, the dreamed-of place" the Llewelyns were thinking of on the bus.

A month after this story was mailed, when the Lowrys were ready to sail for France, they heard from Matson that *Harper's Bazaar* wanted them to make some revisions, but Margerie refused.

2 . SECOND VERSION: BETWEEN ERIDANUS
      AND GABRIOLA

The fourteen-month trip to Europe had its happy moments (especially the visit to Italy, in the spring of 1948), but the long stay in France gradually turned into an alcoholic nightmare. At a certain point Margerie even feared that Malcolm was losing his mind and would need prolonged psychiatric treatment – which they could not afford.

In despair they returned to Dollarton, in January 1949, in the midst of the winter. Immediately, an almost miraculous recovery took place. For a year Malcolm had been unable to "move or think without vast quantities of alcohol." But three weeks after his return he wrote to his French translator, Clarisse Francillon, that "the craving, the absolute *necessity* for alcohol, has stopped in a way I cannot account for; in fact it had virtually ceased a week from leaving Paris." What surprised him even more was that the transition had been "virtually painless," without the dreaded deliriums (SL 168–9). His shack on the beach was, once more, paradise regained.

In the fall of that year (10 October 1949) Margerie mentioned in a letter to Matson that she would "have another stern look at 'October

Ferry.'" The next six months, however, were spent almost exclusively on a filmscript of *Tender Is the Night*, a very original – and highly unorthodox – treatment of Fitzgerald's novel. It was a work, however, they were neither asked nor paid to do, and in the meantime their financial situation had become very precarious: the year in Europe had exhausted their funds; the expected royalties from France and Germany did not arrive; and the devaluation of the pound reduced Malcolm's monthly income from England to about ninety dollars. His letter of 17 July 1950 to Matson was the first of a long series of embarrassing "begging letters."

In these circumstances Lowry decided to postpone his long-term novel projects *Dark As the Grave* and "La Mordida," and he started to work on short stories inspired by the trip to Italy: "Sooner or Later or So They Say" (an early version of "Elephant and Colosseum"), "Strange Comfort Afforded by the Profession," and "Present Estate of Pompeii." On 23 October 1950 he informed Matson that he was "working like mad" to get "half a dozen" stories finished by Christmas, hoping that they would earn him enough money to rent an apartment in the city. Margerie had been ill and was still too weak to stay on the beach during the winter. Three weeks later (14 November) he wrote that a new version of "October Ferry to Gabriola" "should be in the post in a week. This we decided we couldn't collaborate on. So I have completely rewritten it by myself and finally I'm extremely pleased with it" (SL 216).

Among the mass of Gabriola mss there are many notes, suggestions, and hand- and typewritten intermediate drafts of various passages, but not a complete text of this period. Lowry started his new draft by making revisions on the carbon copy of the 1947 typescript, changing lines and adding marginal notes and inserts. When he reached the section in the beer parlour (now called the "Ocean Spray"), he rewrote the text in longhand, again and again, each time adding new elements, until a long insert about his present home on the beach in Eridanus (Lowry's fictional Dollarton) made a quick completion of the story virtually impossible.

In the first version the Llewelyns are simply looking for a new place to live. Neither their previous home nor their reason for leaving it is mentioned. Everything is aimed at the future; the central issue is whether to buy a house or to build one, and Ethan's thoughts often deal with practical construction problems, such as putting in foundations and using the right kind of wood.

In the second version, however, the Llewelyns are looking for a new house because they have been *evicted* from their old one in Eridanus. They are thinking not only of the future but also of the happy past they

have to give up. In the new draft of the beer parlour section, Ethan is
no longer sitting by himself in the Men's Bar while Jacqueline looks for
the ferry (8). They are enjoying the beautiful harbour view from the
big window together. This moment of happiness is the starting point
for a long flashback to Eridanus. Lowry first sketched the outline in the
form of a scenario, a technique he had developed while working on the
filmscript of *Tender Is the Night*. Because this passage is typical of Lowry's later writing technique, an extensive quotation may prove enlight-
ening:

"Ethan," she said, taking his hand. "Yes," he said.
Shot 1 – The Llewelyns, beyond the light in the sky, see their little house for
the first time.
Dissolve to 2 The Llewelyns enter the house
Cut shot 3 The Well
Cut back to Jacqueline in the bar dissolving into her delighted nods (shot 4)
that it can be lived in.
Shot 5 And what they begin to make of it.
Shot 6 The pier – And it was Jacqueline's brilliant suggestion that it should have
a light structure ...
Shot 7 And then, because it is night, a shot of them looking out of the window
at the pier in the moonlight ...
8 Shot of the dogwood blossoms
9 From Margie's notes, the awakening of other life, + the love of nature ...
[up to the fire]
10 Fade into St Malo Cathedral
11 Fade back to the house. Cut to the incinerator of the sawmill. (UBC SC
20:31, 7)

The inspiration for this flashback is, of course, Lowry's own experience
in Dollarton. (The reference in Shot 10 to St Malo Cathedral implies a
visual link between his own burned shack and the war-damaged French
cathedral he saw in France in 1948.)

Writing out the text of this scenario must, for once, have been easy
for Lowry. This whole evocation of the charm of Eridanus and the
happiness of its inhabitants is written in a very small but clear and fluent
hand, without the usual revisions and restarts.[12] Lowry realized that this
flashback was too long to fit the story and therefore drafted a shorter,
seven-page "Corollary." The original text was later typed separately as
the fifty-one-page typescript "Material Mostly for Eridanus" (UBC SC
22:6).

At this point Lowry was still very uncertain of the direction of his
story. In a note to Margerie he wrote: "Our old page 18 [in the carbon

copy] now follows ... But many of the following pages ... must remain in doubt until you, so to speak, have caught up with me. Whatever I do with it here I shall probably fail in part, because of my lack of clarity as to the *anterior* exposition, even though I know *musically*, as it were, what should be done" (UBC SC 18:2, 29). This uncertainty may explain why the new version, which Lowry had promised in November, remained incomplete. Their financial problems forced the Lowrys to stay on the beach through the "lowest March temperatures in Vancouver's history" (*Vancouver Sun*, 6 March 1951). In the meantime Margerie had become ill, and Malcolm had to borrow money again, this time from Albert Erskine (see SL 227).

When spring finally arrived, Lowry used the Eridanus material that had grown out of the flashback in the beer parlour of "October Ferry" for the first draft of "Forest Path to the Spring," his hymn of praise to simple life in nature. The threat of eviction from Dollarton was still there, however, and while working on "Forest Path" and the new versions of "Elephant and Colosseum," he wrote to Erskine: "our chief remaining anxiety is about the house, though this is only indirectly an economic problem: no amount of money perhaps can help us keep it, should they start to "develop" the land ... Scares of eviction come and go, and it is a situation of some universal significance I have always meant to develop in the novel; but that is a whole lot easier to write about than enduring, and while enduring for that matter as hard to write about as it is not to write about" (SL 243).

In October he sent "Elephant and Colosseum" and "The Bravest Boat" to Matson, and at the end of November he mailed a long outline of his work-in-progress ("The Voyage That Never Ends"), together with copies of the stories "The Forest Path to the Spring" and "Through the Panama,"even though the latter two still needed revision. "The trouble is cash," he explained to Matson; "the wolf is howling again on the Path itself, not to say on the porch." Lowry hoped that by completing a number of short stories he would be able to get a publisher's advance for a collection of stories called *Hear us O Lord from heaven thy dwelling place* and thus avoid another winter on the beach. In this volume he would include "October Ferry."[13]

Lowry's publishing company – Harcourt, Brace – first maintained, then released, its option on his work. This blow left him and Margerie stuck in a rented city apartment, and they had to survive the month of March on money borrowed from their friend Einar Neilson. In April Albert Erskine was able to arrange a contract with Random House on the basis of the completed stories and the outline of "The Voyage That Never Ends." Lowry was expected to complete three books within two and a half years and would receive an advance in the form of a monthly income. From the beginning, however, he was concerned about the terms of the contract. He explained to Matson that he could guarantee two books (*Hear us O Lord* and *Lunar Caustic*), and a volume of poems within this period, but he could not "absolutely promise" a third novel (*SL* 311).

Lowry informed Erskine (12 April 1952) that he planned to "finish up some of the shorter stories first, none of which have anything to do with writers or writing," then turn to the longer story "October Ferry" ("also having nothing to do with writers"), and finally to "finish off the Path + Panama." The reference to "writers and writing" is a response to Erskine's "misgivings," in his 21 March 1952 letter to Lowry, about Lowry's plans for *Dark as the Grave* and "La Mordida." Lowry objected that "there is an artist, a poet in every man" and that it is, therefore, easy for anyone to identify with a writer.[14] Nevertheless, he did take Erskine's advice to heart when he started revising "Present Estate of Pompei" in the spring of 1952, and he decided to change the protagonist from a writer to a language teacher (based on his friend Downey Kirk).

Something similar happened when he subsequently turned to "October Ferry." In the original Eridanus material (of the flashback in the beer parlour) the protagonist was a "retired engineer doing free lance journalistic work about nature observation." In his working notes for "October Ferry" Lowry pointed out which Eridanus passages could be used "if we cut the reference to his being a journalist" (UBC SC 22:1, 15C).

Lowry decided to make his protagonist "a sort of cross between Einar, Bill O'Connell [sic], and myself" (UBC SC 20:31). Einar was the already mentioned Einar Neilson, whose place on Bowen Island was an open house for many artists. William McConnell was a young Vancouver lawyer and writer with whom Malcolm loved to talk, not only about literature but also about criminal court cases and legal issues (including capital punishment, on which McConnell had prepared a CBC program).[15] In this second version of the story the protagonist has interrupted his career as "a successful lawyer" and retired to the beach in Eridanus for health reasons (3). This background, however, is not yet elaborated; only a few one-line allusions are made to Ethan's "professional experience" (13; see also 23 and 44).

While Lowry was musing about his protagonist's background, he rechecked the various batches of fragmentary (and often overlapping) handwritten drafts, indicated the passages he wanted to use with such headings as "Wonderful Stuff," "Ocean Spray for Men's Bar," "Appendix," etc., and linked them up in a new holograph draft consisting of texts, notes, and references. The typewritten transcript of this mixture (hereafter called TS 2) will serve as our basis for the further discussion of the second version.

As was pointed out in connection with the intermediate drafts of the Ocean Spray section, the protagonists of this new version are caught between Eridanus and Gabriola, between past and future. But Lowry introduced other oppositions as well. The beauty of nature and simple life is threatened by the "progress" of civilization; the charm of the Ladies and Escorts side in the beer parlour finds a counterpoint in the ugliness of the Men's Bar; a reprieve for the squatters overturns the eviction. There is also a difference now between Ethan and Jacqueline in their attitudes towards Eridanus and Gabriola.

Ethan knows that Jacqueline is very eager to get to Gabriola, and is already dreaming of the skipper's house and hoping that it will have "modern conveniences": "telephone, radio, washing machine, gas stove, and for the first time in so many years running hot and ... cold water" (2). Although he understands and accepts her needs, he is more concerned about the negative side of "progress" and "the inferiority of contemporary materials." This may be reflected in small details such as his new pipe with "its intricate yet absolutely pointless nicotine trap" (6). But it appears in a more elaborated form in the appalling vulgarity of the "improvements" in the Men's Bar of the Ocean Spray: "The floodlit scene of the improvements that now struck his eyes was one of the most horrifying in his experience. It smelled like a recently but not very well disinfected public lavatory. The color scheme seemed to be composed of vomit-yellow and ashes of raspberry, little shit-brown, sick salmon, and a subtlety [sic], decayed salmon, neon cerise, criminal grey, exhausted orange and the same effect repeated interminably in columns of mirrors carefully designed to look broken, under a ceiling of dried blood" (17). At the end of this page-long description of the ghastly interior of the Men's Bar, Ethan concludes that "there was only one reaction possible to this – hatred. Nothing so well expressed the soulless hideous ferocious and frightening horror of North American latter day civilizations than this" (17–18). He fears that "pretty soon the 'improvements' this bar represented would have extended to the beautiful Ladies and Escorts next door" (19); the implication is that Gabriola also might be threatened.

In this version Ethan is often thinking about fate and destiny. The level crossing becomes an important symbol. It is a place "where two distinct forms of destiny, as it seemed to him, under separate control, each fractionally traversed the other's medium, (why did they bury suicides at the crossroads?) each perhaps bound toward the same goal" (5). The death symbolism, implied in the question about suicides, is not yet elaborated here, but the past and future are combined in the sound of the disappearing train: in the first version it was "folding up like a concertina into the future" (TS 1, 3); in TS 2 the musical terms are elaborated, and the sound also evokes now "that protracted powerful chord of the emotions known as nostalgia" (5). The search for a new home becomes a spiritual quest: "Deep and old as love itself was man's desire for a home ... It was a home for his love itself, for the soul must enclose the body, not be within it. And to understand it you had to lose it, both your soul and house, then, even if you found it, to be still, somehow, looking for it at the same time" (UBC SC 22:1, 15C).

In the second part of the story the deeper symbolic implications of the journey are immediately reflected in Ethan's thoughts when he looks at the newly painted ferry: "So must Charon's boat have appeared ... when hell was nearly bran-new [sic]" (28). His "sense of adventure" is mixed for a moment with "cold fear," and the unsuccessful petition for the installation of electric light on Gabriola, which elicited a "chuckle" in the first version, now evokes "a pleasure mingled with sharp pain" because it reminds them of "their old shack in Eridanus" (30). A similar ambiguous feeling is present when the ferry finally leaves: "A joyful moment. And yet – now really they were saying goodbye to their old shack, to Eridanus –" (34).

In the first version the incident of the sick woman was already seen as a warning; at this point in the second version Ethan sees an albatross, which precedes them towards Gabriola "like some embodied symbolic fusion of an angel with its sword" (40), and he experiences a moment of illumination in which "all of a sudden everything that had happened during their day seemed suffused with an extraordinary significance, seemed interrelated, as if part of a series of some unknown system of logic" (44). This leads to a deeper awareness of a mysterious order beyond life:

It is rather as if, on our journey through life, some guardian spirit causes our attention to be drawn, at such moments, to certain combinations, to remind us that we are not altogether unwatched. ... We have not the temerity to call this spirit God even when, at the bottom of our being, we are convinced that it is He. At worst, it is true, we fear it might be the devil. But if beneficent, if not diabolic, what is it, if it is not God, or of God, this eye that hears, this voice that thinks, this heart that speaks, this embodied hallucination that foresees, with more than christal [sic] clarity, and divine speech?   (42)

After this spiritual experience, the protagonist is confronted with a final test. In this second version the ferry returns all the way to Nanaimo to let the sick woman off the boat. There the Llewelyns learn, from an evening paper thrown on board, that the Eridanus squatters have been given a reprieve (45). Immediately their minds turn to Eridanus, but Ethan and Jacqueline now have to resist the temptation to return to their cabin. From a conversation with a Harbour Board inspector (in an Eridanus flashback earlier in the story), Ethan knows that buying the property in Eridanus would not be a solution because that would subject them to zoning laws and destroy the natural charm of the place (15A). The reprieve is a spiritual catharsis; Ethan now realizes that he needs "a house more than ever in Gabriola": "His sin has been to treat something that was God's gift as his own personal property. The more he looked on it as his own personal property the more anguished he became at the thought of losing it. The more he fretted about losing it, the more he tended to spoil their life there and in this way perhaps they've lost some years of happiness" (46).

The rest of the story now follows the line of the 1947 version, except that the choice between buying a plot or building a house has become irrelevant and is kept open. The protagonist has come to "the realization that the Kingdom of Heaven is within" (52). This is symbolically underlined when Ethan, in his imagination, anticipates the evening walk with Jacqueline on Gabriola under a sky full of meteors falling through a "silver midnight of driftwood and burning trees" (54). For the description of this imaginary walk Lowry goes back to parts of Margerie's notebook entry about the forest fire. After Ethan's spiritual experience the fire is no longer threatening; it is, on the contrary, "purging away the rubbish of the past" (55). Ethan Llewelyn is ready to reach his destination.

3. THIRD VERSION: IN SEARCH OF PERMANENCE IN THE FOURTH HOUSE

The next step in the chronological development of "October Ferry" is a new typescript of fifty-nine pages that incorporates revisions and inserts made in TS 2 and also elaborates the notes into a running text. This third version, moreover, includes new background material on Ethan, copied from separate holograph drafts.[16]

Most of the expansion of the story still takes place in the Ocean Spray section. The "scenario" for the Eridanus flashback is now worked out and evokes the happiness of the past in an Edenic setting: "One year ago last spring, in May, Ethan and Jacqueline, having followed the path through the forest, saw the light in the sky and there below them, beneath a wild cherry tree in full bloom, its chimney capped by a bucket, shingled roof needing repair, its strong cedar foundations standing right in the sea, stood the house" (17).

The Ocean Spray section also expands because of *new* exposition. We learn that the Llewelyns have already lost three houses and are now longing for "permanence and stability." They bought their first house near Oakville, when they were just married, "twelve years ago," in 1934. "Jackie had been nineteen and he himself twenty-seven, and not long accepted into [an] old Toronto Law firm." In this home, where their son Dick was born, they had been happy "for four years, until in June, 1938, they began to build the soup factory: 'Mother Gettle's Kettle-Simmered Soup. Mmmm! Good!'" (22) Their second house was a large ten-room stone house built by his great-grandfather in Niagara, which he inherited in 1939. In contrast to the war-built and mass-produced houses seen in Nanaimo, this was a house built to last; yet it went up in flames.

The Llewelyns had hoped to find permanence in their third house, a simple cabin in Eridanus, but the threat of eviction made it psychologically impossible for Ethan to go on living there. This version does not explain why Ethan "finally resigned from the Law firm in Toronto" and came to Eridanus – except for a vague reference to "his last big case, so ignominiously lost" (24). That negative experience is symbolically redeemed when he meets in the Dantesque environment of the Men's Bar the client of "his first big case, ... Henry Knight, whom he had defended and proved innocent of a charge of murder, in Toronto, in 1936" (24). For Ethan this is "a good omen ... It was as if he had suddenly come upon his own brother (though that brother was himself in relation to the past)" (24). The rediscovery of the past leads to an acceptance of the self.

The rest of the story follows and elaborates the texts, notes, and suggestions that have already been discussed for the second version. Special attention is paid to the reaction of the Llewelyns immediately after the reprieve. When Jacqueline hesitates, Ethan tells her: "It's better to go of your own will than to be thrown out." And when she assures him "I loved it, I do love it, Ethan –" he repeats: "But it's time to leave, however much it hurts" (21).

4. FOURTH VERSION: BEYOND HANGMAN'S POINT

In the outline of his work-in-progress Lowry had written that "'October Ferry to Gabriola,' one of the best, should it be included, would take me another six weeks, for it already exists in another form" (UBC SC 32:1, 10). But eight months later the story was still not completed. On 12 August 1952 he informed Erskine: "I am having to rewrite – for the umpteenth time – the penultimate novella in *Hear Us*, due to the appalling difficulty of trying to render overlapping material consistent: the number of false restarts and hen tracks on the page I have made has me half dead with discouragement" (SL 322).

With his peculiar concern for dates of good and bad omen, Lowry wanted to finish "October Ferry" by 1 October 1952. On 9 September he informed Erskine that the end of the novel was "well in sight." But two weeks later, on 26 September Margerie wrote to Dave Markson that Malcolm was "practically incommunicado" because his story kept resisting completion. "I don't know anything more sickening, wildly exciting, despairing and generally frantic than the Battle of the Blank Page," she said. Malcolm added, in an ironic footnote, that this was still not so bad as the "Battle of Bulge or over-stuffed glowering illegible and anyhow totally incomprehensible page."

At that moment, Lowry explained to Erskine, he became "uneasy lest the whole work itself was in places not consonant with the best mental health and spiritual economy of its benighted author so I took some weeks off to read nothing but psychology. What I learned about myself was not very encouraging" (SL 335). In November 1952, when the Lowrys moved into a city apartment for the winter, "October Ferry" was still expanding; by the end of February it had grown into "an unscheduled novel, about 150 or [1]60 pages," which Malcolm would mail before the "end of this month" if he were not "held up a little because of typing" during Margerie's short visit to her mother in Los Angeles.[17] At this point Lowry could only estimate the size of his work because no complete typescript copy had yet been made of this version, and his own handwritten draft was a combination of batches with at least ten different foliations. The typewritten transcript turned out to be almost two hundred pages.[18]

The story had not only grown in size but also changed in focus. In the new version (hereafter called TS 4) the ferry trip is a passage through the subconscious, and Gabriola has become completely symbolic: a search for equilibrium, a choice between life and death, between suicide and spiritual rebirth. The background of the characters is further elaborated, and part of the exposition is shifted from the Ocean Spray section to Ethan's reflections in the bus at the beginning of the story, where the comical figure of Jacqueline's father, the cabbalist Angus McCandless, is also introduced. In the course of the revisions for this fourth version the date of the ferry trip changed twice: from 1946 to 1947, and then (in a later version of the Ocean Spray section and in the second part of the story) to 1949. Also the other dates and the ages of the characters changed. Several important new motifs were introduced in the fourth version: the contrast between life in Eridanus and that in a city apartment, Ethan's drinking problem after the eviction and the resulting quarrels with Jacqueline, and finally, the hanging motif.

Ethan is now a man who retired from a successful legal career to life on the beach in order to find his equilibrium. He gave up practice after the loss of his second house and "the protracted ordeal of one of the most gruesome and complicated cases he had ever defended" (3), a murder case in which his client, whom he believed innocent and had saved from the scaffold, turned out to be guilty. Ethan had been "close to breakdown" (10), but through nature he discovered a new world; he became interested in the stars; he read astronomy, philosophy, literature, and "felt as if he'd been reborn – mentally and physically." "It was as if a new aspiration had come into existence, a longing to be a better, a more worthy man" (11). But "when for the first time in his whole existence he had found this ecstatic joy simply in living," all this had been destroyed by the threat of eviction: "Sometimes he felt they were a bit like William James's people who might have been so happy living on their frozen lake, merrily skating in the sparkling sun, had they only not known, – his tragic image for man living without faith – that the ice was slowly melting beneath them" (14).[19]

Ethan reacted to the news of the eviction as if he "had heard the dread voice in the garden: Adam, where ar[t] thou?" (15). After a few weeks in a city apartment he "often felt like killing himself from sheer boredom" (16). This led to quarrels with Jacqueline, who was "only too glad to get away from your goddam shack!" (16). She told him that his "attachment to the place [was] absolutely pathological!" (20) and accused him of burying her "out there in that god-forsaken hole" in the wilderness (18).

At this low point in their relationship they hear about the house and the lot on Gabriola via their friend Angela, but in the bus Ethan doubts whether any place can be a substitute for Eridanus. His hatred of civilization, already present in earlier versions, is now intensified into an apocalyptic view of the decline of the world: "Your poor little bit of property won't be safe from desecration wherever you are. And when they've totally ruined most of the beauty of the country with industry and thoroughly loused up the watersheds and the rainfall, and the last old sourdough has traded in his gold sifting pan for a geiger counter and staked out the last uranium claim, some fool will drop an atom bomb on top of the whole business" (22). In Eridanus Ethan had "little by little, without deliberate discipline on this point, ... dropped the habit" of drinking (27). But under the pressure of city life it has become a real problem: "the desire for a drink had suddenly overlaid any decision, or thought of any other goal, save a pub. A glass of beer ... now

seemed of more importance than a house. Even than Gabriola" (27).
The grade-crossing section serves in TS 4 as a catalyst in Ethan's consciousness: the "maddening" noise of the passing train makes him aware
of the fact that he has a hangover.

In previous versions the passing log train led to Ethan's thoughts
about the trees he would cut (for his timber) without "desecrating" the
forest; in the fourth version these thoughts are in contrast with the
setting: the bus is driving through a whole area of burned and dead
trees. And in the middle of this "abomination of desolation" (31) appears
an advertisement for Mother Gettle's Kettle-Simmered Soup. The symbol of industrial progress and the cause of the loss of their first house,
in the east, seems to have reached the western edge of civilization.
Before arriving in Nanaimo, Ethan first has to pass through rows of
billboards: on the surface of the narrative they are just "some awfulness
peculiar to American civilization," but on a deeper level they represent
different aspects of man's quest for happiness. These signs have a spiritual meaning for him: "Everything on earth seemed suddenly part of
a miraculous plan ... Even the billboards and advertisements suddenly
took on a n[e]w significance, seemed even to be existing on another
plane, as if man's spiritual pilgrimage on earth too were eternally
between these hoardings, these advertisements for spiritual soup, and
the soul's rest, these drastic remedies for the spirit's anguish" (37–8).

Signs for the Ocean Spray Inn (where Ethan will have to make an
important decision) keep reappearing along the road, as if urging the
visitor to go on. Painkillers offer oblivion in the Coca-Cola age, and
real estate agents are subdividing the Garden of Eden.[20] Other signs
warn the pilgrim: "What shall it profit a man if he gain the whole world
and lose his own soul?" (35) And when the bus enters Nanaimo, which
advertises itself as the "City of the Future," it has to slow down for a
funeral. The spiritual quest continues at the Nanaimo bus station, where
the newsstand is stacked with astrological magazines. Ethan's own problems are now associated with the astrological "Difficulties of the 4th
House." The answer offered by occult knowledge is tempting for
Ethan, but he feels too embarrassed to look at the magazines (49–50).[21]

The Ocean Spray section is, once more, an opportunity for Lowry
to expand his story: the Eridanus flashback, which was entirely positive
in TS 3, now carries connotations of pain and loss. Originally, the sound
of the train on the other side of the inlet was "associated in their minds
with the unearthly beautiful chiming of a church bell in the mist" (TS
3, 18–19). That sound is, in turn, linked to "the carillon-sounding Sunday mornings of Niagara-on-the-Lake" (77). But this sound now hurts,
because it is linked with the eviction from Eridanus (their third house),

the fire of the second house (via the cathedral bell of St Malo), and finally, via "Mother Gettle," the loss of their first house.

The Eridanus section is further elaborated with a long, beautiful description of the sunrise, the winter, and the tides of January.[22] But this too ends on a sad note when Ethan thinks of the empty house on the beach: "Nothing is sadder than a deserted house" (80[A]). These beautiful images of light ("Twilight of the Dove") in the Ladies and Escorts side are contrasted with the ghastly pictures of an imaginary hanging and trial scene in the Men's Bar ("Twilight of the Raven").[23]

From the exposition at the beginning pages of this fourth version, we know that Ethan still occasionally "lectured on Canadian law, to the changing of which, in certain horrendous items he hoped to contribute" (5): "He composed a defense of a seventeen year old boy sentenced to hang for rape that was not based on any point of law but upon a psychological passage in Hermann Hesse's *Damien* [sic] and liked to feel it not impossible he had helped to secure his reprieve" (13). This passage, and the imaginary murder trial in the Ocean Spray (which plays a crucial role in the development of the novel), were inspired by a controversy that took place in Vancouver in 1951, when a young boy, Francis Sykes, was condemned to the scaffold (at Oakalla prison in nearby New Westminster) for the rape-murder of a thirteen-year-old girl. An editorial in the *Vancouver Sun* of 11 October 1951 provoked a flood of reactions, and the death sentence was eventually commuted. Lowry wrote at that time to Dave Markson (1 November 1951): "I have been preparing a public objection to a local injustice where a 16 year old boy was sentenced to hang (in a disused elevator shaft, painted yellow) for a rape he had not committed. Fortunately they reprieved the poor fellow (apparently to please the visiting Princess Elizabeth) but neither the ritual pardon nor the near-ritual murder on the part of our barbarous public, who has now sentenced him to life imprisonment, is something you would leave alone ... *much as one hates to risk one's position in it*, even if one hasn't got one" (SL 269; italics added).

The controversy about hanging flared up again in Vancouver when the *Sun* of 11 December 1951 carried a stark description of the execution of John Davidoff and protested against this "hideous, barbaric and medieval" form of execution. Its cruelty was made palpable two days later in a column by Harold Weir, who described in ghastly detail the hanging of Arthur Campbell, which he had witnessed, and the equally barbarous execution of Benny Schwamm.[24]

The brief allusion to the Sykes case at the beginning of the novel was inspired by Lowry's own letter to Markson, and stated that Ethan had prepared a defence and that the reprieve had already been granted. In the new and far more elaborate version of this incident presented in the beer-parlour section, the sentence has not yet been commuted, and the boy (called Roy Davies here) will hang on 13 December unless somebody will stand up in defence of the murderer or in protest against this form of capital punishment. Ethan so far has done nothing for fear of drawing public attention to Eridanus and his own precarious situation. In a terrifying imaginary trial scene in the depressing setting of the Men's Bar, Ethan finally takes up his responsibility and defends the boy, quoting extensively from Weir's column to create an emotional atmosphere and from Hesse's *Demian* to explain the anxieties of puberty, when suddenly the childhood world of innocence is destroyed – an experience so traumatic that some "cling their whole life long painfully to the irrevocable past, the dream of a lost paradise, the worst and most deadly of all dreams" (98).[25]

In an hallucinatory scene, however, this argument is turned against Ethan himself, and he is accused of clinging to his "own lost Paradise, [his] own irrevocable past, in short, that of Eridanus itself." The final verdict is "Hang Ethan Llewelyn!" (101) On a symbolic level this means that Ethan is faced here with his own guilty conscience; even his own mirror image, in the restroom, accuses him of lacking the courage "to make any decisions at all" (102). Through this experience Ethan comes to a new understanding of himself: "All you think about is the next drink and perhaps all you're looking for, all you long for, is your own death. Perhaps essentially he was afraid even of finding his real self, afraid of discovering himself to be a criminal, a murderer even, or one whose destiny was suicide, in which case there'll be no need to hang Ethan Llewelyn, he'd do it for them" (103). Precisely at this moment, when Ethan feels "almost as if he were dead already," he recognizes the waiter in the Ocean Spray as Henry Knight, the man he had saved from the scaffold. This gives him the strength to make an important decision: he will organize a public protest in the case of Roy Davies; "he would do something, not do nothing, cost what it might" (108). This decision breaks the almost magical spell of the Men's Bar: Jacqueline returns with the news that "there *is* a ferry" and, in contrast to her attitude about drinking in the apartment, joins him for a beer while they wait for the ferry to leave.

In the *second part* of this fourth version Lowry further developed the drinking motif and the search for redemption and spiritual values. At the same time he intensified his protagonist's feelings and tribulations on his way to Gabriola. This second part still starts, as in the 1947 short story, with the Llewelyns going down the ramp to the ferry at quarter to five; but Ethan now feels guilty because he did not help a drunken young man in Nanaimo who talked compulsively about fire and suicide.

The gin bottle he is now carrying will play an important role in the symbolic development of the novel. When he wants to drink to forget his misery, he is unable to open the bottle; later, when he tries to help the sick woman by offering her a drink, it opens without any difficulty. But before he can perform this act of charity, which redeems his earlier failure to help the drunken man, he has to go through a conversion experience.

Ethan's need of faith is commensurate with his need for alcohol. He tries to accept his personal agonies "as the working of a higher will" (28). When he is unable to cope with his "fear of the future, fear of himself" (35), "the bowwave [foams] up to meet him" (37), but he resists the temptation of suicide by asking a priest to pray for him. This scene forms a structural counterpoint to the earlier hanging scene in the beer parlour: Ethan feels like a man on the scaffold with a priest standing next to him for the last prayers. At the end of this scene, the albatross (which was already present in TS 3) appears; like the ancient mariner, Ethan is finally delivered from his guilt. He is ready to ask the fundamental question: "What is faith?" The priest's answer, "Try thinking of it as a messenger" (42), leads Ethan to "a measure of acceptance," and "for the first time in a long while, he felt in tune with his destiny and that of the universe" (44). He also promises Jacqueline "not to have a drink until something really wonderful happens to us. Then I'll celebrate with you" (57).

His resolve to change his life and become a better man and a more considerate husband is tested in a last challenge – the news of the reprieve. In the thematic structure of the previous version it was essential for Ethan to give up Eridanus entirely: "Even if we could stay another year, in the end they'll get us" (TS 3, part 2, 21). But in the fourth version the link with Eridanus is not completely broken. Ethan still tells Jacqueline that they would "have to find a house sooner or later. And that you can't *own* a place like Eridanus." But he adds: "We *could* have another summer or two, perhaps more – we can *go* there whenever we like, a week, a month, two months, it *sounds* too good to be true!" (67–8) Their boat passes "Hangman's Point" without evoking any negative thoughts, and soon approaches Gabriola.[26]

Lowry did not write a complete holograph draft for the part following the reprieve, but he used most of the pages of the previous typescript, with only some revisions and inserts. This creates an ambiguity, however, because in that older typescript the Llewelyns are still looking for a place on Gabriola and asking questions about the captain's house, whereas the new draft of their reaction to the reprieve suggests that they will return to Eridanus, at least temporarily. The unresolved ambiguity in this version may be a sign of the contradictory feelings in the author himself, but it also indicates that, in this fourth version, the symbolic meaning of the journey has become so dominant that the choice between Gabriola and Eridanus is no longer the main issue. The real theme of this voyage through the deeper regions of the inner self is to get beyond suicidal self-hatred and self-torture, to accept life and love.

Writing this fourth version of "October Ferry" must have been a harrowing experience for Lowry. Above almost every page of the murder-trial scene and of the conversation with the priest, he wrote a short prayer ("God, help me," "The Holy Spirit, please help me") or an invocation. The page on which Ethan is accused by his own mirror-image (after the trial) starts with "St Jude, this is harder than ever, sweet Saint of the Impossible, please help me" (UBC SC 17:10). But the inserts he wrote for the next version were an even greater ordeal.

5. FIFTH VERSION: BETWEEN SUICIDE AND THE PERILOUS CHAPEL

After reading an article on the Grail quest in Thomas Mann's *The Magic Mountain* in the January 1953 issue of the *Atlantic Monthly*, Lowry had become aware of the symbolic parallels between his protagonist's (and his own) anxieties and the "frightful and mysterious ordeals" that the seeker of the Grail has to undergo in the "Perilous Chapel" before he can reach his goal. This, he told Erskine later, had given "a terrific fillip to my imagination while going through a Perilous Chapel of my own."[27]

What had happened was that Margerie's visit to Los Angeles, in February 1953, had not only delayed the typing of "October Ferry" but had also broken the precarious equilibrium that enabled Lowry to go on writing. His friends Norman Newton and Gloria Onley received a desperate phone call, and they had to rescue him from a skid-row hotel room, where he lay "in a state of emotional turmoil" and "advanced alcoholism"; the quiet and familiar environment of the Neilsons' home on Bowen Island was needed to calm him down.[28]

In an unpublished letter to David Markson dated 21 April 1953 he wrote, in a very shaky hand, that he had made "a trip through one of the worst of the perilous chapels of my stricken life ... in which I seem to have had all the griefs anxieties worries guilts miseries & terrors of the entire universe thrown at me." After seven lines the letter breaks off, and Margerie had to finish it; she added that the story had turned into a "bloodsucking monster."

During this period Lowry wrote two long inserts: for part 1, the Cordwainer scene (a continuation of the hanging motif); for part 2, a mystical experience of horror and redemption in the Perilous Chapel.

Margerie had made a new copy of the story (TS 5), incorporating the revisions and inserts on TS 4, so that Malcolm could do the finishing touches. But he did not get beyond the grade-crossing section (TS 5, 28)[29] because the hanging and suicide motifs of the fourth version had revived in him the traumatic memories of the suicide of his Cambridge friend Paul Fitte. Lowry had been the last to speak to Fitte and felt a lifelong remorse because he had failed to prevent his friend's death. Fictional allusions to this tragic event appear in several of his works, and it was the central motif in his lost novel "In Ballast to the White Sea."[30]

In the new insert for "October Ferry" this suicidal friend is presented as Charley (later Peter) Cordwainer, the son of the owners of the Mother Gettle soup factory, whose portrait as a boy appears on a billboard at the grade crossing. With this element Lowry links up the various motifs of his novel and gives them a deeper meaning. On the billboard Cordwainer has the same age as the condemned boy Roy Davies; the knots in the timber of the log train, originally part of the building motif, are associated with the knots in the rope with which Cordwainer committed suicide – and with which Davies will be hanged, unless Ethan protests. The warning bells at the grade crossing are associated with the fire of the second house (via the bells of the ruined St Malo Cathedral), with the train bell in Eridanus, and with the university bells on the night of Cordwainer's suicide.

Lowry introduced the Cordwainer insert at the point in the original TS 5 (before the revision) when Ethan, while waiting at the crossing, suddenly became aware of his hangover. In the new draft the confrontation with Cordwainer's portrait leads to a shock of recognition; through a "second consciousness" he becomes aware not only of his hangover but also of the fact that he has been "*consciously* deceiving himself all morning, actually suppressing and misrepresenting the very events of his life for the sake of making them fit into a bearable pattern" (UBC SC 16:17, 3).

The loss of the previous two houses had revealed to him a pattern of doom, a form of divine retribution. Ethan's self-hatred and remorse, his fear of life and the future, now have a concrete and fundamental explanation. In Eridanus he had been happy again, but since the threat of eviction he has been haunted by "the new obsession with destiny: the feeling that he is destined to commit suicide himself" (UBC SC 16:16, 15). His drinking is a refusal to face the facts and accept responsibility, and he has created "a kind of death in life" (16). Their marriage is deteriorating; the only thing left is to wait for "the five o'clock gin" that gives meaning to the whole day (UBC SC 16:17, 13), but this drinking is without joy and leads only to "bickering quarrels" (14).

On his way to his fourth house he is now symbolically stopped at the grade crossing (which had already developed into a death and suicide symbol in the previous versions) by Cordwainer, who thus can be linked with the astrological "Keeper of the Fourth House." His responsibility for Cordwainer's death by hanging can only be redeemed by preventing another death by hanging. Ethan must speak out in defence of the boy Davies, even if that results in his loss of Eridanus, his Garden of Eden.

This Cordwainer insert in the first part of the story is balanced by another insert in the second part: the Perilous Chapel section, placed just before the end of the novel (UBC SC 21:17, E–W). Ethan's happy daydream about his evening walk with Jacqueline on Gabriola now finds a contrast in Ethan's nightmarish climb to the Perilous Chapel, perched high on a crag and surrounded by vultures. This is "the most dreadful thing he had ever experienced" (E); it is the last and final test on his quest for spiritual rebirth.[31]

The whole nightmare is allegorical: Ethan is pushed forward by the sea wind of death, climbing up the gigantic slippery steps of the future, trying to get away from the horrors of the past. In the chapel he experiences a long and violent battle going on in his mind between good and evil. This battle against self-destruction is described in imagery inspired by the horrors of *delirium tremens*, with "appalling crashes, tumult, knockings, groanings," and "even sounds of breaking bones" (J). In this unbearable situation suicide becomes all but irresistible, but at that moment he has a vision of "the eyes of the Virgin piercing through the gloom and what he seemed to see, for a moment, was a look of compassion so divine that his soul leapt out of his body ... And a cool hand lay in his and was offering him a drink, though it was no earthly drink he was drinking and its taste was of ineffable bliss and even of life eternal" (J).

Strengthened by this mystical experience Ethan is able to take the even more dangerous descent, back to the present, although he feels "as if he stood blindfold [sic] on a scaffold at every step" (L). But at the end the terror returns, because "suddenly each step downward had become like a day, a long day of wrath and grief, with nothing to look forward to" but the oblivion of the bottle of gin at five o'clock, and at night "the phenobarbital and more oblivion and then one day finally ⟨and even mercifully⟩ death" (N). He realizes that "there could be no going back [to Eridanus] under these terms" because he could not "live with himself without *drinking* ... unless he once and for all had slain that principle of death in himself" (N). But when "the waters of his mind" rise, and he and Jacqueline are drowning in them, they are saved by a giant with a Christ-like face and by Charley Cordwainer, who assures him that he has been forgiven. The nightmare ends in a picture of warmth and music and human voices, and then moves back into the dream of the evening walk with Jacqueline on the beach. The text moves from total spiritual and psychological isolation, via a religious experience, to an image of social acceptance.

This second insert, "The Perilous Chapel," a nineteen-page holograph in extremely difficult handwriting, crammed with inserts, was never typed out. While Margerie was still typing TS 5, Lowry had already started off on a completely new version of the first part of the novel. "The Perilous Chapel section obliged me to rewrite the exposition," he explained later to Erskine (SL 334). When Ethan realizes that he has been lying to himself about the events of the day and the past, the whole exposition is put into question. The central issue now is the question of identity: Ethan Llewelyn is a man not only in search of the future but also in search of himself, of his own lost identity. He tries to find an answer to the question "Who am I?"

6. SIXTH VERSION: THE QUEST FOR IDENTITY AND TRUTH

This time the return to Dollarton, in April 1953, did not bring the necessary peace of mind for Lowry. In an unpublished letter of 11 April he wrote to Erskine that "living here at all now, still under the shadow of eviction, & at the same time trying to write about just that ... is a situation that must call for ... some major psychological renunciation & acceptance & some super-stendhalian act of will: – in short I have to accept, at the same time disengaging so far as possible all latent death-wishes from the acceptance."

When Erskine received this letter, he became concerned and asked "for some kind of bulletin, no matter how brief, as soon as you can conveniently send it" (22 April 1953). In his answer Lowry said: "So far ... I have willed one thing and the daemon has decided another ... and in 'Gabriola' he has turned out what set out to be an innocent and beautiful story of human longing into quite one of the most guilt-laden and in places quite Satanically horrendous documents it has ever been my unfortunate lot to read, let alone have to imagine I wrote." "October Ferry to Gabriola" had become for Lowry a challenge to his "personal salvation." If he could not finish the work "right *now*, and in these exact and excruciating circumstances of being on the one hand damned Ahab-wise in the midst of Paradise and on the other still mysteriously given the grace to live here," he might as well "admit complete defeat [and] abandon writing altogether" (SL 338–40). He knew that "October Ferry" would no longer fit in the *Hear us O Lord* volume, and he feared that it could not be completed as an independent novel before the November first deadline. In this letter he mentions "buying time" – asking the publisher to stop payments and extend the deadline; but that would only be possible if money from the family estate in England or from a Canadian government fellowship came through.

In the new exposition for the sixth version Lowry elaborated upon the background of his main characters. In the earlier version Ethan was accused of clinging to his dream of the lost paradise. A new insert evokes "a beautiful toy model of Moscow" or St Petersburg, "a city of magical gold domes" that "seemed in memory built on little piles in the 'water,' like Eridanus."[32] This image, which is "nearly the only happy memory of his entire childhood," harmoniously combines two elements, the city and Eridanus, which are diametrically opposed in the present. This toy was taken away by his father, just as his present dream is taken away by fate or a higher force.

Other inserts expand on the first meetings of Ethan and Jacqueline. In this context the beer parlour, the Niagara, functions as a structural counterpart to the "Ocean Spray." In both bars Ethan is plunged into gloomy reflections when he moves over to the Men's side. The exposition about Cordwainer's suicide, which was first developed (in TS 5) at the grade crossing, is now moved forward to the Niagara insert. In both beer parlours Ethan is haunted by remorse and accused by his own mirror image. In both places he is delivered from his despair by the return of Jacqueline, and both times she brings a message about Gabriola. The suicide motif now appears throughout the text, not only in direct allusions but also through associations with Mother Gettle billboards, the Judas tree, a painting by Cézanne, the suicide of a client, and the suicide of Jacqueline's mother.

The return to the past also leads to long inserts about their previous homes in Oakville, Niagara-on-the-Lake and Eridanus. Through these descriptions Lowry stresses the contrast with their present apartment in the city, where the noise is unbearable and the last beautiful things are destroyed in the name of progress. But the threat of eviction has also broken the magic of Eridanus. In former days the Shell refinery on the other side of the inlet could be seen as a "fairy city of dawn" (158), like that "innocent toy model city" of his childhood dream, but it has turned into a "City of Dis"; and the tides of Eridanus are now becoming an "avenging sea-monster ... creeping inch by inch upon the cabin" (77–8).

Ethan's return to the past is not only a search for his lost innocence but also for his lost identity. He is "Llewelyn, meaning unknown" (47), and he is a stranger even to himself. Ethan tries to understand himself through identification with other characters. In the fifth version Ethan saw resemblances between himself and Poe. In the sixth this resemblance is elaborated by shifting the date of the story from 1947 to 1949, so that the new date of the Gabriola trip coincides with the centennial of Poe's death. The school that Ethan and Cordwainer attended is now Stoke-Newington, the place where Poe went.

Ethan also strongly identifies with characters in movies. For this section Lowry was inspired by the old movies he and Margerie had seen, as members of a film society, during their winter stay in Vancouver. The first movie used in "October Ferry", *Outward Bound*, introduces the motif of suicide, on the "spectral ferry between earth and the unbeholden land" (13), a "Charon's boat," which later is associated with the ferry to Gabriola. In the second movie, *Isn't Life Wonderful*, love is purified by fire and tragedy and is stronger than death. This picture functions structurally as a foil to the reaction of the Llewelyns when their own house burns down. Ethan realizes, however, that the power of hatred can also transcend death, when he identifies with Heathcliff in *Wuthering Heights* and with Claude Rains, the criminal lawyer of *Crime without Passion*.[33]

By mid-August 1953 Lowry knew that he could not possibly finish "October Ferry" before the deadline of 1 November, and because of time pressure it was not possible to make a complete working typescript of all the newly written material. A first batch (TS 6, 1–88) was typed out in working draft, quickly revised, and retyped into clear copy (TS 7, 1–102) before the rest of the handwritten material was typed. Under these circumstances there was little opportunity for the critical distance necessary to tighten the structure and straighten out inconsistencies in the chronology. On 14 October Lowry sent the first instalment of 102 pages; on 31 October the next 10 pages were mailed, and another instalment (TS 7, 113–59) was promised for "the beginning of next week." After that, he said, "there will still be another fifty pages or so to go till I reach my old final draft, which will need some overhauling too when – touch wood – I overhaul it" (SL 345).[34]

Lowry was greatly relieved when he heard that Random House had given him a ninety-day extension of the deadline. But in December the omnibus edition of *The Books of Charles Fort*, which Margerie bought as a wedding anniversary present, set his imagination reeling again. In 1940 he had already written to Margerie's mother: "I know of no writer who has made the inexplicable seem more dramatic than Charles Fort" (SL 26).[35] This book, with all its descriptions of strange coincidences of unexplained fires, brought back to Lowry's memory the "fifty other odd senseless sad terrifying and curiously related things" that had happened to him after June 1944, when his own house had burned down in Dollarton. "Fire itself seemed to follow us in a fashion nothing short of diabolical," he wrote to Aiken when describing all the coincidences, and he added, "maybe I am the chap chosen of God or the devil to elucidate the Law of Series" (SL 48–9).

Lowry now used these coincidental fires to search for the hidden reason behind the chain of disasters in Ethan's life. From Charles Fort he learned that fires "had actually been *feared* into existence," and that "feelings of sheer hatred or revenge toward other human beings had been sufficient to cause ... disaster otherwise inexplicable to others" (*October Ferry* 139). In that case, Ethan concludes, his disaster could also be caused by his self-hatred. In the long insert "The Element Follows You Around, Sir!" the protagonist is struck by a "collision of contingencies" that lead to a mystical illumination, a visualization of Poe's "unparticled matter," an experience of "some spiritual region maybe of unborn divine thoughts beyond our knowledge."[36]

At the end of December, Lowry informed Erskine that the book would take him beyond the extended deadline: "I hadn't counted on ... inspirations such as last week's. Where it insists on growing I have to give it its head." At that point Random House decided to wait till the whole typescript was available and to suspend monthly payments. "On the basis of what we have read," Erskine wrote in an official letter on 6 January 1954, the "fear is unavoidable that you may be trying to cram more into the vehicle than it can possibly carry." Lowry felt rejected and was completely shattered. When he mailed the clear copy of "The Element Follows You Around, Sir" (TS 7, 160–206), he replied that if he could not "make his novel move horizontally," this section proved he could "do it vertically" (SL 362).

When the Lowrys returned to Dollarton in April, the bulldozers had pulled down all the shacks up to the light-beacon, just a few hundred yards away. Their shack was unharmed – for the time being – but the situation was now untenable, and when they finally received money from England, Malcolm gave in to Margerie's wish to go to Sicily.

To Erskine he wrote: "Though this oasis last forever, sanity and health dictates we should this time go ... We of course hope to come back, but all preparations have to be made as if we would not ... I honestly don't know at the moment whether I shall cut 200 pages out of *Gabriola*'s 500-odd and I won't know until it's finally (sic) typed" (SL 371). Margerie typed out the fifty pages that were almost ready at the end of October (TS 6, 196–246), but not much more work was done on the novel. The spring that kept Malcolm going had snapped. On 30 August the Lowrys departed from Dollarton, leaving behind in their cabin and in their storage shed a lot of books and manuscripts they would not need. Children later broke into the shed, and manuscripts were strewn all over the ground before friends found them.

7. VERSION SEVEN: CHARRED SMITHEREENS AND BRIGHT ILLUMINATIONS

Sicily was for Lowry "a first rate disaster," as he wrote to Markson in the spring of 1955 (SL 397). When he and Margerie moved to England in the summer of 1955, Malcolm required urgent medical treatment. The doctors feared that brain surgery was necessary, but he recuperated, and one of the first things he did from the hospital was to restore the "umbilical cord" with Random House. He told Erskine that he had "to write off much of the last 18 months as a dead loss" but would start working again on "October Ferry" (SL 381). First, however, he submitted to a gruesome aversion treatment at Atkinson Morley Hospital. In February 1956 he and Margerie settled down in the White Cottage in Ripe, and he started working on "October Ferry." TS 7B, the carbon copy of the text that was sent to Erskine in October 1953, shows suggestions for cuts and some marginal notes; the text is subdivided into small sections with tentative chapter headings, but not much writing was done before he went to Atkinson Morley for a second (and even worse) aversion treatment.

A key to the situation of the work at this time is a note for Margerie written at the end of his second stay, in August 1956: "Preeminently the task here while at Atkinson Morley should be to force my way through to the end of the level-crossing bit with Cordwainer – even if it's not *finally* written I should be able to see & hold the thing clearly in my mind thus far: for after that it's relatively plain sailing, that is, to 'and now it has clasped the wheel forever.'"[37] At that moment he was struggling with overlapping versions of the "The Tides of Eridanus" (chapter 13 in *October Ferry*), of which he had three different typescript drafts (all made in Vancouver in October–November 1953). In the hospital memo he wondered: "How to disentangle The Tides of Eridanus section ... I don't remember the order of the thing either. Did I split it originally, & have two chapters under that heading? One on each side of "The element follows you around, sir!?" (UBC SC 18:7) Lowry had also noticed inconsistencies in the dates: "[I have] to reacquaint myself with the time scheme etc. – I haven't done any work on it for 2 years." In a marginal note he wondered, "WHEN was Tommy born?" (TS 7B, 108)[38]

After his return from the hospital, in early September, Malcolm's mind was better than it had been for years, and he returned to "October Ferry." Five months later, however, in an unpublished letter dated 22 February 1957 he wrote to Markson that it was difficult work "picking up your charred smithereens or even bright illuminations and piecing them together, especially when they often seem to mean bugger all."

Most of the parts written in England are "tangential" flashes of inspiration. They are situated in Eridanus but deal with the problem of drinking: the physiological process of alcohol, its relation to mysticism, its habit-forming aspect, and the consequences of trying to break the habit either by force or by will-power. Some pages are almost illegible scribbles, but others are carefully revised and rewritten in longhand four or five times. The longest text with continuous foliation to be reconstructed from the scattered bits and pieces consists of sixty-six tightly written pages (with extensive revisions and alternative drafts) dealing with the beach in Eridanus during a visit by Angus McCandless; the conversation soon moves into a discussion of Lamb's essay "Confessions of a Drunkard" (in *The Essays of Eliah*), which claims that, in the case of drinking, "the remedy [is] simple. Abstain!" But Lamb also knew from experience that the first steps might be "a process comparable to flaying alive" and that, therefore, "the weakness that sinks under such struggles" cannot be "confounded with the pertinacity which clings to other vices." Another holograph text of thirty-six pages (UBC SC 18:8), with the heading "Either for dialogue or imagery," was later mixed up with other fragments and not recognized as a unit when the posthumous edition was prepared. Other, more legible excerpts were typed out and inserted in the novel.[39]

Standing on the porch of his cabin in Eridanus and looking out over the inlet, Ethan opens his speech to an imaginary audience of Alcoholics Anonymous with a variation on the first chapter of St John: "In the beginning in some sense was Alcohol." Ethan considers himself "a poet set aside to proclaim God's revelation" and to warn the people against the coming of the "Alcoholocaust" (11C). As soon as he starts speaking about the situation of Eridanus, the tone of Ethan's speech becomes very serious:

Señor, Lord, I wish to be your disciple, I say to you passionately, you are in need of disciples, or at least interpreters ... the birds had their nests you said ... but here they cut down the trees with the young birds in them ... Has not this landscape a right to exist? ... Do not they kill you when they pollute the water ... needlessly evict a fisherman from the little shack he loves. Hear Us O Lord From Heaven Thy Dwelling Place. Is it well ... that because the suffering is unendurable ... we take to drink to stop the suffering?   (11E-12)

Of the holograph pages from the England period, only a few are real revisions of the existing drafts of "October Ferry." One such text is a new draft of the grade-crossing section, the passage where the real trouble for Lowry started when he added Cordwainer's suicide to TS 5; this caused the first 27 pages to proliferate into the 246 pages of the unfinished TS 6, which ended with the grade-crossing section. In the new draft for this seventh version of "October Ferry" Lowry inserted the horror of "death-in-life," a motif in the Perilous Chapel section: "The Five o'clock gin gave the meaning to the whole day. At night there were barbiturates and perhaps even benzedrine." "He felt like a man who is told by a fortune-teller that he is going to commit suicide one day" (UBC SC 21:5, 13). The holograph now includes pages with Malcolm's own old letters of apology to Margerie, his excuses, his promises of a new start – with the names Malcolm and Margerie barely changed into Ethan and Jacqueline, and the date untouched in an "Oath to Higher Self" of Easter Sunday 1951. The critic may wonder what this has to do with the ferry trip to Gabriola. But for Lowry the book, in its own idiosyncratic way, was also a story about love drowned in oceans of alcohol and guilt.

Some people have seen Lowry as primarily an alcoholic or a psycho-path who, in his later years, kept writing as a form of occupational therapy. The "October Ferry" manuscripts, however, show him as a romantic who tried to express, through the magic of language, his glimpses of immortality, as well as the horror and pain in the human heart and soul. Like the Consul he knew that "right through hell there is a path," and in the Perilous Chapel the suffering became "almost like ecstasy." Lowry considered himself an outcast in this world, a rejected page of God's unfinished novel, "crumpled up into a tight little ball and hurled overboard into a kind of whirling cosmic waste-paper basket ... together with bits of the discarded scenery we perhaps originally existed in" (England notes, 11A). His only defence against the failure of his existence was to rewrite his life. In "October Ferry" the protagonist is in search of a new paradise, but he has boarded Charon's boat, the "spectral ferry between earth and the unbeholden land."

If the novel itself did not become what Lowry had hoped for, and what the critics had expected, then perhaps it is fitting at the conclusion of this study of the "October Ferry" manuscripts to allow the author to say what he *tried* to do. He did this in the form of a prayer, when he reached a complete impasse in his writing:

Dear Lord God, I earnestly pray you to help me order this work, ugly chaotic and simple though it may seem to be, in a manner that is acceptable in Thy sight, thus, so it seems to my imperfect and disordered brain, at the same time fulfilling the highest canon of art, yet breaking new ground, where necessary, & old rules: it must be tumultuous, stormy, full of thunder, the exhilarating works of God must sound through it, pronouncing hope for man, yet it also must be balanced, grave, full of tenderness & compassion, & human: the writer himself being full of sin he cannot escape occasionally false paranoiac concepts, following will-o'-the-wisps down wrong paths, if left to himself: please – I feel you need writers – let me be truly that servant in making this a great and beautiful thing, & if my motives for writing it be obscure, & the words at present scattered & often meaningless, please forgive me for this.   (UBC SC 20:23)

NOTES

1 Unless otherwise indicated, the information in this study of the "October Ferry" mss is based on research conducted in the Malcolm Lowry Manuscript Collection at the University of British Columbia during two extended investigations in 1970–71 and 1984 and a shorter period in 1987. Documentation for the general chronology of the manuscripts is presented in Victor Doyen, "Fighting the Albatross of Self: A Genetic Study of the Literary Work of Malcolm Lowry," PhD Katholieke Universiteit Leuven 1973, and deposited in the Lowry Collection.

   Sincere gratitude is due to the late Mrs Margerie Lowry for permission to quote manuscript material, to the Belgian Nationaal Fonds voor Wetenschappelijk Onderzoek for financial assistance, to the Katholieke Universiteit Leuven for research time, to Anne Yandle and the staff of UBC Special Collections for turning the scholar's den into an Eridanus, and to Sherrill Grace and the participants of the 1987 Malcolm Lowry Symposium for their encouragement to continue on a voyage that never ends.

2 Winters in Dollarton were not always as mild and idyllic as the first one in 1940. From 1944 the Lowrys left the beach during the winter each time they could afford it.

3 Unpublished letters are identified by date and addressee, and can be located in "An Inventory to the Malcolm Lowry Manuscript Collections in the Library of the University of British Columbia – Special Collections Division," prepared by Judith O. Combs, 1973, revised by Cynthia Sugars, 1985.

4 See Alfred McKee's reminiscence in Sheryl Salloum, *Malcolm Lowry: Vancouver Days* (Madeira Park, BC: Harbour Publishing Co. 1987), 44–51, and Salloum's maps with keys to Lowry's Dollarton and Gabriola Island.

5 A later draft of this passage appears in the chapter "Ocean Spray" of *October Ferry to Gabriola* (New York and Cleveland: World Publishing 1970), 252. Subsequent page references to this edition (abbreviated *October Ferry*) will appear parenthetically in the text. To make a distinction between the constantly growing manuscript story and the published text, the former will always be given between quotation marks ("October

Ferry to Gabriola" or, abbreviated, "October Ferry"). The chart in Appendix 1 indicates the corresponding page numbers in the different manuscript versions as well as the 1970 hardbound edition and the 1970 Penguin edition. The two- by five-inch notebook can be found in the Malcolm Lowry Collection (UBC SC 20:34). The pages are unfoliated; 9 are in Margerie's hand, 37 were written by Malcolm, including (at the end of the notebook) a 17–page outline for a story entitled "October Ferry to Gabriola."

6 The oldest story draft is a 26–page rough typescript on brown paper (UBC SC 21:1, 1–26). A clear typescript of this text (21:2, 1–28) was sent to Matson. Both the rough ts and the clear copy were made after the trip to Haiti, as is clear from a text reference to Porte-au-Prince.

7 *October Ferry*, 204. Only in later versions will the negative connotations of some of these names be explored.

8 The text says (without further explanation) that, after years of separation, Ethan now "really was back, they were miraculously together" (8); in the later versions they have been separated by the war.

9 According to Canadian law at the time, a "beer parlour" was strictly divided into a "Men's" bar and a "Ladies and Escorts" section; therefore, Ethan has to move from one side to the other.

10 A detailed description of this ferry, the Atrevida, with its "capacity of 70 tons or six cars and fifteen tons," can be found in June Lewis-Harrison, *The People of Gabriola* (Cloverdale, BC: Friesen & Sons 1982), 211–13.

11 The association in Ethan's mind between his first sea voyage and the present ferry trip might suggest a subconscious fear that the romance of Gabriola could turn into "platitudinous reality," but that is not worked out in this story. In later versions of this passage it is not Ethan himself but his younger brother who made that first voyage to Norway; and from the fourth version onwards this voyage led to his brother's death (*October Ferry* 312–13).

12 The flashback starts on page D of a new draft of the beer parlour section ("Nine years ago in the spring, the two figures having followed the path") and continues for 38 pages, up to "H after Z." On page "F after Z" the flashback stops and the text returns to the present situation in the Ocean Spray.

13 See unpublished letters to Matson, 29 Oct. and 23 Nov. 1951, and SL 266–8.

14 Letter to Erskine, late March 1952, not Spring 1953, as stated in SL 330.

15 From personal communication with William McConnell; see also McConnell's reminiscence in Salloum, *Malcolm Lowry*, 110–22.

16 This typescript has a (typed) heading "(Margieversion)" on the first page. Since practically all the material of this ts can be traced to sources in Malcolm's hand, this does not mean that Margerie actually "wrote" the new

text. It rather seems to indicate that she was allowed here to choose between existing alternatives. Normally she would literally follow Malcolm's latest handwritten draft and comment on this text on separate pages.

17 Letter to Erskine, 22 Feb. 1953, not 1952 as Douglas Day suggested in "Malcolm Lowry: Letters to an Editor," *Shenanandoah* 15, no. 3 (Spring 1964): 10.

18 The second part of the ts was made after the February 1953 letter to Erskine: Margerie typed page 14 on the verso of the rough draft of this letter (UBC SC 20:6). In this ts 4, part 1 covers 118 pages, part 2 79 pages.

19 Lowry's text is a free paraphrase from a passage on "The Sick Soul" in William James, *Varieties of Religious Experience* (New York: Modern Library 1902), 13. In this context James stresses the contrast between the positivistic outlook and the religious experience, a view that corresponds to the new thematic development of "October Ferry."

20 In his clipping files Lowry kept a selection of real-estate advertisements. The text of his "Garden of Eden" and "Sound of the Sea!" (*October Ferry* 244) "ads" are taken, almost literally, from the *Vancouver Sun*, 25 October 1952, 45 and 47. In Lowry's presentation the hyperbolic advertising language acquires an ironic twist: "GARDEN OF EDEN! THIS WON'T LAST LONG!"

21 This whole page about astrology was accidentally dropped from the posthumous edition, so that the reference to the McCandless appears out of context (*October Ferry* 223).

22 On 8 January 1953 Lowry mentioned to Matson that "October Ferry" had "to be prevented from greedily gulping the material" of "the short intermezzo *Eridanus*" (SL 328).

23 In TS 4, a fragment of the section "Twilight of the Dove" (already typed on 79–80) is accidentally retyped in the section "Twilight of the Raven," in the middle of the description of the last morning of the condemned person. This explains the overlapping in the published version, *October Ferry* 225 and 263–4.

24 Lowry kept some of these newspaper reports in a clipping file (UBC SC 20:36). The imaginary hanging scene at the beginning of the "Twilight of the Raven," where Ethan identifies with a condemned murderer rising to a summons on his last morning, is an almost literal quotation from the *Vancouver Sun* description of the execution of Frederick Ducharme on 14 July 1950. The idea to use them in "October Ferry" may have been triggered by another execution taking place on 20 January 1953, while Lowry was writing this fourth version of his novel.

25 In the fictional transformation the boy and the girl are both fifteen, so as to fit the picture of adolescence described by Hesse. The real date of 11 December is changed to 13 December (a more ominous date for Lowry). In a working draft Lowry changed the real name Francis Sykes into Hugh

Sykes-Davies, the name of a Cambridge friend. He preserved part of that private joke in the name Roy Davies, which he used throughout the rest of the manuscripts. (The other names appearing in the published edition are posthumous changes.)

26 The posthumous edition does not have this new reaction to the reprieve (see *October Ferry* 325); the text follows TS 3, 1–8, for the beginning of the second part, then continues with TS 4, 25–74, and concludes with TS 3, 26–9 (see the chart of the mss in Appendix 1). The name Hangman's Point is Lowry's fictional variation on Gallows Point, the real name of the southernmost point of Protection Island, which the Gabriola ferry has to pass. When the Llewelyns were looking through the window in the beer parlour the waiter told them that Gabriola was "just beyond Hangman's Point – nice name isn't it?" (TS 5, part 1, 66).

27 Letter to Erskine, 11 April 1953 (not 1952, as suggested by Day). The Perilous Chapel allusion refers to Thomas Mann, "The Making of *The Magic Mountain*," *Atlantic Monthly* 191 (January 1953): 41–5.

28 For a lively account of this week (as perceived by an outsider), see the reminiscences by Gloria Onley, Norman Newton, and Noel Stone in Salloum, *Malcolm Lowry*, 80–94.

29 TS 5 was copied directly from TS 4 without an intermediate holograph draft, and consists of part 1:1–109; part 2:1–39, and TS 4:45–79. The second part of TS 5 is not completely retyped. TS 5:39, is a half-page of which the last line corresponds with the last line of TS 4:44.

30 See M. C. Bradbrook, *Malcolm Lowry: His Art & Early Life* (Cambridge: Cambridge UP 1974), 113–16. The fictional character Cordwainer is a composite of Fitte (who gassed himself) and a Cambridge amateur conjurer who accidentally strangled himself when experimenting with knots. For the echoes of the former incident in Lowry's unpublished manuscripts, see V. Doyen, "Fighting the Albatross of Self," 15–16 and 191–3.

31 Lowry himself entitled this 19–page holograph "The Perilous Chapel" (UBC SC 21:17, E–W). A detailed description of Einar's house at the end of the text (V) indicates that this fictional transformation of his own alcohol-inspired ordeal in the Perilous Chapel was written after his recovery at the Neilsons' place.

32 *October Ferry* 158. Where the text remains unchanged, page references will from now on be given to the published version.

33 See TS 7:11–26; the structural and symbolic function is less clear in the printed version, where large parts have been cut. For a further discussion of the role of films in "October Ferry," see Sherrill Grace, *The Voyage That Never Ends* (Vancouver: UBC Press 1982), 88–90.

34 There is so little difference between TS 6 (working copy on brown paper) and its clear copy (TS 7) that for practical purposes we consider them the same *version*. But the *carbon* of this clear copy is the basis for the revisions

and refoliations of *version seven*. To solve this terminological problem, TS 7 is used for the clear copy sent to the publisher, while TS 7B refers to the carbon copy on which Lowry makes revisions (in Dollarton in 1954, and England in 1956–57) for version seven.

In TS 6 the numbers 89–102 are missing, but the text is complete. This indicates that Margerie first typed TS 6 up to 88, and then later continued with the foliation of TS 7. The following chart illustrates the correspondence among the TSS 5, 6, and 7 (see also Appendix 1):

TS 5	TS 6	TS 7	
1	1	1	TS 7: 1–102, mailed on 14 Oct. 1953 (later chaps. 1–11)
↓	↓	↓	
8	88	102	
	103	103	TS 7: 103–112, mailed on 31 October 1953 (later chap. 12)
↓	↓	↓	
	112	112	
	113	113	TS 7: 113–59, mailed in November 1953 (later chaps. 13–17)
9	↓	↓	
	152	159	
↓	153	160	TS 7: 160–206 ("The Element Follows You"), mailed on
11	↓	↓	26 January 1954 (later chaps. 18–21)
	191	206	
	192		TS 6: 192–246, working ts typed after 22 May 1954; no
↓	↓		clear copy was made of this ts (later chaps. 22–26).
27	246		
28	247		TS 6: 247–56D, covers the revised version of the grade-
↓	↓		crossing section (later chap. 27).
30	256D		
31			TS 5: 31–109, covers the rest of the original part 1 (later
↓			chaps. 28–32).
109			

35 Charles Fort, *The Book of Charles Fort* (New York: Henry Holt 1941). This omnibus contains *The Book of the Damned* (1919), *New Lands* (1923), *Lo!* (1931), *Wild Talents* (1932), and an index that makes it possible to check which events happened on the same day. Margerie's dedication in Lowry's copy refers to their 1953 wedding anniversary.

36 *October Ferry*, 146–7. In Poe's essay "Mesmeric Revelation" the dying Mr Vankirk reveals in his hypnotic sleep that "there are gradations of matter of which man knows nothing" and that "the ultimate or unparticled matter" is God. Therefore "thought" is "matter in motion." *Complete Works* v, ed. J.A. Harrison (New York: A.M.S. 1965 [1902]), 241–54.

37 Lowry here quoted the last line of "The Wheel of Fire" (TS 5:54), the chapter that followed immediately after the grade-crossing section.

38 In version 3 the ferry trip took place in October 1946; the protagonists
were married in 1934; their son was born in 1936; the second house burned
down in April 1945, after Ethan's return from a short trip to France for his
law firm; they moved to Vancouver in May 1945 and settled down in Eridanus in June 1945. In version 4 the date of the ferry trip was 1947; the
second house burned down in November 1945; they moved to Vancouver in
January 1946 and to Eridanus in July 1946. In TSS 6 and 7 (which covered
only the first section of the novel) the ferry trip took place in 1949, the
marriage in 1938; the son was born in 1940; the house burned down in May
1946, after Ethan's one-year stay in France as a soldier; they then immediately moved to Vancouver and, one year later, in May 1947, to Eridanus.

39 The following fragments of this text were inserted, rather haphazardly, in
the posthumous edition of the novel:
   • 4 appears on 170–1 ("Colleagues, Criminals and Escorts");
   • 11B appears on 84 ("It is an esoteric lightning");
   • part of 11C appears on 84–5 ("Dear Universe");
   • a paragraph of 11E appears on 83 ("Señor, Lord").
In the posthumous editing process (started in 1963) some smaller sections
were edited as short stories or separate chapters: the grade crossing, the
beer parlour, the section about the mysterious fires (the latter was published
as "The Element Follows You Around, Sir" by *Show* magazine in March
1964). For legal reasons the name of the boy, Roy Davies, was changed
three times. This is still visible in the book version (46: Chambers; 93–4:
Richard Chapman; 162, 168: Richard Chester). For the later part of the
novel TSS 5, 4, and 3 were used, but they had a different chronology. This
problem was not completely straightened out in the book version (for
example, the age of Tommy). For the conclusion of the novel TS 3 was
chosen rather than 4, so that the separation from Eridanus is more final
than in the latest version Lowry wrote. This was probably not a mistake
but an editorial option.

APPENDIX I: SIMPLIFIED CHART OF "OCTOBER FERRY" VERSIONS

	Different versions 1946–1957						Posthumous edition						
	1946	1947	1950–51	1952	1953–54	1956–57	1963–64	1969	1970	1979	Chap.	Title
	0	1	2	3	4	5	6	7	[8]	[9]	World	Peng.	Chap.	Title

PART 1

NOTEBOOK	1946 (0)	1947 (1)	1950–51 (2)	(3)	1952 (4)	1953–54 (5)	(6)	1956–57 (7)	1963–64 [8]	1969 [9]	1970 World	1979 Peng.	Chap.	Title
N		1–2	1–2	1–2	1	[1]	[1]	1		1	3	9	Ch. 1	Greyhound
O					6	[6]		4		5	7	12	Ch. 2	Magician
T							11	10		10	12	16	Ch. 3	Outward
E							20	12		13	14	18	Ch. 4	Isn't Life
B							31	24		19	19	23	Ch. 5	Devilishe
O							43	35	11	27	26	29	Ch. 6	Niagara
O							53	49	17	35	33	36	Ch. 7	Grey Hair
K							63	62		45	41	44	Ch. 8	Really
							68	74		53	48	51	Ch. 9	Called
					7	[7]	80	81		60	52	55	Ch. 10	Hound
					8	8	87	94	21	72	62	65	Ch. 11	Eridanus
							113	101		80	68	71	Ch. 12	Niagara
								113		92	76	79	Ch. 13	Tides
					9	9	117	119	21	99[A]	83	85	Ch. 14	Bottle
					10	10	126	129	29	111	93	95	Ch. 15	Isn't Life
							137	142		124	102	104	Ch. 16	Lake
							148	155	39	138	111	113	Ch. 17	House
						11	152	159	41	142	114	116	Ch. 18	Element
							161	171		155	124	125	Ch. 19	Fire
							169	181		166	132	132	Ch. 20	Wandering
							191	206		192	151	151	Ch. 21	Go West

1946 (0)	1947 (1)	1950–51 (2)	1950–51 (3)	1952 (4)	1953–54 (5)	(6)	1956–57 (7)	1963–64 [8]	1969 [9]	1970 World	1979 Peng.	Chap.	Title
						192	MSS 1–66		193	152	152	Ch. 22	A Little
					12	204			206	164	164	Ch. 23	Adam
				11	16	213	1–36		215	173	173	Ch. 24	Wretched
				15	17	222	MS inserts		223	181	181	Ch. 25	But Still
	2		3	17	18	231			231	190	190	Ch. 26	Stalked
	3	3	4	25	28	247–56	MSS 1–18	1–13	247	205	205	Ch. 27	Knots
*	5	4	6	31	31				257	217	217	Ch. 28	Wheel
*	8	8	9	48	55			1–9	272	233	232	Ch. 29	Bastion
		11	16	68	65		1–8	1–17	286	247	245	Ch. 30	Ocean
	11	15D	21	79	74				298	255	253	Ch. 31	Raven
		19	23–30	101–18	94–109				317	272	270	Ch. 32	Dove

PART 2

1946 (0)	1947 (1)	1950–51 (2)	1950–51 (3)	1952 (4)	1953–54 (5)	(6)	1956–57 (7)	1963–64 [8]	1969 [9]	1970 World	1979 Peng.	Chap.	Title
*	15	26	1	1	1				330	285	283	Ch. 33	Dock
*	21	34	9	27	24				340	294	292	Ch. 34	Outward
		(34)	12	38	33–39				350	303	301	Ch. 35	Perilous
*	22	36		48					358	311	309	Ch. 36	Not the
	26 27–8	45–56 27–8	20–29	64–79		[MS] E-W			369–379	323–333	320–329	Ch. 37	Uberimae

Different versions 1946–1957 · *Posthumous edition*

KEY TO APPENDIX I

Readers familiar with the published version of *October Ferry* will recognize, in the last four columns of this chart, the chapter headings,
chapter numbers, and page numbers of two book versions (World Publishing Co. 1970, and Penguin 1979).

The *first* column of the chart refers to the *notebook* in which Malcolm
and Margerie jotted down their impressions during the 1946 trip to
Gabriola Island. (Asterisks in this column refer to notebook entries used
in the story.)

Version 1 is the 28-page short story jointly written by Malcolm and
Margerie in 1947.

Version 2 (58 pp) is Lowry's revision in the fall of 1950, incorporating
the eviction theme and lyric descriptions of Eridanus. For the conclusion
he used the last pages (27–8) of the previous version.

Version 3 (30 + 29 pp) redistributes the exposition and adds the
protagonist's legal background and the loss of three previous houses.

Version 4 (118 + 79 pp) is written in the summer and fall of 1952
and elaborates especially the hanging and drinking motifs.

Version 5 (109 + 39 pp) is an incomplete TS, made in the winter of
1952–53 and using the text of TS 4:45–79 for the later part of the story
(see n29). It was meant as an "almost clear" copy of TS 4; but then Lowry
added the suicide motif to the grade-crossing section (28–30), and the
Perilous Chapel motif to the end of part 2 (see version 6, E–W).

Version 6: These inserts forced him to rewrite the entire exposition.
Throughout 1953 the first 28 pages of version 5 expanded into a TS of
more than 250 pages (TS 6) and turned the voyage to Gabriola into a
quest for identity and truth. Lowry's energy broke when Random House
ended the contract, in January 1954, and Margerie stopped typing the
clear copy (TS 7) after page 206.

Version 7: In England Malcolm made tentative revisions on his carbon
copy of TS 7 and wrote new holograph sections about Eridanus and
alcoholism (MS 1–66; 1–36) and new versions of the grade-crossing section
(MS 1–18; 1–8), but was unable to revise the later part of the work.

Posthumous versions (8 and 9): Margerie began the posthumous edition
of *October Ferry* in 1963. In a *first* stage she worked on Lowry's annotated
carbon copy of TS 7, retyping some of the pages but mostly using
refoliated pages of the old TS.

In a *second* stage (version 8) Margerie apparently considered the possibility of publishing parts of the book as separate stories or sections:
– Drastic cuts in the first 159 pages of TS 7 reduced this part of the novel
  to one-fourth of its original length (TS 8:1–41).

– The rest of TS 7 (159–206) was edited as the story "The Element Follows You Around, Sir" (published by *Show* magazine in March 1964).
– The grade-crossing section (TS 6:247–56) was edited from several over-lapping drafts into a 13–page story.
– Also parts of the Ocean Spray section (TS 5:65–93) were edited as separate stories: 1–9; 1–17.

In a *third* stage (version 9) Margerie went back to the original 159 pages of TS 7 for the first 17 chapters of the novel. For chapters 18–20 she used the edited TS of the story "The Element Follows You Around, Sir." The rest of part 1 is based on TS 6:191–256 (for chaps. 22–7), and TS 5:31–109 (for chaps. 28–32). In this later part of the new TS 9 she incorporated the pages that had already been typed out as short stories (but this led to the confusion of names described in n39).

When Margerie reached the original part 2 of the novel she was con-fronted with a new problem. Not only did this part use a different chronology for the story (see n38); the various drafts had become so mixed-up that it was not easy to find out what belonged together and what came first. As a result the posthumous edition does not use the latest version (TS 5:1–39, completed with TS 4:45–79) but a mixture of TS 3 and TS 4: chap. 33 is based on TS 3:1–8; chaps. 34–7 follow the text of TS 4:25–77; but the conclusion of the novel goes back to the earlier version of TS 3:26–9, with its more radical separation from Eridanus.

The chapter titles of part 1 are based on handwritten suggestions made by Lowry, but at the time of his death these titles were still tentative. Those of part 2 are editorial additions. Although the title of chap. 35 seems to suggest that "The Perilous Chapel" section is included in the posthumous edition, this crucial holograph (version 6, E–W) was never typed out. Of the handwritten revisions and inserts made in England (listed in italics under version 7) only a few excerpts are included in the published book (see n39).

Insert for "October Ferry" written in England, 1957 (UBC SC 18:8)

APPENDIX III: TRANSCRIPTION
OF HOLOGRAPH PAGE 11A
FROM THE "OCTOBER FERRY" MSS

TRANSCRIPTION OF THE MAIN TEXT

It is perhaps curious to note that Alcohol, on the purely chemical level (and which one might remark reasonably is so productive of biological & neurological breakdown in man) is itself produced by the biological breakdown of larger molecules found in nature, the agents being the enzymes, living catalysts, present in bacteria or moulds, so that the process of fermenting is similar to decay, rotting, composting etc (Kenneth Hutton, Conquest of Materials) but is more carefully controlled. But while we are talking about the breakdown of molecules, & before we get back to grandmother's penicilline, this might be the point to raise the question how life, on this chemical level may be held to have begun on earth at all. The Cabbalists hold that life descended from God, Kether, to Man, or the Earth, Malkuth, by a flash of lightning and that man's task is to retrace that path of God's lightning back again to God.

[Insert] On the face of it there seems about as much sense in this as saying it is the moon's task – and some people are afraid she may indeed feel it to be so – to retrace her path back to the earth with catastrop[h]ic results to both concerned. Yet indeed, for once having created us, and left (discarded) us here, typographical errors, dirty dusty unfinished pages and sentences, rejectementa of every kind that we are, all crumpled up (as) into a tight little ball and hurled overboard into a kind of whirling cosmic wastepaper basket (that is at the same time a sort of compost heap) condensed around us to make sure, incidentally, we don't come bouncing back together with bits of the discarded scenery we perhaps originally existed in, given us to provide us maybe with the illusion that we still do, what possible use we can dream of would God have for us, & what possible purpose would there be in the coming back, unless it was to take revenge, or to give thanks, which given in this manner might seem (were) a worse revenge still: something like reminding a novelist of his first novel he hoped everyone had forgotten & their adding insult to injury by saying we still thought it was brilliant [end of insert].

It has been the case, I gather, – or may be allowed to assume. The few Cabbalists who, on their own terms, & according to the special reality of the Cabbala itself, however, may have performed this titanic task, which is one of huge self-sacrifice & discipline, without having succumbed to the use of black magic on the way (known in the Quabbala as sod, a Hebrew word meaning the abuse of wine) have found that they

have, far from having drawn any nearer to God, much less approached Him, succeeded in creating a kind of world within this one on their own account; a world that works, as it were, but nonetheless an imaginary one: no matter how ostensibly selfless the motive, or ascetic the discipline, as with Roland in the Valley of Roncevalles somehow or other the blot of personal pride & vanity has finished the sentence that was beginning to be fair: spiritually these men became hugely developed, developed powers beyond our knowledge, but once having achieved the goal their only reward was to have to wait for other less gifted to catch up; (in this state of suspension) those of us (of you) who are going to catch up at all that is, and what they may do, in that state of suspension aloft, half Gods and supermen but more powerless than an imbecile, one cannot know because their human intelligence has [been] cast off from them as ballast by these most intrepid of all precarious & dangerous – yet who is one to say vain? – of all bal[l]oon ascents ([variant] by these most intrepid of all aeronauts on that most precarious & dangerous – yet who is one to say vain? – of all voyages [bal(l)oon ascents]):
but meantime we have been left with the lightning. It is an esoteric lightning too, like the magical powers, and there is the danger that in talking of it we may seem to be trying to render the esoteric exoteric which, while seemingly the most human, it maybe is in fact the essential proliferating folly of man, though how shall we be sure of this if we take as anything like fact what I have described as actually happening to an esoteric individual who practises sternly what he preaches only to his initiates? Be this as it may, fortunately for my logic, the lightning no longer scrawls in the void whose secrets are known only to mystics, who, as Barbey d'Aurevilly said, like the lobster know the secrets of the sea & do not bark – but via Dr. S.L. Miller, of Columbia University – ah, that mystic world Columbia that will keep cropping up ...

Hear us O Lord and Lowry's Micro/Macro Text

ELSA LINGUANTI

Like most devoted readers of Lowry I have developed my own opinions about which have to be considered the important and definitive works among all the many and often mixed-up papers he left when he died. After a few years of work on his published and unpublished works I find that I am ready to consider *Under the Volcano*, a couple of versions of *Lunar Caustic*, and the collection of short stories *Hear us O Lord from heaven thy dwelling place* as *the* bulk of literary production that Lowry has left to his readers, a bulk to which the papers so admirably collected at the Special Collections Division of the library at the University of British Columbia only add an impressive amount of material that makes the reader aware of the tremendous potential the man still had. This does not mean that I think it not worth working on those materials – I am sure that I have not yet finished with "Ghostkeeper," for example, and I would still like to work on the script for *Tender Is the Night*. It only means that the works I have mentioned are not only individual works of interest, success, and beauty, but also that they constitute a macrotext. I leave aside the unprofitable question of what the macrotext would be like if Lowry had completed other works, which he did not, and of how the "case would be altered" by them.

A collection of works can be considered a macrotext when elements belonging to different organizing systems within the individual works – diegetical, structural, formal, ideological, linguistic, semantic, rhetorical, etc. – are so combined in the collection as to produce an integrated unity, and when there is a form of process and progress in the discourse so that every single text can only be where it is and not anywhere else in the succession.[1]

If we start by thinking about *Hear us O Lord*, it is easy to see, and everyone has noticed, that, as Lowry wrote to Giroux, "it is a canon, or roundelay, with everyone taking up his part, dropping out, new voices joining in and dropping out, without beginning or ending" (UBC SC 3:1). It is also true, as Lowry explained, that the seven stories are "interrelated, correlated ... but full of effects and dissonances that are impossible in a short story" (SL 28). The movement is like that of a jazz suite and is based on an irregular, not linear, development of the themes, on the repetition of refrains, on occasional improvised a-solos, on self-quotation and self-parody, sonorities and brooding passages, sophisticated harmonies and strutting syncopations. The reader is given a series of clues that key him or her in to some of the codes operating through the collection.

At the beginning and at the end jazz is evoked: in the first "ouverture" story (I think it was Christine Pagnoulle who so titled it in her beautiful chapter "En terre de miracles"),[2] after the strident discord of a loud-speaker "enthroned on a wagon" which "barked from the city," and the sound "as of a wailing and gnashing of teeth" of the sawmills, the Suspension Bridge comes into view as part of a musical score: "the road now mounting towards the Suspension Bridge in the distance much as a piece of jazz music mounts towards a break" (HOL 16) – and then: "through whose branches ... could be made out, from time to time, suggesting a fragment of music manuscript, a bit of the Suspension bridge itself" (HOL 17).[3] At the end in "Forest Path to the Spring," of course, the protagonist is a jazz musician and music becomes the all-embracing energy, drive, the model of all movement, transformation, integration, and even the tides and currents in the sea become analogous to music: "not music but having the effect of music" (278), substantiating the protagonist's symphony and the jazz opera he writes.

Between the first and the last story there are more links: the young couple of "Bravest Boat," "laughing and stumbling ... arm in arm" (25) anticipate the anonymous couple of the final story whom we last see in a similar way: "laughing we stooped down to the stream and drank" (287). The subjects stated at the outset in one voice are taken up again by other voices until striking themes of strongly marked character pervade the entire fabric, entering now in one voice, now in another.

After the softness of "Bravest Boat," "Through the Panama" strikes a jarring note, but it does so while at the same time imitating or duplicating, in contrapuntal thinking, the themes presented in the first voice: we have again the voyage of a ship, a man and a wife, the new beginnings at the end ("out of the past finally to safety and a home" and, all around, "a seething of spring" [25] become, by permutation, "dawn, and an albatross, bird of heaven, gliding astern" [98]), and repeated mentions of hell and paradise. Within "Through the Panama" the repetition of the phrase "the whole is an assembly of apparently incongruous parts" refers to the ship engaged in the voyage from Vancouver to England through the canal (the ship is French, built by Americans, with a crew of Bretons), to the canal (built by Frenchmen, Englishmen, Americans, and the eight hundred Chinese who, deprived of opium for "moral" reasons, have let themselves die along its banks), to the protagonist, who is a Scot and a Norwegian, who is Wilderness, Trumbaugh, and Firmin, who progressively identifies with a voice, a lock of the canal, and the ship itself. This key phrase, of course, also refers to "Through the Panama" as text.

"Through the Panama" is a tremendous achievement: nowhere else is the dictum we all believe in today that form is content so perfectly embodied. The text is the voyage as it unfolds, organized but also subject to many unexpected events; it is a diary that is a work-in-progress; it is the novel the man is writing, which is still subject to changes; it is the canal, which is also transformed into fiction by both the historian and the novelist. Also the text parades its texture, the apparently incongruous parts of which it is made slipping past one another: fragments of the *Ancient Mariner*, a history book, the two columns unfolding with reciprocal substitution from left to right, the independent lines flowing alongside each other as happens in polyphonic music. But as the ship has a ceinture put around it, so the story is there, and exactly where it is, gliding on, the tortured form still containing it. In following the different planes of movement, the reader becomes aware of the illusion of space which it is the unique capacity of counterpoint to create, and of the tensions brought into being by the simultaneous unfolding of the lines.

The three following stories all take place in Rome, but the protagonists come from and will go back to Eridanus, with the exception of the protagonist of the central story – the central story of the three and of the collection – Cosnahan, whose topological reference points are the Isle of Man and Nantucket, the first a variant of Eridanus and the second an allusion to Melville.

The first story of the three is an a-solo from an artist away from home; the third is about a man away from home who is feeling ready to go back; in the middle is Cosnahan, completely lost in the maze of the streets of Rome and out of touch with himself. "Elephant and Colosseum" is the pivotal story: sheer fun, pure comedy. It is again a virtuoso piece, like "Through the Panama," and it is a self-parody. While *Under the Volcano* produces and exalts contradictions, and is tragic,

"Elephant and Colosseum" shows that any attempt to reconcile them is comic.

Here again we find the voyage on a ship and the tempest, the artist abroad, the dying-dead mother motif that "Through the Panama" had introduced; here the theme that had come to the fore in "Through the Panama," of the artist enmeshed in his own creation, is taken up in a different register in "Strange Comfort" – where the artist finds a moment of liberating amusement in his own notes and in the similarity of idiosyncratic attitudes and poses between himself and other artists before him: Cosnahan is enmeshed in himself, has illusions and delusions about himself. At the beginning of the story Cosnahan is sitting with a glass of milk and an expression of "sombre panic" (114) at the bar of the Rupe Tarpea restaurant in Via Vittorio Veneto in Rome; at the end, at sunset of the same day, he is sitting at the same place with a bottle of sparkling wine, and he laughs. All through the afternoon the "lone man" has been talking to himself, trying to rationalize his problems, to unravel perplexities, cogitating in a language slow, well-built, logical, almost Ciceronian. Cosnahan has difficulties of various types: linguistic incompetence; antagonism with the traffic in Rome; inability to write (even the letter to his mother, postponed until it is too late, or the letter to his wife); absent-mindedness (he is in Rome to get in touch with his publisher for a translation of his book into Italian, but has forgotten to bring the contract, has forgotten the publisher's name, remembers their address but has got the wrong city); difficulty in recognizing himself and in making himself be recognized: "Nobody recognized him at home (191); those dreamed-of moments of recognition (132); What on earth was he after? (139); What did he know of himself? (146); was he a writer?" (146)

The comedy sets in because of the fundamental predicament of Cosnahan, which consists in the contrast between the illusions he has about himself and the reality of life imposed on him: the appearance is that his book is exceptionally successful, for a high-class audience, that he is a successful man and unique; reality shows to him that his book is one among others, that no one knows it or him either, that he is like everybody else. Forms of "serene confidence" and "quiet elation" make him "entranced by himself" (155), give him a sense of "his own extraordinary rarity" (160): "he smiled pleased by his intelligence and felt much better" (161), but very quickly he begins to feel mean.

Cosnahan's predicament is aptly imaged in the "logical crossing" of the Roman streets he cannot face: illusion/reality, rationality/magic (something running in the family) are divarications that he illusorily tries to mediate.

The mental behaviour the text attributes to Cosnahan, counting on the reader's connivance, is quite naïve, and the syntax obviously organizes it: the syntax of Cosnahan's sentences shows a succession of logical connectives: causal (because, since, for), correlative (both ... and, not only ... but, not merely ... but, no sooner ... but) and comparative (as, so, thus, than), each of which emphatically joins together segments in an apparently faultless organization (125–6). What happens, however, is that many segments introduce diversions regardless of their semantic relevance: the irrelevant diversions engender a perception of the dissociation between the devices and contrivances in Cosnahan's reasoning and the pretence of artlessness and straightforwardness of his prose. The reader sees the process as artificial and funny, while the character produces his statements naïvely. The comic effect is not produced by puns or by the tensions that generate irony in the *Volcano* but by the attempt at rationalizing in an innocent unsophisticated way, with the naïveté and the blindness necessary for the comic element to be born. Cosnahan's discourse operates in the absence of any acknowledgment of possible objections and within a syntactic structure that takes for granted that the chosen techniques of argumentation are adequate to reach logical consequences.

Cosnahan's narcissistic axiologies, whose starting point is, in Aristotelian terms, the "locus of quality," give value to the elite over the mass, to the exceptional over the normal: while considering the possibility of being a "unique case," Cosnahan meets the "endless mirrored reduplications" of his figure among all the others in the street, of his novel among all the other novels on the publishers' bookshelves (but his own is actually missing). At the same time, Cosnahan also gives value to the "locus of quantity" because he thinks that to be appreciated by the greatest number is preferable to being known only to a few.[4] Lowry's decision to make Cosnahan meet the elephant Rosemary and be recognized by her, and to make Cosnahan appreciate the value of the meeting and of the anagnorisis that follows on the basis of a causal link starting from magic intuitions, is so overtly and blatantly discordant and incongruous that the text becomes metalanguage of itself in a transparent way. The comic element sets in in such a gentle fashion that it is as if Lowry were showing himself using the incongruous element to his own ends.

The divarications between the "locus of essence" (according superiority to individuals who best represent the essence of genus) and the "locus of existent," between man and nature, the improper hierarchy among the elements that Cosnahan accepts uncritically, are definitely overthrown when humour replaces seriousness: "Naturam expellas pitch-fork, something or other recurret! Throw out nature with a pitch-fork but back she always comes! It was as if God, with that all-wise sense of humour that Cosnahan respected increasingly the longer he remained as a guest upon His earth, had kept Mother Drumgold ... up His sleeve" (HOL 125). The Latin quotation first mentioned in relation to Cosnahan's mother and her magic powers reappears in the zoo before the elephants' cage. Between tautologies ("Because an elephant, by the way, is an elephant," 163) and hyperboles ("the marvellous juxtaposition of the grotesque and the sublime," 162) the text shows Cosnahan pre-paring to praise the elephant in philosophically constructed sentences:

And an elephant, as itself, within its own paradisal and thundery being as an elephant, among other elephants ... had its own elephantine virtues which ... simply attested ... to a common divinity. Since must there not have been some principle of goodness and sagaciousness first, existing in the elephants' percep-tions, that the elephant was able to recognize too ... some principle of tolerance, or above all pity, for his captor, who could not help himself, and a certain sense of interest in sportive adventure about whatever he was doing that he recognized as amusing and instructive to his elephantish faculties?   (HOL 163–4)

The elephant is proof of God's existence and testimony to God's sense of humour ("his wild wild humour," 162); the elephant is endowed with reason, intellectual powers, and a profound sense of humour ("Freedom was of the spirit. So reasoned the elephant ... with a practiced intellec-tual swirl of [its] trunk ... Moreover watch elephants ... smiling softly to themselves, enjoying at the same time some transcendental joke," HOL 162–4). Above all, "an elephant may serve man, or as a spectacle for man, or as a friend of man, but what he really serves is elephant, his higher elephant" (HOL 164). Cosnahan is ready to reconsider the quotation about "naturam" when Rosemary suddenly welcomes and hails him by trumpeting: "No preposterous recognition in literature ... could have been more complete" (HOL 168). The anagnorisis, "a meet-ing in its gently buffoonish manner nearly sublime" (172), enables Cos-nahan to disentangle himself from his dilemmas, to discover the inconsistencies of his premise, to see the way his own arguments inter-act: he feels himself to be "translated – his mother's son at last – into a conscious member of the human race" (174). The syllogism – all men are unique, all men are similar, then their uniqueness consists in their similarity – becomes explicit in the final litany: "But man was Quayne and man was Quaggan, man was Quillish, man was Qualtrough, man was Quirk and Quayle and Looney, and Illiam Dhone, who had been hanged. And yet lived because he was innocent" (HOL 174).

According to Butor every literary work is a parody of the ones that have preceded it.[5] "Elephant and Colosseum" is obstreperous, flagrant self-parody of the writer of *Under the Volcano*: the protagonist here mentions a brother and a friend; his wife is an actress. There are also the death of the mother, an obsession with the past and the occult, the cat as Lares (Citron-le-taciturne substituted for the Oedipus, Priapus, etc., of the *Volcano*), and the magic cabbalistic elements, although coincidences that were fiendish in *Volcano* become benevolent here. Self-parody can be identified even in small segments of the text: the "broken pillars among which the grass was green" (HOL 129) remind the reader of the "broken pink pillars that might have been waiting to fall down on him";[6] the "truckloads of Italian soldiers" (HOL 148) call up the "boys standing at the back of lorries" (UV 18); the "discovery of Rosemary ... bringing back those days of longing for home at sea" (HOL 170–1) echoes the phrase "his passion for Yvonne had brought back to his heart" (UV 18). Because of its position at the centre of the collection, the comic character of "Elephant and Colosseum" has momentous consequences for the second half of the book: there will be no more "gnashing of teeth" after it, and a gentle mood will set in.

The repetition of themes distributed among various voices and in different registers safeguards the unity of the work, while the constant transformation supplies the element of variety: *Hear us O Lord* has a horizontal narrative implemented by the devices of augmentation, diminution, inversion, and canonic imitation.

After the two minor pieces of "Present Estate" and "Gin and Goldenrod," the form of the canon really sets in with "Forest Path," which is the "triumphant ending" of the collection (SL 266) and "a novella of great seriousness [that] starts gently, so gently" (SL 340). Cosnahan's final choice in favour of the value of the simple human being reappears here even more clearly: the protagonists of the story do not even receive a name. The man is reaching for some meaning that may be grasped subliminally, by means of slow approximation, in a language deliberately clumsy, interspersed with questions, with a subdued discourse scrupulously mimetic of the stages of interiorization. And Cosnahan's nature ("back she always comes") is in the foreground. The writing registers days and nights and seasons as they follow one another, the tempests and the calms, frost and thaw, snow and drizzle and all sorts of weather happenings, real close-ups of illumined surfaces with shafts of pearly colours.

The similes only touch on a series of hieratic-mystic elements: churches, cathedrals, votive lamps (recalling the "alabaster lamp illumined from within" of the dream of the northern paradise in *Volcano*).

The naming process concentrates on flowers and colours, stars and constellations, crystals, diamonds, jewels. The habit of repetition, almost obsessive in *Volcano*, is toned down so that the occasional anaphoric repetition becomes all the more meaningful: "I soon learned," "Eventually I realized," "I learned," "We found," "We discovered." The search for meaning, which is the exact centre from which Lowry's writing radiates, meets the gratification of the slow, progressively diminishing resistance of the external world to the consubstantial appropriation of man. Syntax shows a high frequency of co-ordinated sentences that, at short intervals, introduce elements that are included and integrated in the process, as happens in a canon:

At dusk ... And at dusk ... And on other days   (HOL 216)
But apparently ... But now ... but we   (HOL 239)
And then ... And I thought ... And then I thought   (HOL 258)
And we remembered ... And they seemed ... And the ships ... And the snow
    storms ... And ourselves   (HOL 279–80)

"Less an ordinary book of tales than a sort of novel of an odd aeolian kind itself" (SL 320), *Hear us O Lord* is a kaleidoscope, the same elements reappearing in all the stories in different voices, registers, in contrapuntal form. But it is also an exploration in the process of writing, showing the narrator before the choices he continually has to make in order to give form to his materials: this happens in a dramatic fashion to Wilderness in "Through the Panama" and is shown in a metafictional parodic way in "Elephant and Colosseum," while the artist musician of the "Forest Path" makes use of fragments stranded on the beach (the canister and the ladder are converted to use), despite his declaration that he "lacked spiritual equipment to follow such thoughts through" (282). As if to prefigure the "odd aeolian" form of *Hear us O Lord*, Lowry had written to James Stern in 1940 that, "the best kind of novel ... is the shortish one perfect in itself, and without being full of inventories (like Joyce), or poems (like Faulkner), or conjunctions (like Hemingway), or quotations from quotations (like me 7 years ago) ... a satisfactory work of art by simple process of writing a series of good short stories" (SL 28).
   It is true that intertextuality had been one of the main characteristics of the *Volcano* and of the first version of *Lunar Caustic*. Already in the second version of *Lunar Caustic* many references, allusions and quotations from other texts are dropped, and in their place Lowry uses occasional self-quotation: this will become systematic in *Hear us O Lord*.
   But for all that there is one text that Lowry cannot stop alluding to: Dante's *Divine Comedy*. A miniature reproduction of *The Voyage That Never Ends*, *Hear us O Lord* follows Dante's stages, stopping on the

threshold of earthly paradise. From the "selva selvaggia ad aspra e forte" to the "divina foresta spessa e viva," the journey moves through the hell of "Through the Panama," the purgatory of "Strange Comfort," "Elephant and Colosseum," and "Present Estate," towards paradise in "Forest Path": "it seemed that we were in heaven; there was everywhere an intimation of paradise" (HOL 264). "Bravest Boat" shows the whole pilgrimage in a diminutive form, while Sigbjørn and Primrose of "Through the Panama" are similar to Adam and Eve dismissed from paradise, and Fairhaven, in "Present Estate," suffers from a longing for his lost Eden, which the anonymous protagonist of "Forest Path" has regained.

In the same way as in Laruelle's chapter in the *Volcano*, where the reader can follow Dante's steps down to the Malebolge, so in "Forest Path" the twenty-seventh canto of the *Purgatorio* is always present behind Lowry's choice of material: as the path seems short and less tiring to Dante as he moves towards his Beatrix, so the path seems shorter to the man as he goes back to his wife; Beatrix is made perfect and immortal, and the man's wife does not change and the passing years do not seem to affect her at all. The woman has a Matelda function in the story, teaching the man, showing him the things he cannot see or understand by himself; the protagonist, seeing his own threatening shadow, which appears to him as a projection of the dark side of his being, recalls Dante's shadow appearing as a gloomy stain in the sunlight of purgatory, a dark and sorry recollection of the world. As Dante bathes in the Lete and Eunoè, so the man at sunrise, in the inlet, is transformed: "suddenly transilluminated by the sun's light, so that I seemed to contain the reflected sun deeply within my very soul, yet a sun which ... was in turn transformed ... into something perfectly simple" (HOL 272). He becomes consubstantial with the sun and the light in the water of the bay.

The three Lowry works that I consider central (*Volcano*, *Lunar Caustic*, and the stories) are interrelated, correlated, full of reciprocal effects and dissonances. It is impossible to forget that the dream of a northern paradise in *Volcano* appears in exactly the same terms through *Hear us O Lord*, from the first description in "Bravest Boat" to the nostalgic memories of Wilderness in "Through the Panama" or the vivid presence in "Gin and Goldenrod" and the triumphant, almost word-by-word echoes in "Forest Path." A scene from a Canadian landscape on a calendar set to the future (because it shows the month of December) hangs on the wall in the bedroom of the prostitute in the last chapter of *Volcano*, and even in *Lunar Caustic* there are elements in the description that remind us of "Forest Path."

Also, the macrotext of these three works does show the voyage in its three main stages. If *Volcano* is obviously hell, *Lunar Caustic* is the passage through purgatory, because the man enters the hospital at the beginning – and the door opens with "a dithering crack" – and comes out at the end accompanied by the "roar of the building," which sounds like the earthquake that shakes the purgatorial mountain when a soul is ready to leave it. Plantagenet's predicament could be described as being like Dante's in the *Purgatorio*: "questi non vide mai l'ultima sera / ma per la sua follia le fu si presso / che molto poco tempo a volger era" (1:58–60). From the crowd of patients, two people move towards Plantagenet: in the same way two souls move towards Dante in canto v; Garry and Kalowsky ask Plantagenet to intercede for them ("ombre che pregar pur ch'altri prieghi," vi:26). Like Dante's *Purgatorio*, *Lunar Caustic* is a passage during which the protagonist cauterizes himself (with silver nitrate).

The whole journey is taken up again in *Hear us O Lord*, which ends in an earthly paradise, but the three stages must not be taken literally because experience is always flowing back on itself and starting all over again. The end of "Forest Path" reverses the order of the stages, once again with a contrapuntal technique: "if someone had charged us with the notion that we had gone to heaven and that this was the after life we would not have said him nay for long. Moreover if we had been charged with formerly having been in hell for a while we would probably have had to say yes too, though adding that on the whole we liked that fine ... and were sometimes even homesick for it" (*HOL* 284–5).

The reader, through the experience of the three works mentioned, is enabled to see other shapes taking form in Lowry's macrotext. The associating impulse, the analogical obsession, confines man to a form of indefinite existence in *Under the Volcano*; everything is like everything else and there is no place from where to start again. Incapable of dominating experience, the Consul clings to reality, while reality is introjected in *Lunar Caustic* and possessed by means of consubstantial appropriation in "Forest Path." The whole function of the negative drive (infernal confusion, chaos, discomposure) in *Under the Volcano* is to focus attention on the extenuation of all cultural codes and the radicalization of all contradictions: the wheel, movement without advancement, is the unstable structure from which multiple meanings hang.

Centred on a state of disequilibrium, *Lunar Caustic* is a characteristically incomplete segment, an iterated attempt at finding a way out of the vicious circle; it does not organize meanings in forms of knowledge but projects them into visions that strategically assail the rigid frontiers of conscience, of rationality. In *Hear us O Lord*, however, tensions and conflicts gather and disperse, and the exalted rejoicing of the last story is so organized as to offer a kind of direction by means of the path to the spring and at the same time make clear that no process is ever ended.

NOTES

1 Maria Corti, "Testi o macrotesti?" in *Il viaggio testuale* (Torino: Einaudi 1978), 185–200.

2 Christine Pagnoulle, *Malcolm Lowry: Voyage au fond de nos abîmes* (Lausanne: Editions de l'Age de l'Homme 1977).

3 All references are to the 1961 Penguin edition of the stories and are included in the text.

4 See Lucie Olbrechts-Tyteca, *Le comique du discours* (Editions de l'Université de Bruxelles 1954), and Chaim Perelman & Lucie Olbrechts-Tyteca, *Traité de l'argumentation, La Nouvelle Rhétorique* (Presses Universitaires de France 1958).

5 Michel Butor, "La Critique et l'invention," *Critique* 23, no. 247 (Dec. 1967): 982–95.

6 All references are to the 1963 Penguin edition of *Under the Volcano*.

The Emergence of an Authorial Figure in the Manuscripts of Lowry's Poetry

SUZANNE KIM

In a postface to *Essais de critique génétique* Louis Hay attempts to define the origin and prospects of a new approach to textual criticism through an examination of the various documents, manuscripts, drafts, and typescripts concerning literary text-production.[1]

He first notices that the term *manuscriptologie*, that is, the discourse about manuscripts as *avant-textes*, appeared only recently in lexical terminology, that is, only when the development of a new field in textual research started to yield its fully fledged experts. This definition came rather late, even if interest in "philosophy of composition" or in the initial conditions and the dynamic evolution of what Joyce called "work in progress" was not a new thing in literature. From Goethe, Coleridge, and Poe to T.S. Eliot, literary interest ranged from the inner mental compulsions to the very writing processes that were involved in text-production, in order to reach a deeper comprehension of the secrets involved in the making and meaning of a literary text.[2]

The impetus given to genetic criticism eventually gathered speed with such progress of textual analysis as the New Criticism and "la nouvelle critique" proposed, and also with new methods in the treatment and description of manuscripts. This allowed literary criticism to consider manuscripts as "inscriptions" towards the making and meaning of literary texts. In France this approach to literary criticism took a new turn when a type of Battle of the Ancients and the Moderns, with Raymond Picard and Roland Barthes as respective champions and Serge Doubrovsky as arbiter, raged in Paris in the early sixties. In this debate Barthes' *Sur Racine* (1963) became the butt of Picard's pamphlet *Nouvelle critique ou nouvelle imposture* (1965), to which Doubrovsky rejoined with *Pourquoi la nouvelle critique* (1966). Such disputes about finalities and processes in literary criticism could only be beneficial to the advocates of genetic criticism, who were now able to steer their course between the concepts of totality and transformation, *avant-texte* and text, text and context, necessity and chance or genesis and structure, that is, somewhere between Structuralism and the former practices of literary criticism. Henri Mitterand quite relevantly closes the debate when he concludes his article in *Essais de critique génétique* with the following statement: "Genèse et structure sont des notions non pas contradictoires mais solidaires."[3]

Genetic criticism, therefore, does not mean to deal only with the linguistic aspects of textualization; it also makes use of such concepts and notions as are provided by various epistemic systems endeavouring to define mental cognitive processes or deep psychology, logical patterns or sociological facts and historical events. Thus, rejecting no possibilities, from whatever directions they may spring, genetic criticism is in a position to highlight the interrelationship between text generation and the problems of representation at work in literary manuscripts that are considered adequate fields of investigation because they are both texts in the making and texts likely to describe an unstable reality. A genetician's task might lie, first and foremost, in the recognition of the fundamental flexibility of texts in order to take into account the tricks and traps of thought and work, the organic tension between words and their adequation to endopsychic intentions, as well as to external realities, and to steer a course between this flexibility and scientific rigour in an attempt at defining textual production.

Louis Hay then proceeds, not without a sense of humour, to set down the necessary requirements for a literary genetician to apply his or her talent: first, he or she should be able to pry into a writer's workshop/ backstage/laboratory or whatever word he or she chooses to use to define a place for text-production; second, in order to be able to interpret what is found, he or she should have the proper rhetorical equipment to permit a refining of knowledge about the activities governing text-production. Finally, Hay raises one question and a corollary that, in spite of their simplicity, involve the working methods and the operating efficiency of his original approach: what does a genetician mean by the term "manuscript" and what material does he or she use? In practice the materials are mostly, though not exclusively, handwritten, or manuscripts. For the purpose of a thorough analysis, any kind of "text" prior to the final version will be examined: these include points of documentary research, worknotes, outlines, sketches or scenarios previous to the writing of the text, or intermediate states of the final version consisting of copied drafts or typescripts. The corollary to what material is used is: how does the critic use it? A proper answer requires, besides the examination of minor changes (for example, grammatical corrections) or more important additions (such as marginalia, overwritings, erasures or emendations in succeeding versions), a consideration of more lengthy inserts or new arrangements within blocks of meaning evincing a purposed clarification or even a recasting of the pattern of the "work-in-progress" towards total or partial rejuvenating effects.

Lowry's poetic *avant-textes* are no exception to the rule. All kinds of documents have to be scrutinized and can be, but as far as the poetic manuscripts are concerned, specific problems come to light. Some poems for which the manuscript version is missing altogether appear only in typescripts or as published versions. Other poems show a writing stage that compels the genetician to consider them as last copies before typing, whether the typescripts exist or not. Another category of poems still stands only in manuscript form, having never reached completion either in typescript or published versions. Fortunately enough, Lowry wrote a number of poems on exercise books of the type used by schoolchildren. These yield a profusion of pages corresponding to the puzzle of the various stages in text-production and suggest worthwhile remarks that contribute both to the definition of Lowry's creative process and to the conclusions that can be reached about Lowry as a person.

When attempting to reconstruct such a highly structured imagination as Lowry's, the genetic critic cannot simply rule out the problems of synchrony and/or diachrony. He or she will, therefore, be confronted with the task of date evaluation. Only a few poems were dated by the author himself at the time of production. Margerie Lowry and Dr Earle Birney, when they worked on the manuscripts for the 1962 publication, endeavoured to ascribe dates wherever they could. But human memory is far from reliable; it must be mistrusted, just as on the critical level guesswork is taxed with irrelevancy. In dating manuscripts, two lines of attack can be pursued: analysing the objective material or looking for internal evidence, trying to search for such referentials as the practical allusions, names, and episodes that are echoes of actual experiences or real facts.

With Lowry, looking for internal evidence proves to be most unsafe. Lowry did not always start writing under the pressure of circumstance, however traumatic, and yet this kind of incentive can no more be totally disregarded than the Wordsworthian "recollection in tranquillity" incentive. Also, as Lowry was a perfectionist, he revised most of his poems again and again over many years. The second method, restricted to paper identification through its nature, colour, or watermarks and submitting samples to chemical treatment, yields a meagre crop of dates.[4] So far, no method holds any hope for a permanent dating system for the type of material in hand.

Less disappointing, however, is a comparison of various items interrelatedly or with such prose manuscripts or typescripts as are undisputedly dated. This can be done by comparing poetic manuscripts, letters (published or unpublished), and various typescripts. For example, Lowry's draft copy of "The Lighthouse Invites the Storm," as it stood in 1939 (UBC SC 6:51), can be compared with the material donated to the archive by Harold Matson in October 1973, which shows the typescripts of poems sent to James Stern in 1940 (UBC SC 6:55) and those sent to Albert Erskine in November 1947 (UBC SC 7:42). Also, the poems given to Dr Birney or sent to A.J.M. Smith and James Davenport for publication in 1947 through 1949 (groupings appearing in UBC SC 33:26 to 33:33) provide interesting comparisons.

The poem entitled "Grim Vinegaroon" in the published version of the *Selected Poems* (SP 27) will serve to show how manuscripts can be used in the genetic criticism of literary texts. Its composition unfolds along a line of nine manuscript versions and three typescripts that are clean copies for editing work at various stages of text-production (UBC SC 4:20; 4:93; 5:35). Thanks to Lowry's writing habits, it can be safely assumed that the recto versions are first attempts and the versos intermediary drafts. Now, recto 1 (see Plate 1), the longest version, gropes with the cat theme in the marginalia, plays with the term "vinegaroon" by means of the words "vinegar" and "vermigaroon," and dwells, at some length, upon the theme of hypocrisy. The cat figure, an animal Lowry associated with Conrad Aiken, appears in *Volcano* chapter 5 manuscripts as early as the 1940 draft, and the emphasis on hypocrisy relates the draft to a 1939–40 Vancouver context. The verso of the recto 2 version (see Plate 2), developing a love of earth together with a loathing for his "ugly" ship, points to an early Dollarton period. The recto sides of versions 4 and 6, showing a letter written to Aiken in the early forties with a definite 1940 publishing context, suggest a later Dollarton period for these versions. The intermediary verso 5 has on the recto page a poem entitled "A Sailor sees the world The Long Voyage Home" and bears in the margin the name of "Mr Weeks" (in Margerie Lowry's hand), which refers to the 1941 letters about the publication of "In Memoriam" in the *Atlantic Monthly* (UBC SC 1:5). Again, the recto 8 version develops the delirium-tremens-of-the-world and I-am-ashamed themes under the title of "Hey Young fellow," which might refer to what Russell Lowry called the 1942 "prodigal son" episode in Lowry's life.[5]

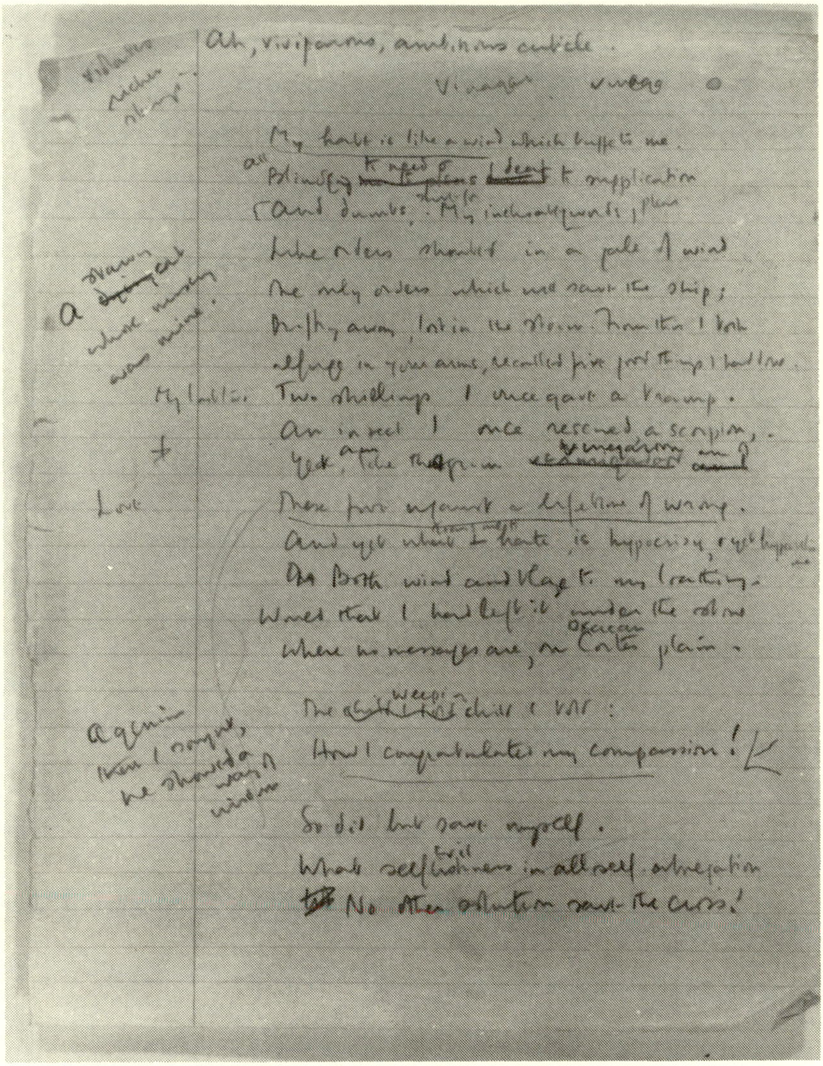

PLATE 1 "Grim Vinegaroon" recto 1

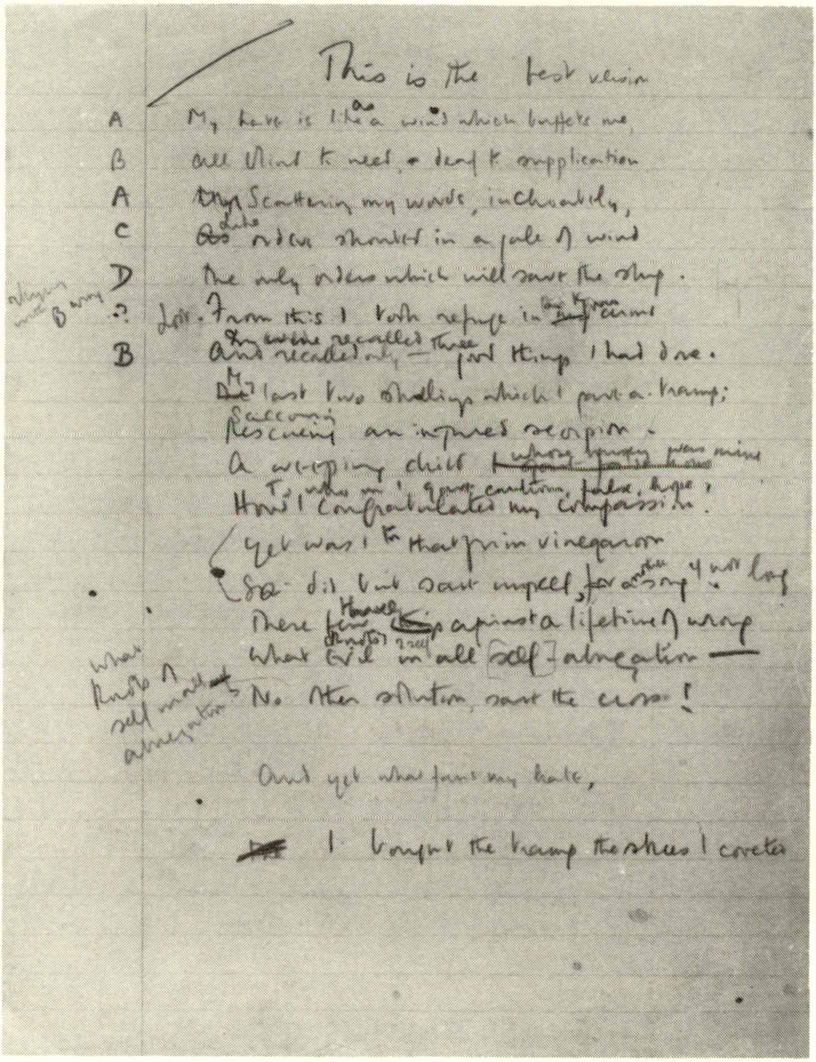
This is the best version

My hate is like a wind which buffets me,
all blind to need, & deaf to supplication
Scattering my words, incoherently,
Like orders shouted in a gale of wind
The only orders which will save the ship.
From this I took refuge in
And recalled only — past things I had done.
The last two shillings which I gave a tramp;
Rescuing an injured scorpion.
A weeping child
How I congratulated my compassion!
Yet was I to that grim vinegaroon
So — did but save
These few against a lifetime of wrong
What evil in all self abnegation —
No other solution, save the cross!

And yet what fans my hate,

I bought the tramp the shoes I coveted

PLATE 2 "Grim Vinegaroon" recto 2

(Grim Vinegaroon)

My hate is like a wind that buffets me,

All blind to need, deaf to supplication,

Scattering my words, inchoately,

Like orders shouted in a gale of wind,

The only orders which will save the ship,

Lost! From this I took refuge in your arms.

In wine recalled three good things I had done:

Succoring an injured scorpion;

My last two shillings I once gave a tramp,

Which bought him but the chaos I coveted;

A weeping child whose misery was mine

I gave false hope to, knowing there was none.

How I congratulated my compassion!

Yet was I too that grim vinegaroon,

So did but save myself, if not for long.

These three, against a lifetime of wrong.

What knots of self in all self-abnegation –

No other solution save the cross!

PLATE 3   "Grim Vinegaroon" typescript showing Margerie Lowry's 1962
editing of the poem

A close examination of the three typescripts suggests the dates 1941 to 1947; the version chosen by Margerie Lowry in 1960 goes back to versions 2 and 3. Version 2 she calls the best (see the top of Plate 2) on the basis of the manuscript itself, and she reinserts the two lines from version 3 about the scorpion that stings itself to death under a stone (see Plate 3). All these details permit a final date evaluation: the poem must have been written in the very early days at Dollarton. It evinces traces of a transitional stage between the Mexican writings and the 1942–43 revisions of *Volcano*. Margerie Lowry's editing posture directed her choice towards the most significantly symbolical meaning. That she was eventually right in her editing decisions I hope to show.

Recto 1 (see Plate 1) can hardly be called a poem, the less so as some lines lack initial capitalization altogether. But as it stands it contains nearly all the themes and images the poet had in mind to express in a striking manner. After Lowry hit on the syntagm "knots of self," as early as verso 2 (see left margin, Plate 2), the first and last lines were already complete and did not change throughout the sequence. They frame, so to speak, the poem's general theme: this provides illustration for the biblical text that charity will redeem a multitude of sins. At first sight it may appear that salvation can be earned only because it was heavily paid for in advance, yet the argument is less optimistic. Love cannot counterbalance hatred, for mercy here aims first and foremost at one's own salvation, so that "knots of self" are tied up with all redeeming acts. The hate motive, linked to the soul's uneasiness, is present from the start: hate is like a storm that deprives the poet of all understanding. He cannot see, he cannot hear; his voice also is muted and cannot give the orders that might save his ship; refuge in his beloved one's arms permits the memories of acts of compassion to rise up to clear consciousness again, yet he finds they cannot compensate for "a lifetime of wrong" because hatred and love, selfishness and abnegation are but faces of hypocrisy. The cross remains the only way to salvation.

Again, the major metaphors connected with the self are neatly defined. A net of corresponding figures runs through the text: the poet is the lost word, the drifting ship, that scorpion, and that vinegaroon; he is no better than a tramp, cat, or insect. Versions 2 and 3 take the shape of poems with the delineation of rhymes and lines. New figments, places and acts, are modulated. The original five "good things" to be memorized are reduced to two. The cat of recto 1 turns into a "weeping child," and the poet's need for salvation becomes less egotistical since the production of "another song" justifies it now. The places of refuge vary from "arms" to "inn" (versions 3 and 4 and published text) to "house" (versions 5 and 6) to "sanctuary" (versions 7, 8, and 9). The arresting nature imagery disappears altogether: "words ... Like orders shouted in a gale of wind" (line 4), and more damagingly the scorpion/ vinegaroon "That stings itself to death beneath the stone / Where no message is, on the mescal plain" (recto 3). The scorpion/stone/death *symboliques*, so essential to Lowry's personal imagination, give way (after recto 3) to the more sentimental images of the "weeping child" and of the "last two shillings" offered to the tramp.

But, as if to compensate for the loss, later changes throw a new light on the darkening of the thought by single word alterations: the drunkard's "skies" are transmuted into a chaos and hell "coveted" by both giver and receiver; the "last shillings" are metamorphosed into a "Saturnian" shilling whose sumptuous qualifier cannot screen the stress put on the themes of illusion and delusion that replace the initial hypocrisy motive, even though the progressive catastrophe might be concealed behind the tendency to sentimentalize tone and rhythm through substituting a word such as "sanctuary" for "inn" at the end of a line or the phrase "against a lifetime of wrong" for "for another song / of fretful tenderness, in a world of wrong" (in version 4 to the end). These latter changes constitute a rather deceptive way of qualifying the rough kind of "song" produced by Lowry's poetry.

Strangely enough, the loss of vigour and vision stems from a need for rigour, in Lowry's governing posture, concerning formal matters, which postulates, under Aiken's influence, the need to tighten up a poem as a disciplinary rule at the presumed time of composition. At the same time, the castrating clipping of a flowery poem into shape must be seen as symptomatic of Lowry's inner compulsion for order. The critic might well be entitled to raise the question whether the unhappy fate of a poem, doomed to reduction for the sake of form and order, does not point to writing habits that Lowry would adopt later in the fifties – the piling up of pages and pages of notes, documents, drafts, and copies for a minimal text-production. A close examination of this sequence of nine manuscript versions of one poem shows how and why writing for Lowry became a never-ending process, hindering him from ever reaching any clear definition of the self as unified, even though with *Under the Volcano* he had achieved a formidable recognition of something fundamentally constitutive of both his writing and his phantasmal life.[6]

From the outset to the bitter end of his poetic writings, a repetitive pattern of figures of the self appears, regardless of time and place in the manuscripts. They can be listed as follows: the sailor and the drunk; the son and the lover; the child and the wrestler; the poet and the comedian; the ailing man and the mirthful buffoon; the derelict and the deserter; man in prison and madman in a mad world; sinning man and man sinned against; the wrecker and the rescuer; the victim and the victimizer; he who consumes himself, yet is threatened by others; at times the corpse, but also the ghost.[7]

These oppositions in contrasting pairs do not derive from some arbitrary love for rigid structures on the critic's part; they quite naturally come to mind due to Lowry's obsessive iteration. Moreover, by syncretically grouping those manuscripts that reveal a temporal progression in the different stages of their writing, it becomes possible to identify the existence of what might be called "clusters of nuclear *topoi*" that might refer to topical events or cultural themes or phantasmal elaborations, all of which tend to testify to a rigidly structured imagination whose potential could claim to have victimized both Lowry's person and his writing.

Some figures bear names: Vigil Forget (*SP* 20), Tashtego (*SP* 19), Tom and Bill (*SP* 13), "the Sweeney Tod of improvisors" (*SP* 56), Saint Malcolm and Saint Francis (*SP* 52), Legion (*SP* 41–4), and Lowry's own name.[8] Some of the names intervene only as terms of comparisons, such as Friday, Crusoe, and Columbus (*SP* 41–4), Christian (*SP* 14), Redburn and Ahab (*SP* 11–12), or Antipholus (*SP* 21). Other figures are allegorical representations, now implied, now explicit: the rider (*SP* 33), the voyeur (*SP* passim), the wrecker (*SP* 65), the pilgrim (*SP* 70). In "Sestina in the Cantina" (*SP* 41) "Legion" denotes multiplicity connected with evil in the Bible and sums up all the other poetic identities ever worked out before or after its composition, while still referring to the "other" on the dramatic level of the poem.

The writer's own name appears only on rare occasions, one being in the poem entitled "Epitaph" (*SP* 62). Here the use of the social referential name is once more related to death, but in a different way. The figure is not of a doomed man, in spite of the title; not that the relation of a Lowry figure to death (which is predictable enough) can surprise, but the nature of the representation is uncommon in Lowry's work. For once it is the figure of a happy rascal enjoying life and showing it. Nomination here points to a rare moment in a man's life when a perfect adequation of the subject to the *imago* of the ideal "I" has been reached. This permits Lowry to accept the real: for once the self, rid of guilty representations, can refer to the self under its patronymic, attached to the "Father's Law." Exorcised, self-absolved, Lowry can define himself as a happy clown. Such coming to terms with reality is rare in the poetic manuscripts, which demonstrates that Lowry's discourse on self does not follow the "smooth" path that could have led him from a multiple self to a single unified figure. Such ideal progress might have been possible for Bunyan's Pilgrim, but it cannot express Lowry's experience of life and self, for Lowry's self was closely related to Shakespeare's "naked ape" or Saul Bellow's "dangling man." Usually, however,

nomination with Lowry is less obvious. Then, some metaphorical process is at work, ranging from comparison to identification with ship,
tree, lighthouse, seagull, vulture, salmon and eagle, wolf and scorpion
– the last two playing the role of genuine totems linked to taboos.

The poetic manuscripts show that the emerging of the figures does
not proceed from metaphor to symbol and/or allegory. The act of naming, that is of pinning down the very essence of being, very often
intervenes after a long groping for definition. Not so here; it soon
appears in the very titles, because there seems some a priori representation at work. Then names are transmuted into signs; the flexible metaphor and the far-reaching symbol are frozen into monolithic emblems
plumbed with a terrifying reality. Then symptoms and signs are let
loose. The figures are necessarily corollary to the "knots" that tied up
Lowry's predicament: they epitomize conflicting situations of disappointment and hatred, loathing and horror, self-derision and histrion-
ism. They pin down the image repeated ad infinitum of a being,
whether man, beast, vegetable, or thing, bowing to the burden of
doom, perilously pursuing identification and salvation in highly fic-
tionalized representations of the self peering into the gulf that yawns
between the imaginary and the symbolic, the real and the imaginary.
The very profusion of hypostases involved in the process of plural nomination, which could have originated a release from the self by way of
dissémination, in fact deceitfully conceals the tragedy of a man desperately in search of a single self, groping for definition by means of an
almost naïve Cratylism against the odds of a multiplicity of reeling
selves.[9] The title of the first poem in *Selected Poems* significantly epit-
omizes this struggle for single identity through Cratylic nomination:
"No Kraken shall be found till sought by name" (*SP* 11).

NOTES

1 My general introduction to genetic criticism, a new approach to literary
   textual criticism currently discussed in the seminars and research groups
   of l'Institut des Textes et Manuscrits Modernes, closely follows Louis
   Hay's "La Critique génétique: origine et perspectives," postface to *Essais
   de critique génétique* (Paris: Flammarion 1979).
2 In search of filiation, Louis Hay cites the following authors, works, and
   schools: Novalis and his late eighteenth-century *Fragments*; Goethe's "Letter to Zeller," dated 1804; Schlegel's *Pensées et maximes de Lessing* (1801);
   Kleist's *L'Elaboration progressive de la pensée au fil du discours* (1806); Coleridge's *Biographia Litteraria* (1817); Poe's *Philosophie de la composition* (1846);

T.S. Eliot's *De Poe à Valéry* (1948); the New Criticism and "la nouvelle critique" close the list.

3 "Genesis and structure are concepts less contradictory than interrelated" (my translation), *Essais de critique génétique*, 226.

4 At the University of British Columbia's Special Collections Lowry Archive the conditions for genetic criticism are fully met because scholars have generous access to Lowry's backshop and front window. The substantial MSS and TSS located in the archive can be considered a near-complete collection of rough drafts or neat copies, intermediate or final.

5 See "Preface: Malcolm – A Closer Look," *The Art of Malcolm Lowry*, ed. Anne Smith (London: Vision Press 1978), 9–27.

6 During the summer of 1983 the poetic MSS were examined by Mr Harold Sault, member of the International Association of Paper Historians. But this type of investigation was an exercise in frustration.

7 For a definition of most of Lacan's terms used here, see Lacan's *Les Quatres Concepts fondamentaux de la psychoanalyse*, Seminaire de Jacques Lacan (Paris 1973).

8 The overwhelming number of figures that crop up in the unpublished MSS collection or even the published selection of poems prevents any attempt at citing them all in this paper.

9 For "reeling selves," see the 1 July 1949 letter to Frank Taylor, in which Lowry speaks of himself as a "Pirandello in reverse" (SL 180).

Under the Shadow of the *Volcano*: Malcolm Lowry's Poetry

MARK ELLIS THOMAS

Clearly, everyone agrees that *Under the Volcano* is Malcolm Lowry's greatest and most famous work. Some would go further and claim that it is his only work of consequence, that, as Dale Edmonds has said, Lowry is a "one-book author."[1] Just as clearly, not everyone agrees about that. Critics of *Lunar Caustic*, of the short stories, and of the posthumous novels have argued convincingly that those works of prose fiction deserve attention independent of the masterpiece novel. In fact, the trend in Lowry criticism is increasingly to account for more of his writings rather than to exclude from consideration everything but *Under the Volcano*.

Yet despite the relatively small number of Lowry texts, even the more accommodating of Lowry's critics conceive of him only as a writer of prose. That this is true would be easy to prove, if my thesis were only that Lowry's poetry has been overshadowed by the prose fiction.[2] This conception of Lowry is demonstrably an error in fact; my thesis is that it is also an error in judgment.

In the next few pages I shall approach various poems by five different critical *topoi*, since for me one of the hallmarks of interesting and worthwhile literature is its capacity to sustain analysis from a number of critical perspectives. Let me briefly outline my plan: my *topoi* proceed from referentiality to biography to typology, intertextuality, and on to what I call intratextuality. Touching briefly on each *topos* and using examples from the poetry, I shall demonstrate that this portion of Lowry's work rewards critical examination and requires further study.

From the perspective of the referential *topos* I consider Lowry's poems as reflections of the writer's physical world. Many of the poems are set in geographically identifiable locations, from Rosslyn Park in Vancouver to a waterfront tavern in Vera Cruz, from the Bowery of New York City to the jail in Oaxaca. But not all the objective references are self-evident. The poem "In Tempest's Tavern," for example, refers to "The *Ohio* smoking in Frisco on a sharp pen / Of rock" (SP 94). What most readers do not know is that the s.s. *Ohioan* was stranded off San Francisco in October 1936, just before Lowry sailed from San Diego to Acapulco.[3] I can iterate the need for further referential scholarship with this story. Recently I came across the Spanish translation of Lowry's *Selected Poems*. While flipping through, I noticed that in the short poem "Prayer for Drunks," the word "Pontefract" is translated as "*puente cortado*," which I would render in English as "broken bridge."[4] What the translator failed to realize, because no commentator on Lowry's work has mentioned it, is that Pontefract refers to a town in the Wakefield district of West Yorkshire:[5] once known as Pomfret, it is the site of royal murders in Shakespeare's *Richard III* (3.3.9–14). These pieces of information are clearly important; without them a reader cannot understand even the literal level of the poem, which begins in referentiality.

Lowry's poem "Xochitepec" does more than locate and describe a setting, though it does that. The poem is grounded objectively by its references to Xochitepec and Tlalpám, communities near Mexico City, but it also reflects the speaker's psychological state, depicting the events of Lowry's last night in Mexico with his first wife, Jan Gabrial.[6] Here we see the grey area between referential and biographical readings of the poems. Specific referential features sometimes coincide in a single image with more vague associations of autobiographical expressiveness, as here:

> – Just before we left Tlalpám
> Our cats lay quivering under the maguey;
> A meaning had slunk, and now died, with them.
> The boy slung them half stiff down the ravine,
> Which we now entered, and whose name is hell.   (SP 25)

The town, the cats, the boy, and the ravine all belong to the objective world; the dead "meaning" and hell are essentially subjective. The violent imagery signifies the turbulence of the marriage's disruption and points to a biographical, expressive reading. A formalistic, intratextual approach might focus on the phrase "under the maguey" as an echo of the novel's title, to associate the Consul and the cats. But it is the referential reading that notes the precise linkages of Lowry's details: the cats are apparently poisoned by the maguey plant, maguey is the source of mescal, and mescal was Lowry's drug of choice. This chain connects the destruction of animals with Lowry's fears for his own mind and body.

Many of Lowry's self-expressive poems depict the fears that impelled him to drink self-destructively: for example, "No Company But Fear," "Without the Nighted Wyvern," its companion "The Drunkards," and others. But none of them expresses the increasingly difficult achievement of joyful drunkenness better than "Without the Nighted Wyvern" (*SP* 39). This poem begins with a brilliant reworking of Robert Burns's "Freedom and Whisky gang thegither!" which Lowry may have read either in the original or as it appears in Earle Birney's novel *Turvey*.[7] Lowry's ironic first line, "Notions of freedom are tied up with drink," associates freedom with alcohol, while freedom is paradoxically "tied up." "Wyvern" presents a hierarchical series of taverns, each more ideal than the last – from one with "unlimited beers" to another with "a finer, ah, an undistilled wine / That subtly intoxicates without pain." The drinker in "Wyvern" is a writer, a creator not only of the Platonic ladder of taverns but of "Tracts of a really better land." The ultimate, idyllic "inn / Where we may drink forever without owing / With the door open, and the wind blowing" is an impossibly idealized vision that invites, by its plurality and openness, all people to join him.

When Lowry's self-involvement (or our reading of the poems) gets beyond the level of strict biography, then his persona achieves universality. As Lissa Paul Bubbers writes, even though "the alcoholic ('Cantina') poems appear to be highly solipsistic since they deal with the particular experience of one man [n]evertheless they are extremely compelling because of the way the poet transforms the internal vision into a universal one; the despair of the drunk becomes the despair of mankind."[8] When Lowry approaches his readers this way, his poems allude to archetypes and icons. But Lowry creates his types contextually as well as allusively, by repeating similar situations. Aficionados of the prose should not be surprised to find in the poems "the specific figure which concentrates and intensifies a much more general reality."[9]

Primal scenes appear typically in Lowry's poems – for example, in the group of poems that share the theme of drowning, in which both swimmers and ships founder. These poems, individually and even more so as a group, convince their reader that sinking is but a watery Fall of Man. It is not the unique individual who drowns; it is every one of us, collectively and alone. My next example shows this universality while also finding that Lowry participates in what George Landow describes as "the older Christian uses of the situation [of crises, which] ... always rely on a dual perspective that presents both the abandonment and the presence of God."[10]

Lowry's "In the Oaxaca Jail" (*SP* 28) imposes a Christian *telos* on to the atheistic statement of James Thomson's "City of Dreadful Night." "Oaxaca Jail" begins by quoting Thomson's poem, which is stridently atheistic and which ends with an appeal to a secular icon, Dürer's *Melencolia 1*.[11] In Thomson's poem there is no God, so the reader finds no reason to mourn his absence. Lowry, by contrast, employs a religious type to apotheosize himself as Christ: "And I crucified between two continents." The same poem also inverts the typological effect to undermine the archetype, ironically describing a cathedral's cross as "Wires and the tall pole moving in the wind." This double-edged use of a type increases both the pathos of the immediate crisis (incarceration) and the ironic deflation of the cross. Lowry sees suffering in God's universe as the only suffering that is significant beyond the individual. He therefore rejects the atheistic aestheticism offered by "The City of Dreadful Night" and reinvents Thomson's poem according to his own theistic typology.

One type appearing often in Lowry's poems is the familiar literary type, one in which Lowry's experience reinforces the legacy of such writers as Thomson, De Quincey, Poe, and many others: the dissipated artist. This inheritance leads me to my next category of consideration: intertextuality. Some poems explicitly connect with other writers; Nordahl Grieg, Conrad, Rilke, and Yeats are mentioned in poem titles, and at least sixteen other authors are mentioned either by name or by the name of one of their characters. These intertextual references, deserving further study than is possible here, are important to understanding the poems. For instance, as I have already noted, "In Tempest's Tavern" uses Ernest Dowson and Wordsworth to establish a polarity by which we can assess that poem's protagonist.[12] In general, though, Lowry was less capable of answering his precursors in poetry than he was in prose. His characteristic prose style bespeaks an authentic voice the like of which breaks through only occasionally in the poems.

The whole issue of intertextuality and influence raises the issue of plagiarism, a vice Lowry feared and one he addressed in "The Plagiarist," which explores the barrier between experience and language. That barrier becomes a muddle when, after we read, literature *is* our personal history. Poems and our past become difficult to separate finally.

Before I quote the poem in its entirety (as it appears in *Selected Poems*, not in manuscript – a different and rich area for investigation), let me note that it opens with an image for plagiarism that captures both the interplay of presence and absence and the problem of loss – regarding the duplicate, not the original. Quickly, the poet makes a self-reflexive, metatextual remark before developing a new image of a dying man using another's words to explain the inexplicable:

> ... See the wound the upturned stone has left
> In the earth! How doubly tragic is the hollowed shape –
> It is a miracle that I may use such words
> As shape. But the analogy has escaped.
> Crawling on hands and sinews to the grave.
> I found certain pamphlets on the way.
> Said they were mine. For they explained a pilgrimage
> That otherwise was meaningless as day
> But twice as difficult, to explain away ...   (SP 76)

The poem begins by turning words into wounds, and ends by asserting their capacity to explain. Unlike Macbeth, whose words became him as his wounds, Lowry's words and wounds do not smack of honour but of guilt. Indeed, the image and tone of Lowry's poem are more reminiscent of Milton's description of the earth when Eve eats the forbidden fruit: "Earth felt the wound, and Nature from her seat / Sighing through all her Works gave signs of woe, / That all was lost."[13] Furthermore, the implications of the rolled-away stone of the Resurrection show how this event is "doubly tragic," since the poem in that case is not about Adam's original sin but about the second Adam and the failure of the word, that is, man's failure to grasp a credible salvation as well as the failure of language to redeem our mundane experience. The upturned stone of the Resurrection is an emblem of repetition, just as a plagiarized text repeats or returns to a prior text.

Lowry's "Plagiarist" involves us in an indictment of identification with literature. The "certain pamphlets" are the canonical, ideological texts that co-opt culture and so finally shape the reality they initially try to reflect. We see the central figure's guilt, which is due to his dependence on another's words to explain his life for him. And we may be implicated in that guilt, for in the act of identifying with him, we run the risk of plagiarism. Whenever we turn to literature only as a confirmation of the world or our lives in the world, we buy what William Gass has called "Brand Name Realism" and become plagiarists too.[14] This means that we are responsible for the meaning and for explaining the meaning of our own lives. To turn to another's words is to participate in the inevitability and guilt of our belatedness.

"But," says Lowry, "the analogy has escaped," showing that what is fleeting is ultimately the relationship between the word and what it signifies. What escapes is the analogy, the association between one writer's words and another's, between words and what they mean. Appropriately for such a self-consuming poem, "The Plagiarist" is a fragment.

I turn now from the intertextual issue of other authors' influence to the intratextual phenomenon of the co-existence of Lowry's poems with his prose. When the poems have been discussed in the past, this was the usual justification – that they illuminate the prose. The first Masters thesis on Lowry's poems, for example, was titled "The Poetry of Malcolm Lowry in Relation to Fiction" (Bubbers 1976). Now, this is not a bad reason to study Lowry's poems, but because it finds its end outside itself, this approach is doomed to second-class status. Still, the fact remains that many of Lowry's poems take the prose as their subject or subtext.

For example, it is useful to know, as Lowry explains in his 23 May 1957 letter to Ralph Gustafson, that "Xochitepec" was composed in the margin of a manuscript page of *Under the Volcano* (SL 412). The reader (of either the novel or the poem) who knows this is a better reader for knowing it. Unsurprisingly, the poem "For *Under the Volcano*" (SP 23–4) shares images with the novel – such as that unforgettable one of a huge sea turtle bleeding to death on the sidewalk outside a seafood restaurant – but it shares themes with *Volcano* as well. The poem's distilled expression of the fear of venereal disease and the impossibility of sex rivals the novel's non-event of the Consul's impotence: "the flute of my weeping, / betrothed to the puking vacuum and the unfleshible root."

Several poems share phrases or situations with *Under the Volcano*. "The Volcano Is Dark" (SP 26) juxtaposes creation and destruction in a phrase that recurs during the Consul's episode with the prostitute, Maria: "And the cries which might be the groans of the dying / Or the groans of love –."[15] The sexual liaison of *Under the Volcano* is also recreated in "Thirty-five Mescals in Cuautla":

The girl ... pours a glass of death,
And if that death's in her it's here in me.
On the pictured calendar, set to the future,
The two reindeer battle to death, while man,
The tick of real death, not the tick of time,
Hearing, thrusts his canoe into a moon,
Risen to bring us madness none too soon.   (SP 35–6)

The sexual imagery and the threat of madness and incipient death from syphilis make the poem interesting for its own sake. Still, through the connection to *Under the Volcano* (and because this poem is dated ten years

before the novel was published), we become better readers by comparing them. Furthermore, "since soma is not mentioned at all in the text
of the poem [but is explained in an authorial footnote], it is the responsibility of the reader to recall that Lowry identifies soma with mescal
and the moon in *Under the Volcano*" (Bubbers 64). The intratextuality
becomes even more tortuous when we note that the line "*the tick of real
death not the tick of time*" is cited by Sigbjørn Wilderness, in Lowry's
later novel *Dark as the Grave Wherein My Friend Is Laid*, as "his first
poem."[16] The problem of priority belongs to the textual scholar, and
the questions of full interpretations are too involved for the scope of
this essay. I can suggest, however, that one effect of this repetitive pattern is to defeat time, to defy closure – and that this is an appropriate
technique for a fragmentary group of poems Lowry planned to include
in his magnum opus, the cyclical *Voyage That Never Ends* (Day 426).

Finally, I want to mention the poems apart from the imposed concerns
of the previous *topoi*. The readers of Lowry's poetry do not need to
justify their activity on the basis of subservience to any critical method,
or to Lowry's biography, or to the prose. The capacity of the poems to
entertain the several means of inquiry employed in this paper is one
more reason to consider Lowry's poetry worthwhile. But as I hope my
examples demonstrate, it is the poem itself that is interesting, not the
means of approaching it.

Lowry's poetry does not need to be rediscovered by general readers.
The *Selected Poems* has an outstanding history as a book of poetry. In
print continuously since 1969, printed sixteen times as of January 1985,
it has been translated into French, German, Spanish, and Italian. General
readers are already familiar with Lowry's poetry, but academic, professional readers, even of Lowry, have largely overlooked and undervalued
it.[17]

Because of its independent worth the poetry should be accepted as a
part of the main body of Lowry's work. The poems require further
scholarship, as I have suggested with regard to intertextual references,
textual bibliography, and so on. But study will not end there. Because
of the unity of Lowry's work, each discovery affecting the poems will
be a boon to the field of Lowry study as a whole. Lowry's poetry is
the virgin land of his works. Coming out from under the shadow of
the *Volcano*, it is the remaining frontier for Lowry scholars and critics.

NOTES

1 See Dale Edmonds' review of *The Voyage That Never Ends* in *Malcolm
Lowry Review* 12 (Spring 1983): 3–7.

2 Let two examples suffice to prove the point. The Lowry entry in *Twenti-eth-Century Literary Criticism*, ed. Sharon K. Hall (Detroit: Gale Research 1982), is representative: in a twenty-page compendium of commentary, one-half page is allotted to a mixed review of *Selected Poems*. One of the most recent book-length studies of Lowry dismissed the poetry in a sin-gle, misleading sentence; see Ronald Binns, *Malcolm Lowry* (London: Methuen 1984), 17.

3 See Bruce D. Berman, *Encyclopedia of American Shipwrecks* (Boston: Mari-ners Press 1972), and Mark Ellis Thomas, "Malcolm Lowry's 'In Tem-pest's Tavern,'" *Explicator* 47, no. 1 (1988): 36–7.

4 With the exception of "In Tempest's Tavern," all the texts of Lowry's poetry cited in this paper are taken from *Selected Poems*. For this Spanish translation, see M. Antolin Rato, *Malcolm Lowry: Poemas* (Madrid: Visor 1979), 49.

5 See the entry for "Pontefract," *Encyclopedia Britannica: Micropaedia* (1986).

6 Douglas Day, *Malcolm Lowry: A Biography* (New York: Oxford University Press 1973), 230–3.

7 See Robert Burns, *The Poetical Works of Robert Burns* (Philadelphia: John D. Morris, n.d.) 1:121–7, and Earle Birney, *Turvey: A Military Picaresque* (Toronto: McClelland and Stewart 1969), 76.

8 Lissa Paul Bubbers, "The Poetry of Malcolm Lowry in Relation to the Fiction," MA York University 1976, 8.

9 Raymond Williams, *Marxism and Literature* (New York: Oxford University Press 1977), 101.

10 See *Images of Crises: Literary Iconology, 1750 to the Present* (Boston: Routledge and Kegan Paul 1982), 90.

11 See *The City of Dreadful Night and Other Poems* (London: Reeves and Turner 1888), 1–55.

12 See n3.

13 *Paradise Lost*, ed. Merritt Y. Hughes (New York: Odyssey 1962), 9:782–4.

14 William H. Gass, *The Habitation of the Word* (New York: Simon and Schus-ter 1985), 109.

15 See *Under the Volcano* (New York: New American Library 1971), 349, 351.

16 *Dark as the Grave Wherein My Friend Is Laid* (Harmondsworth: Penguin 1972), 210.

17 I have discussed this neglect in "Strange Type: The Shoddy Commentary on Malcolm Lowry's Poetry," *American Notes and Queries* 23, nos. 5–6 (1985): 84–5.

PART FOUR

Swinging the Maelstrom:
An Apostrophe

Lowry, Jazz, and
"The Day of the Dead"

GRAHAM COLLIER

Malcolm Lowry has said that he "learnt to write while listening to Bix Beiderbecke," and he once spoke of trying to write a new kind of novel – "something that is bald and winnowed, like Sibelius, and that makes an odd but splendid din, like Bix Beiderbecke" (SL 28). Lowry's favorite jazz musicians were undoubtedly Beiderbecke, a white trumpeter of German extraction whose lyrical style was highly influential, Joe Venuti, one of the few violinists in jazz, Venuti's partner, guitarist Eddie Lang, and saxophonist Frankie Trumbauer. All worked at various times in Paul Whiteman's orchestra, but there is no significance in that or in Lowry's apparent liking for white musicians. (Other names that appear in Lowry's work or letters are Red Nichols, Benny Goodman, and the Quintet of the Hot Club of France with Django Reinhardt.) Lowry's selection of favourite musicians is presumably accidental, formed through listening to the limited number of records available in his time, particularly in England. Lowry's strong interest in the guitar would naturally have led him to Eddie Lang, and through Lang to Venuti, Beiderbecke, and Trumbauer.

It was the records made by Trumbauer's group (featuring Beiderbecke and Lang) in 1928–29, when Lowry was in his late teens, that seemed to have impressed him most. Ralph Case, a Lowry friend from Cambridge, has said: "to anyone who knew Malcolm intimately it was inevitable that jazz should be tied up with, indeed be part of, his literary output."[1] Lowry refers to jazz often in his fiction and his letters and, as I will show later, he seemed to see some kind of common language too, which Case was astute enough to recognize.

There are three characters in Lowry's writing for whom jazz is a very solid interest. Hugh, the Consul's half-brother in *Under the Volcano*, is given Lowry's own musical background; he talks about Venuti and Lang often, and speaks of "a day like a good Joe Venuti record."[2] In *Lunar Caustic* the protagonist says: "perhaps it was America I was in love with. You know, you people get sentimental over England from time to time with your guff about Sweetest Shakespeare. Well, this was the other way round. Only it was Eddie Lang and Joe Venuti and the death of Bix."[3] Then, in "Forest Path to the Spring," Lowry has his hero say: "One evening on the way back from the spring for some reason I suddenly thought of a break by Bix in Frankie Trumbauer's record of Singing the Blues that had always seemed to me to express a moment of the most pure spontaneous happiness. I could never hear this break without feeling happy myself and wanting to do something good."[4]

Lowry's first biographer, Douglas Day, is among those who have felt that Lowry's relationship with jazz requires further attention. My feeling is that such a study can only be undertaken by somebody who understands jazz fully. In the only published article on Lowry and jazz to date, Perle Epstein describes "the construction of *Volcano* with its twelve chapters [as] based to some extent on the Zohar (a reference to the Cabbala) with its emphasis on the mystical number twelve. Here I would like to note that the blues form in jazz is also based on a twelve-bar construction."[5] True enough, but so what? The twelve-bar blues was formalized from a tradition that could just as well use eight or eleven or thirteen or any number of bars. Taken overall, the blues form simply provides a basic structure for improvising, and it is on the *repetition* of such structures that jazz is traditionally based.

Leaving matters of form aside, it is my feeling that Lowry attached himself to that personal, highly individual look at the world that a jazz musician expresses when he is soloing. What he got from jazz was the kind of oblique thinking one intuits from a good jazz soloist: he speaks of Beiderbecke's "odd but splendid din" (SL 28) and of Venuti's "wild controlled abandon" (UV 158), and there is an obvious link between Lowry's freewheeling language – moving from connection to connection in a kind of stream of consciousness – and jazz soloing. Take this passage from *Lunar Caustic*, for example:

Or – was he dead? Ah ha, watch the surgeon slit the foot of the dead man! What next, Nostradamus? Will blood appear? Or has it clotted, in some vital organ? Bleed, dead man, bleed, set the poor surgeon's mind at rest, so that he won't have to get drunk and go through the jumps and the blind staggers; the horror of the rats, the wheeling bushmills, and the Orange Bitters; bleed, so that he will not have to think how much more beautiful women are when you are dying, and they sway down the streets under the fainting trees, their bosoms tossing like blossoms in the warm gusts; bleed, so that he will not have to hear the louse of conscience, nor the groaning of imaginary men, nor see, on the window blind all night the bad ghosts –   (26)

It does have a kind of sense to it, but it could perhaps best be described as "an odd but splendid din." There is a sense, too, of each of the characters in *Volcano* stepping forward for his or her "solo," in which, as Dale Edmonds has pointed out, "the interplay of thought and action filters through an individual's sensibility, much like a jazz soloist filters the given material of melody, harmony, rhythm and mood through his own sensibility."[6]

"Mosaics of experience" is another phrase used about Lowry's writing that has a relevance to jazz and is, perhaps, a way of explaining how a jazz musician improvises. He doesn't usually attempt to build a structure logically, moving from A to Z through B, C, D, etc.; he explores his subject, uses his experience in a stream-of-consciousness way, moving from idea to idea until his allotted space is up or he has said all he has to say at this time.

Discussing Lowry's later work, Muriel Bradbrook has said that "each book culminates and absorbs the previous books, and its many layers include images that go back to childhood. This combination of fragility and rooted strength arises from the method of writing and the free, almost random mixing of overlapping versions; this allows craftsmanship to combine with spontaneity."[7] Again, there is a definite parallel with jazz: craftsmanship and spontaneity. She also cites the enormous sentence length in Lowry's later work: "He uses what the Greeks termed the 'kai' style, phrases linked by 'and ... and ... and.' It is the style used by children but also by the great jazzmen. The effect is to stress the musical element and to give a unified sweep analogous to that of ..." – and there she spoils it by citing Bob Dylan, who can hardly be called a jazz musician, but I feel that the points she raises do nevertheless have validity. Another parallel to jazz was found in Conrad Aiken's use, in a review, of a quotation about poetry: "The initial stimulus, the stimulus which first set the language habit to work, is soon lost sight of in the wealth of other language associations which are evoked from the subconscious."[8]

However, it is important to realize that the language in today's jazz parallels Lowry's writing style more than the language of that of his heroes such as Beiderbecke and Venuti. There was a formal underpinning to all the music of that era that is not present in Lowry's writing or in the best of contemporary jazz, where the forms used and the freedom offered to the musician allow much more to be said, and for it to be said in a much deeper way than in previous styles. To quote Aiken again, this time from comments about Faulkner: the "purpose [of Faulkner's sentences] is simply to keep the form – and the idea – fluid and unfinished, still in motion, as it were, and unknown, until the dropping into place of the very last syllable."[9] As with the jazz musician there is a subconscious logic to it all, and when it works it is what jazz critic Charles Fox has called the sudden transformation of the unexpected into the inevitable.

Many composers in all areas of music have been inspired by words. Such inspiration can be subdivided into those of title, mood, and text. The first is most common, where a composer may write a ballad and decide that "Tess" is as good a name as any because he has vague memories of reading the Hardy book or seeing the film. The second, being inspired by the mood of a literary work, is much more valid. Here the piece "Tess" has arisen as a direct result of a love of Hardy's work, and the music is closely informed by what the composer enjoyed in that particular novel. Some titles can be literary but indirect, as in my series of fragments "Pebbles Fresh from the Brook," where the music came first but the phrase about Hemingway's style fitted the bill admirably as a title.

Many composers have used texts directly, whether in the setting of a poem or a series of poems, or less often a prose passage. Some of these have undoubtedly worked well, but it seems to me that in most works that have literary aspirations, whether they include text or not, the music side is rarely thought through deeply enough. All too often the music is purely descriptive accompaniment to the poems or prose passages. That can be interesting enough, stimulating enough, but at the end the poem is still there, unchanged, and the music has done little if anything more than just remain in the background. To make it work properly you must find something that has hidden depths, of the sort I found in Lowry, that are capable of being plumbed by the music. My initial stimulus came from the link, which I saw at first subconsciously, between contemporary jazz language and Lowry's, but in each of my works inspired by Lowry I have tried to suggest by the music another dimension of meaning – not simply to use the words as exotic colour but rather to create a whole greater than the sum of the parts. Undoubtedly my composing has developed because of my understanding of Lowry's techniques ("the layers, the depths, the abysses, interlocking and interrelated," SL 421) and my application of them to my own technique of controlling jazz improvisation within a compositional framework where I utilize levels and layers, ranging from completely improvised passages to completely written ones, with finely controlled gradations between.

The earliest of my Lowry works was "Symphony of Scorpions," written while I was heavily immersed in Lowry and his works for the first time. The title comes from that marvellously evocative phrase in *Ultramarine*: "a symphony of scorpions, a procession of flying grand pianos and cathedrals."[10] The work explores in musical terms the co-existing levels, both horizontal and vertical, of Lowry's writing, as well as what he called "the technique of divided attention." Then came "Forest Path to the Spring," where my discovery of the story, and the necessity to find a companion piece for the Scorpions album, made me interested in trying to capture the feeling of the novella in music. As Douglas Day has said, "It is all quite lovely, and described with a simple eloquence that often approaches, but seldom falls into, sentimentality."[11] The obvious musical starting point was the solo break by Bix in "Singing the Blues," which had always struck Lowry as expressing "a moment of the most pure spontaneous happiness" (*HOL* 255). Those few musical notes served me well as the musical germ behind the piece, but the attempt to capture Lowry's feat in the novella in musical terms was to prove one of the most difficult tasks I have ever taken on.

The "Forest Path" theme occurs again in "Day of the Dead," the largest work I have done to date. (I say to date because I still nurture plans for a jazz opera based on *Volcano*, but so far the necessary funding has eluded me.) "The Day of the Dead" was commissioned by the Ilkley Literature Festival and first performed there in 1977, with a subsequent British tour, a record, and the first North American performance at the 1987 Lowry Symposium in Vancouver. It was as a direct result of the recording of this work that I was asked to write the music for the BBC Hi Fi Theatre dramatization of *Under the Volcano* in 1979.

"The Day of the Dead" uses Lowry's words, from *Under the Volcano* and *Dark as the Grave*, as well as some extracts from the letters and short stories. They were selected and assembled to make, with the music, a composite portrait of Lowry and the Consul. I have heard that Margerie respected the choices I made, while admitting that the music was a little beyond her. The *Financial Times*, however, did say that it was "a perfect marriage of words and music!" Although the setting was loosely meant to be a Mexican cantina on the Day of the Dead, I wanted to avoid purely descriptive writing. I could see little point either in recreating *Volcano*, in the sense of using a straight narrative line where literary event would be copied by musical happening. I wanted to add another layer, to utilize voice and music together to make a whole experience. In one section the Consul is asleep in his bathroom, with memories echoing around him. The words, drawn from many parts of the novel and some of the letters, are presented, often in a distorted way, by two simultaneous tracks of the same voice. The musicians, solo or in groups, improvise within some constraints suggested by me as composer/director, reacting to the words swelling around them. In the penultimate section of the work we hear my "Forest Path to the Spring" theme in its entirety after earlier fragmentary, echoing hints. This time it has words from the novel, illustrating what the Consul has given up for drink. (When I came to assemble the record, the narrated words "the sudden O'Neillian blast of a ship's siren" [HOL 258] coincided with a very high, almost distorted saxophone note on the pre-existing music track. What a Lowryan coincidence, matched only by the fact that the original "Forest Path" recording had been done at my engineer's house in Bix, a village in Oxfordshire!)

By such choices and contrasts of music and words I wanted to combine my knowledge of Lowry's life, work, and techniques with the often disregarded resources of jazz techniques and improvisation to present a different aspect of Lowry's genius. In so doing I hoped to present a portrait of Lowry and of his Consul, perhaps of all of us in our struggle between good and evil.

NOTES

1 Ralph Case in a taped conversation.
2 *Under the Volcano* (Harmondsworth: Penguin 1963), 125.
3 *Lunar Caustic* (London: Jonathan Cape 1968), 19.
4 *Hear us O Lord from heaven thy dwelling place* (Vancouver: Douglas & McIntyre 1987), 255.
5 Perle Epstein, "Swinging the Maelstrom: Malcolm Lowry and Jazz," in *Malcolm Lowry: The Man and His Work*, ed. George Woodcock (Vancouver: UBC Press 1971) 150–1.
6 Dale Edmonds, "*Under the Volcano*: A Reading of the 'Immediate Level,'" *Tulane Studies in English* 16 (1986): 66.
7 Muriel Bradbrook, *Malcolm Lowry: His Art and Early Life – A Study in Transformation* (London: Cambridge University Press 1974), 92.
8 Quoted from Nicholas Kostyleff's *Le Mécanisme cérébrale de la pensée* by Aiken in *Collected Criticism* (New York: Oxford University Press 1968), 52.
9 Conrad Aiken, "William Faulkner: The Novel as Form," *Atlantic Monthly* (November 1939): 652.
10 *Ultramarine* (New York: Lippincott 1962), 133–4.
11 Douglas Day, *Malcolm Lowry: A Biography* (New York: Oxford University Press 1984 [1973]), 457.

Hear us O Lord
and the Orpheus Occasion*

ROBERT KROETSCH

Hear us O Lord from heaven thy dwelling place.[1] With this apostrophe, Malcolm Lowry cautions us that his collection of related stories, circuitously and directly, is a meditation on the relationship between a lyric strategy and the narrative desire.

We as readers become eavesdroppers on an address to the sacred. We hear Lowry addressing God. We hear the writer addressing the deafness of God in the only way possible: by narrating the deaf God into the story as hearer. And then, the hero made hearer, we as readers find ourselves written out of all innocence, into complicity, into the violence of the telling. And now we too, in our deafness and in our listening, transgress our way *away* from indifference, proposing ourselves at once as gods and fools.

Geoffrey Hartman, in his "Preface" to Maurice Blanchot's collection of essays *The Gaze of Orpheus*, writes: "According to Blanchot, writing is a fearful spiritual weapon that negates the naïve existence of what it names and must therefore do the same to itself."[2]

Lowry, always, in writing, negates the naïve existence of what he names. His act of writing, always, negates its own naïve existence. And to read that writing is to share the risk that that writing undertook.

I am a reader writing my reading. In typing the title of Lowry's story, I wrote, by accident I believe, Hear us O Lord from *heavy* thy dwelling place. Already, I propose my own signature, and Lowry as mediator becomes in turn usurper, the deaf mediator who will not hear me, and I must write his stubborn story into my story. Hey. Malcolm.

To continue with Hartman's comment:

Literature runs the danger of denying its own desire for presence, although it cannot (as Hegel thought) become anything else – philosophy, for example. Hence writing is a self-disturbed activity: it knows itself to be, at once, trivial and apocalyptic, vain yet of the greatest consciousness-altering potential.   (ix–x)

Fooling around, we god our loins. Transgressing as readers, we speak the title *with* Lowry (Hear Us O Lord), re-citing those words "From the Isle of Man."

We hear, in our own apostrophe, the terror of a double distance. Literature indeed runs the danger of denying its own desire for presence. The very act of speaking announces space. The apostrophe is addressed quite possibly not to God the Father but to the gap itself, the gap that separates the speaking voice from the listener, the mouth from the ear, the spoken word from the longed-for signification.

The boat in "The Bravest Boat" is a small and gone boat, slow in its vast returning. The finding is a treasure beyond all hope of treasure. But the message is gnarled. It is a written message. "Hello," it begins. "Thanks," it ends. "My name is Sigurd Storlesen," it begins. "Sigurd Storlesen," it ends. Against the vast narrative of "Hello" and "Thanks" is posited a solipsism that makes even the ordinary language of communication problematic. The distance inheres even inside the namer naming his own name.

Jonathan Culler, in *The Pursuit of Signs*, writes heroically on the idea of apostrophe. Culler says that apostrophe "makes its point by troping not on the meaning of a word but on the circuit or situation of communication itself."[3]

We live at a time when poetry – Canadian poetry at least – is full of the etymologies of words, as if an earlier version of a word had a privileged status against all the problematics of meaning in our fumbling century. Lowry returns us from that false innocence to the circuit or situation of communication itself. He reminds us, continually and radically, that we are always, as writers, as readers, in the predicament of Orpheus, listening across his shoulder, hearing first and only the silence of Eurydice, who might or who might not be following, behind his uncertain head. Lowry and Orpheus, like few other poets, it seems to me, address compulsively the complicity of eye and ear. Distance is at once our vocabulary and the denial of its efficacy.

Hear us O Lord is somehow full of couples, a man and a woman. Inseparable couples. Joined couples. Page 24:

> "And we've been married seven years."
> "Seven years today –"
> "It seems like a miracle."
> But the words fell like spent arrows before the target of this fact.

The Orpheus predicament speaks its silence. Eurydice announces the life-in-death, the death-in-life concern of so much of Lowry's writing: the will toward the unreachable recovery, the problematics of any action occasioned by that will.

The circuitry of Eurydice's fate includes at once the will toward that unreachable recovery and the act that refuses it. It is the very acting itself, not the not acting, that sends her back to hell. We move from gap to gape to gap. Hear us O Lord. From Heaven. Thy distant place. The indifference, addressed, becomes true *différance*.

Or does the indifference, addressed – given an address – confound all distancing?

Culler goes on to write of a level "at which one must question the status so far granted to the thou of the apostrophic structure and reflect on the crucial though paradoxical fact that this figure which seems to establish relationships between the self and the other can in fact be read as an act of radical interiorization and solipsism" (146).

Lowry is profoundly writing Lowry. Not writing *about* Lowry. Writing Lowry in a way more deceitful and correct than any autobiographical act. It is the very daring to address God's improbable ears that locates Lowry himself as the questing voice in the fictionality of his fiction. He dares the impossible gaze. Inventing outward, he becomes the possibility of himself.

But – does he then run the risk of realizing himself at the cost of losing that very cosmos which he so longs to narrate into visibility?

"This internalization," Culler goes on to say, "is important because it works against narrative and its accompaniments: sequentiality, causality, time, teleological meaning" (148).

It is this very resistance to narrative, this temptation of solipsistic discourse with the other, that gives Lowry's narratives their special poignancy. By our act of reading, we write with him. The journey that never ends cannot end because the story as he conceives it allows, even predicates, its own resistance to story. There is a movement towards the impossible complete cosmology that, centring on the authenticity of thou, reduces the probabilities of "I." There is a movement towards the realized "I" that, by the process of internalization, forfeits the assurance of a cohering and intelligible "thou."

That dance, that quarrel, that play of seduction and resistance in its complexity and contradictions and Don Juanish promises, is what commits us as readers to the embarrassment and the irresistibility of our reading. It is the prospect of our own dismemberment that excites us with that further prospect of our re-membering.

Near the end of the opening story in *Hear us O Lord* we read: "It was like gazing into chaos."

We think of Orpheus turning to look backward, into the night, into that version of chaos which is the underworld. For even chaos, it would seem, has its shapes, its laws of randomness. Orpheus, turning to look back at the ghostly presence he has sung so hard to rescue, looks to his other and by his willing and not willing creates the gap that his other must now become. That gap will bind him to Eurydice as no mere rescue ever might. His gaze is a betrayal, and yet it is a fulfilment too. For it is the task of the artist, as Blanchot tells us, to dare to *look*.

In Lowry we have Orpheus in the moment after he looks back, in that appalling and sacred moment when he believes still in the possibility of union (and unity) and realizes nevertheless that dismemberment is his fate. To look, even to look back, is to look forward. For Lowry, the writing of a narrative becomes the writing of a discourse against his own will to narrate.

The chaos that was a version of other becomes in the apostrophe of Orpheus' gaze a condition of the interior. From the opening of "Through the Panama":

Frère Jacques
Frère Jacques
Dormez-vous?
Dormez-vous?

The sacredness of Frère Jacques and the profaneness of Brother Jack sleep together and at once. If they "give in" to sleep.

The surrogate writers in "Through the Panama" seem occupied chiefly in gazing. And now even gazing doubles on itself, becomes ambiguous. These writers in their gazing threaten to abandon the gift of time, they threaten to confound the narrative whose ends they would pursue.

But ... And yet ...

The duplicity of their "looking" in its confounding of narrative renews the narrative. Lowry, the part of Lowry that is "pure" artist, is tempted by the power of song, as the trees and rocks were seduced by the songs of Orpheus: a diabolic solipsism whereby the artist is tempted out of narrative by the hearing of his own power of narrative.

Page 30:

The further point is that the novel is about a character who becomes enmeshed in the plot of the novel he has written, as I did in Mexico. But now I am becoming enmeshed in the plot of a novel I have scarcely begun.

The "I" threatens to become the merest shadow of the world it would initiate, and even that shadow a hindrance.

Page 31:

– The inenarrable inconceivably desolate sense of having no right to be where you are; the billows of inexhaustible anguish haunted by the insatiable albatross of self.

Malcolm Lowry thinking of Sigbjørn Wilderness thinking of Martin Trumbaugh thinking. The surrogate writers in Lowry's story compounding in their conspiracies the resistance to the seductions of art, asserting the making of art by resistance, the story itself becoming journal entries, asides, marginalia, letters, history; all those forms of non-art discourse that in their discourse make art of art. Art, in the purity of art, sacred or profane, as sleep. That sleep, as night, as the chaos of the underworld, as mere sleep, a sleep that must be entered and broken.

That sleep as other. The other is the not-me that is me. It is also the me that is not me. And that sleep, like chaos, is insufficient, if for no other reason than its refusal to let us share its inexpressibility. For to speak at all, to write, is to render "undecidable" the absolutes of chaos and sleep. The large boat moves, in "Through the Panama," as did the small boat in the preceding story: we deliver our small, absurd messages from ourselves to ourselves. The hermeneutic sleep is somehow break- able, even when art itself becomes the lullaby, when art becomes the endless song against awakedness.

The gaze of Orpheus, in its affirmation and betrayal, recognizes the Lacanian fissure between self and other. The gaze is an act that announces distance, an act that in its announcing turns space into a relentless quality of time. That transformation from space into time allows the narrative to resume its energy. The pressure of narrative, in Lowry, arrested by the gaze, in the instant of its recognition and denial employs that condition of *arrest* to move itself forward.

The past, always, for Orpheus, for Lowry, is the as yet empty sign of the future, a sign that is at once full of the possibility of meaning and full of the potentiality of emptiness. Page 44:

... and even at this moment Martin knew it to be no dream, but some strange symbolism of the future.
– The French government falls again.

Every act of "being there" is at the same time a passage. That passage of course might be to mere death. If death is to be found only in the future. And that too is undecidable.

Lowry and his writers travel in the company of writers: Pirandello, Strindberg, Fitzgerald, Edgar Allan Poe, Robert Penn Warren, Wallace Stevens. A ship of holy fools. Samuel Taylor Coleridge, that earlier Orpheus, having met death in life, life in death, Christ crossified, signs a letter dated 22 November 1947. Wilderness Carlos Wilderness signs a poem.

The passage is down as well as forward:

passing San Pedro, forgetting Point Firmin (sic) down, down, at 404 fathoms at Carsbad on November 16 at 1,045 fathoms off Cape Colnet, at midday on the 17th at 965 fathoms, still going down … (52).

One way or another, we must go down. We must gaze across, and then cross – to chaos. To sleep. To death.

But I almost forgot, Lowry writes.

But I almost forgot the Lighthouse Keeper of Aspinwall. And there he is. Or rather there he once lived. In the imagination of another novelist … he [The Lighthouse Keeper] failed to provide illumination for his lighthouse, in fact went to sleep, which no lighthouse keeper should do even if spiritually advanced enough to have an illumination in Aspinwall (64–5).

Down is up, up down. Future is past, past future.

Hear us O Lord. Hear us O Lord. Circle circle circle.

Inside this book, in this story, we are inside another story, in another book. But the paradox of the book is this: entering in, we are taken outside.

Is the book itself, then, another other?

In the margin of the story, in "Through the Panama," we are in a marginal story that refuses, quite possibly refutes, the notion of centre. The story itself composes itself as stories. Or the stories compose themselves as story.

Dismemberment, Lowry seems to say, is the plentitude of the self; the self is the fissure, the gap that all roads lead from. It is that O that in Lowry's title is the apostrophic O. It is the circle, the O of nothing. Or the O of everything. Naught. Or the naught that is not. Setting out is somehow the setting of *out*, like a gopher trap, a bear trap, those zero jaws of a trap, O-ing. Owing.

Self abounds in its own othering. The Ancient Mariner, for Lowry, is manifold. Page 73:

(Mem: Discuss this a little: problem of the double, the triple, the quadruple 'I'.) Almost pathological (I feel) …

The writer's "I" multiplying out, trapped. Just to begin with, in that same paragraph: De Voto, Thomas Wolfe, Mark Twain, Joyce.

Just to begin with: Wilderness, Trumbaugh, Kennish Drumgold Cosnahan. Stories, again, containing stories, contained in stories.

Page 176:

Roderick McGregor Fairhaven sat listening to his wife describe the scenes from the train yesterday (not this train, which was the Circumvesuviana, but the Rapido, the Rome–Naples Express), how fast it went, past the magnificent Claudian aqueducts, a station, Torricola – och aye, it was a rapido indeed, he thought, as once more in memory, bang: and they flashed through Divino Amore. (No stop for Divine Love.)

Once again, a happy couple. A woman and a man. Listening. Not listening. The gaze.

"No stop for Divine Love."

And yet there is, perhaps. If we allow for that contrary, that rapido exchange of in and other that is the world's only order. Or the world's dream of order, allowing that chaos too has its other, perhaps in its dream of a dreamer.

If the Father is the primal Other (Hear us O Lord), the Mother is that which contains the Father's primacy. That there can be no story that is not embedded in story is amply suggested by now. Why should the father, then, be an exception? (O Dad, poor Dad.) Is the mother really the Terrible Mother, giving all, returning all to herself? the all-giving cannibal source of all?

Page 73:

– frightening thought occurred to me last night, when Primrose says I woke her up saying: "Would they put Mother back in the sea?" What awful thing did I mean?

Was Eurydice, perchance, not Orpheus' wife at all, but rather his Mother? Thus the indiscreet and destructive glance, an outrageous glance in place of gaze, allowing magnificently for the moment of individuation. Even the archetype is made unstable in the postmodern ferocity of Lowry's imagination, let *her* then become the many who will do the dismembering.

Even Mother cannot escape indeterminacy. She too *owes* something to the O that she is. "They" comes to collect. The small puzzle, the riddle, of that shaky pronoun includes all else. Who the hell were "they" and what were "they" up to?

Lowry must have plot and must not have plot. The very will of plot to complete its own circle fills that circle with emptiness. The plot unravels because of plot. The story, even in its pastness, signs the future. What was it you said will happen? What was it you said will happen.

Page 85:

... for example, he has never been able to follow the plot of even the simplest movie because he is so susceptible to the faintest stimulus of that kind that ten other movies are going on in his head while he is watching it.

Not the possibility but the impossibility of completing the story is the force that keeps Lowry writing. Discouraging as that might be. Each telling toward completeness announces itself, belatedly, as fragment. Even the tellers in their election to write share this impossible condition, recognize in the other of chaos, sleep or death the not-me that is me – and the other that is inviolately other.

Dismemberment of the story into stories reflects the dismemberment of Author into authors. And then those smaller names, too, are dismembered.

Page 109:

Kafka – Kaf – and others ... And Flaub – ... George Or – ... hieroglyphics, masterly compressions, obscurities to be deciphered by experts – yes, and poets – like Sigbjørn Wilderness. Wil –

The names themselves become fragments, the authors fragmentary, caught and lost in moments of naming that unname as well.

Lowry's work is full of the impossible and necessary task of the search, the finding, the losing again, the will to assemble, the being enabled to speak by the failures, the being caused by those failures, one's own, the failures of the speaking itself, to speak too late, too soon, in the wrong place, on the wrong occasion, to the wrong listener.

Dissembling. Even to the Mother, dissembling.

Page 124:

I'll write Mother and explain why I couldn't write her before she died ...

He couldn't write *to* his Mother before she died. But further, he couldn't *write her* before she died. The completeness, now, is possible only in her definitive incompleteness. Within his statement of intention are two statements in dialogic contention: "I'll write Mother"; "I couldn't write her." This equivalence of the me and not me is the analogue of his own being. He can only *be* here on this edge of solution and dissolution. And speaking too late, his Mother already dead, preparing again an apostrophe, Hear Me O Mother, he at once recognizes the collapse of narrative into solipsism and the possibility of narrating that predicament. Here again, this occasion is "no dream, but some strange symbolism of the future."

Even to avoid looking is to look, apparently. And Lowry, with Orpheus before him, looks more intently at that predicament too.

As poets have been dismembered into survival, so have cities, so have cultures. In the opening of "Present State of Pompeii" we read (page 175):

Inside the restaurant during the thunderstorm, there was one moment of pure happiness within the dark inner room when it started to rain. "Now thank God I don't have to see the ruins," Roderick thought.

That thunderstorm connects to the end of the opening story, to the statement, "it was like gazing into chaos," where the chaos translates into the world as a violent storm. Roderick, unwittingly and innocently, a "liberal-minded and progressive Scotch-Canadian schoolmaster," believes he has been spared the gaze.

A few pages into the story we hear again that fateful (or fating) song:

Frère Jacques!
Frère Jacques!

Dormez-vous?
Dormez-vous?

The doubled lines of the song, redoubled here, double the occasion as well. The deaf God listens now to Roderick's not listening. And this is the same Roderick who will observe so wonderfully later, "It was a silly place to put a volcano."

Lowry is the poet of ruins. Ruins of place, of culture, of visions of self, of visions of paradise. There was indeed "one moment of pure happiness." Even paradise must submit to the time of narrative. Even Roderick must submit. And the city, in its submission, instructs both paradise and poet. The city, dismembered, enters into the incompleteness and the temptation of completeness that make story possible and unavoidable.

Page 192:

... Roderick found himself suddenly hating this street with an inexplicable virulence. How he loathed Pompeii! His mouth positively watered with his hatred. Roderick was almost prancing. It seemed to him now that it was as though, by some perverse grace, out of the total inundation of some Pacific Northwestern city, had been preserved a bit of the station hotel, a section of the gasworks, the skeletal remains of four or five palatial cinemas, as many bars and several public urinals, a fragment of marketplace together with the building that once housed the Star Laundries, what was left of several fine industrialists' homes (obscene paintings), a football stadium, the Church of the Four Square Gospel, a broken statue of Bobbie Burns, and finally the remains of the brothels of Chinatown which, though the mayor and police force had labored to have them removed right up to the time of the catastrophe, had nonetheless survived five thousand nine hundred and ninety-nine generations whereupon it was concluded, probably rightly, that the city was one of the seven wonders of the world, as it now stood, but wrongly that anything worthwhile had been there in the first place, with the exceptions of the mountains.

Pompeii, its absence, its presence, its ruins, its endurance afflict Roderick at once with loathing and with the need to attend, to pay attention, to *look*. Precisely because (a passage I skipped, page 187) –

... "On the other hand – If you compare it with Bumble, Saskatchewan –"

I was a youngish if not young writer when I first read *Hear us O Lord*. I had earlier struggled with *Under the Volcano* and given up and then been drawn back, and had then discovered its unutterable beauty and my own compulsion to go on looking. But in *Hear us O Lord*, which I came to early in the 1960s, I recognized my own "I," my own will towards utterance.

In so far as I recognized myself as the writer from Bumble, Saskatch-ewan, Lowry was my other. Perhaps because he offered me the ruins that I so badly needed in order to become a writer.

In my version of Saskatchewan – in the rural Alberta landscape where I was born and grew – I mistakenly read that world as original, unwrit-ten, uninscribed. Of course it was those things too. But it wasn't. I believed in a version of newness that came out of what we now, looking back, call the modernist tradition. Lowry pointed me towards the tra-dition we now call, so uneasily, postmodern. Perhaps his task was to sing me, not out of hell, but out of heaven. Or are those *others* of each other simply the boundaries that mark the rift where all writing occurs?

When I first read *Hear us O Lord* my favorite story was "The Forest Path to the Spring," and one day I noticed in that story:

One day when we were rowing we came across a sunken canoe, a derelict, floating just beneath the surface in deep water so clear we made out its name: *Intermezzo*.

I won't pretend to know why that sentence picked me out the way it did. Perhaps I heard in its directness the impossibility of innocence. Perhaps I heard in its duplicity the duplicity of what passes for discovery.

In our strange faith in nature, as nature is practised in North America, we fail to recognize that nature and culture, from the moment when nature is named as nature, engage each other with tenderness and loath-ing. That troubled hold, half stolid embrace, half dance, was apparent to Lowry from the Columbus-moment when first he set foot in the New World.

Christopher Columbus, returned from his voyage, from his voyages, insisted to his dying day that he had sailed to the Indies. Malcolm Lowry proves him half right.

Europe made an easy other of the New World. Lowry complicates that easy binary by going and looking for himself. Lowry, sailing home for that other Columbus, sailing home again and again, sailing home to the essential eviction, the eviction that is all, ever, that allows for entry, delivers again the message that Columbus did and did not deliver. No, I have come to the Indies. Yes, I have not.

If we let go for a moment of that sacred name, New World, we see our familiar world with a startling freshness. Malcolm Lowry invites us, dares us, to take that risk, for a moment to unname what it is we think we are, where it is we think we are.

The ruins were ruins, he tells us, before we so gloatingly ruined them. Before the Spanish and the Portuguese, before the French and the English, death was waiting to recognize itself in the arrival of death. Death had built its earthly cities, as Cortés discovered, even if Columbus would not. To discover paradise is to discover the idea of paradise contained in the idea of ruin that is contained in the idea of paradise.

To read "The Forest Path to the Spring" as conclusion is to resist Lowry's elaborate positing within his book of cities, numerous cities, cities in their multitude, in their incompleteness, in their continuous ruin, in their eternal othering embrace of nature. The city – *polis* – in its sheer inability to complete itself, is the embodiment of the incompletable fecundity of human story-making.

In the strange mathematics of a book, I'm more inclined to look at the middle than at the end.

Kennish Drumgold Cosnahan, the writer in "Elephant and Colosseum," has written the story of his shipping an elephant to the ancient and ruined and vital city of Rome. He could write this story because he did ship an elephant to Rome, he insists on that too. And he trusts us to remember that others before him shipped, marched, drove elephants to Rome and its promise of a Colosseum and glory.

But now Cosnahan has himself come to Rome, as author, not as writer. He is here to discuss with his Italian publisher his novel *Ark from Singapore* – again, the completed book within the incompletable book, the completed book being translated out of completedness first by a literal translation, then by the experience that follows on what was the "end" of the novel.

Kennish Drumgold Cosnahan, in the city, is again the hesitating male come to the gap or fissure, resisting the gaze and tempted to have a look, drinking his way between the narrative of action and the discourse of inaction, obeying and revising Ortega's dictum that he invent himself as he goes along, concentrating on and avoiding the other that is the silence at his back. For this, again, is a love story. Cosnahan, in the complex silence of his life, is tempted to glance just once in the direction of his first great love, Rosemary.

Kennish Drumgold Cosnahan, the author, here becomes reader. He reads the city. He reads the novel he carries with him but won't open. Cosnahan, now, after the lapse of so many years, after failure and success and the ambiguity of both, after his own transport from the Isle of Man to America, reads the elaborate story of his own career as writer.

This Nantucket man (for that is what Cosnahan has become), just as Ishmael learned to love one whale, learned to love by loving an elephant. A female elephant named Rosemary.

He is distracted or instructed in his reading first by the cosmological lure. Cosnahan, we are told, having imagined a flight of angels that became real, then (page 170)

seemed to detect Mother Drumgold floating upwards on her celestial journey. His mother? But the answer came before Cosnahan had time to question.

And now we read the answer that anticipated his question (pages 170–1):

For was not Rosemary a signal *from* his mother, nay, was it not almost as if his mother had herself produced Rosemary or at least guided his steps to her, his meek and impossible elephant, to a meeting in its gently buffoonish manner nearly sublime.

That meeting, buffoonishly sublime, is not only the marriage of heaven and earth. It is also the uneasy marriage of nature and culture, of the elephant and the book about the elephant, of the earthly city and the mother who in her containing is not yet mother, who only in her emptying-out becomes the container of all.

Cosnahan, in his moment of recognition that "now at one of those rare points where life and poetry meet, Rosemary had appeared; Rosemary, so to say, *was* his work –," resorts again to apostrophe.

And now his apostrophe is a promise, not a request, a ritual kind of profane prayer:

Page 172:

Tomorrow, to that uniqueness of yours, I shall make an offering of the choicest Roman carrots, a bouquet of the freshest and crispest cisalpine celery. And sometimes it is true, so hapless does man seem to me, that I feel that if there is evolution, it must be to such as you. But great and wise though you are, Rosemary, I am bound to point out, our star being low, that man is more various.

Apostrophe, finally, is an appeal to the muse. Rose Mary. We remember. Those names name us into Dante's ultimate poem, into the seeming inclusiveness of the Christian story. There in Christian and pagan Rome. The elephant herself, at once tearing loose and imprisoned, naming the writer into the task of writing. In memory and forgetfulness we begin by saying, dangerously:

Hear us O Rosemary!

NOTES

1 Malcolm Lowry, *Hear us O Lord from heaven thy dwelling place* (Philadelphia and New York: Lippincott 1963; copyright Margerie Bonner Lowry 1961).

2 Geoffrey Hartman, Preface to Maurice Blanchot, *The Gaze of Orpheus and Other Literary Essays*, trans. Lydia Davis, ed. P. Adams Sitney (Barrytown, NY: Station Hill Press 1981), ix.

3 Jonathan Culler, *The Pursuit of Signs: Semiotics, Literature, Deconstruction* (Ithaca, NY: Cornell University Press 1981), 135.

Contributors

FREDERICK ASALS teaches English at New College, the University of Toronto, and is the author of *Flannery O'Connor: The Imagination of Extremity* (1982). He has published various articles on American literature and wrote "Malcolm Lowry" for the Profiles in Canadian Literature series. He is currently working on a study of the composition of *Under the Volcano*.

GRAHAM COLLIER, British composer and lecturer on musical composition and the history of jazz, has long been fascinated by Lowry's work. In 1977 he was commissioned to compose "The Day of the Dead," a work inspired by Lowry's texts and letters, and this work was given its North American première at the 1987 Lowry Symposium. Mr Collier, who is director of Jazz Studies at the Royal Academy of Music, has many books, articles, and compositions to his credit, and he was made a Fellow of the Order of the British Empire in 1987 for his services to jazz.

HALLVARD DAHLIE is professor of English at the University of Calgary and author of books on Brian Moore and Alice Munro. His most recent book is *Varieties of Exile: The Canadian Experience* (1986), but he has written articles on various Canadian topics, including pioneer work on Lowry's *Ultramarine* and his debt to Aiken and Grieg.

VICTOR DOYEN is professor of English and American literatures at the Katholieke Universiteit Leuven and a specialist in textual editing. He has published on American and British literature, done extensive work on the Lowry Archive, and in May 1987 he gave a special Western Canadian University Dean's Graduate Seminar on Lowry at the University of British Columbia. He is currently preparing a variorum edition of Lowry's *Lunar Caustic* and a critical edition of *October Ferry to Gabriola*.

DAVID FALK is chair of the Department of English, Speech and World Literature at the College of Staten Island (City University of New York). He has written articles on contemporary writers, including Malcolm Lowry, and is currently at work on a study of Lowry entitled *Strategies of Self-Mastery*.

JAN GABRIAL was a young writer exploring North Africa and Europe when she met Malcolm Lowry in Granada, Spain, in 1933. His letters and her journals attest to the mutual enchantment that led to their marriage some months later. In the years following their 1940 divorce, Jan Gabrial published short stories in a variety of "literary" magazines and in *Mademoiselle*, *Woman's Day*, and *Story*. She has recently completed a book dealing with the life she and Malcolm shared, tentatively entitled "The Volcano and the Rainbowpuss." She is currently working on a novel.

ALBERTO GIRONELLA is the contemporary Mexican painter who designed the cover for the Spanish translation of *Under the Volcano*. He has executed a number of oils and mixed-media works inspired by Lowry, and has exhibited widely in Mexico, the United States, and Europe.

SHERRILL GRACE is professor of English at the University of British Columbia and author of *The Voyage That Never Ends: Malcolm Lowry's Fiction* (1982). She has also written and edited books on Margaret Atwood, and she has published widely on Canadian, American, British, and comparative topics. Her most recent book is *Regression and Apocalypse: Studies in North American Literary Expressionism* (1989). She is currently editing the collected letters of Malcolm Lowry.

D.B. JEWISON is professor and chair of the Department of English, University of Winnipeg, and past president of the Canadian Association of Chairs of English. His main scholarly interest is in twentieth-century fiction written in Canada, Britain, the Commonwealth, Europe, and South Africa. His interest in Malcolm Lowry dates back to Honours and Masters theses written in the 1960s.

SUZANNE KIM is a maître de conférences at the Université de Paris (Sorbonne Nouvelle), where she teaches English and American literature. She is the author of numerous articles on modern writers, including Lowry and James Joyce, co-editor of a recent study of *Finnegans Wake*, and has published a French translation of *The Selected Letters of Malcolm Lowry*. She is currently an attachée de recherche at the Centre National de la Recherche Scientifique, where she is working on Joyce's notebooks for *Finnegans Wake*.

ROBERT KROETSCH, professor of English at the University of Manitoba, winner of the Governor General's Award for fiction, and Senior Killam Fellow, is a leading Canadian poet, novelist, and critic. His works include the trilogy *The Words of My Roaring*, *The Studhorse Man*, and *Gone Indian*, four other novels, several volumes of poetry in his ongoing collected poems, called *Field Notes*, and numerous critical essays.

ELSA LINGUANTI is professor of English at the University of Pisa and a specialist in American, Canadian, and Australian literature and in rhetoric. She is the author of several articles on Canadian and Australian writers and of *L'Itinerario del Senso nella Narrativa di Malcolm Lowry* (1984) and a contributor to *Myriad-Minded Man: Jottings on Joyce* (1986).

JOAN MULHOLLAND is senior lecturer in Communication and Cultural Studies in the English Department of the University of Queensland (Australia). She is a specialist in speech-act theory and has published on nineteenth-century literature. In 1974 she completed a Masters thesis on "Malcolm Lowry's *Volcano*: A Study in Stylistic Method," and she has published articles on Lowry in *Language and Style* and *ACLALS Bulletin*.

CHRISTINE PAGNOULLE teaches English literature and translation at the Université de Liège (Belgium). She is the author of *Malcolm Lowry: Voyage au fond de nos abîmes* (1977) and *David Jones: A Commentary on Some Poetic Fragments* (1987), and organized a panel on translating *Under the Volcano* at the 1987 Vancouver Symposium. She is currently working on translations of Wilson Harris's novel *Carnival* and of various African poets.

CYNTHIA SUGARS is a graduate student at McGill University. For her Masters thesis at the University of British Columbia she edited the Aiken-Lowry correspondence. She has worked extensively with the Lowry Archive and published articles and reviews on Lowry.

HILDA THOMAS is a senior instructor of English at the University of British Columbia, where she teaches Canadian literature and rhetoric. She completed a Masters thesis on *Under the Volcano* in 1965 and has an article on the Lowry letters in *Malcolm Lowry: The Man and His Work* (1971). She has been an active socialist and feminist for many years and is interested in Marxist critical theory.

MARK ELLIS THOMAS is a graduate student and teaching assistant in English at the University of Illinois. He wrote his Masters thesis on Malcolm Lowry and is now at work on his doctorate. He has begun to publish short studies on poetry and on Lowry in journals such as *Canadian Literature*, *Explicator*, and the *Malcolm Lowry Review*.

SUE VICE is a lecturer in English at the University of Sheffield. She is the editor of *Malcolm Lowry: Eighty Years On* (1989).

Index